SUGARLESS COOKERY FOR THE GOURMET

Sugarless Cookery for the Gourmet

Delectable Dietetic Dishes for Sugar-Restricted Diets

Elsie Maye Peckham, R.N.

Foreword by JAMES R. HILL, M.D.
President, International Academy of Metabology, Inc.

An Exposition-Banner Book
Exposition Press
Hicksville, New York

First Printing, February, 1976
Second Printing, August, 1976
Third Printing, January, 1978

LIBRARY OF CONGRESS CATALOG CARD NUMBER: 76-5635

ISBN 0-682-48359-1

Printed in the United States of America

To James R. Hill, M.D., Dallas, Texas,
and William C. Smith, M.D., Lubbock, Texas,
whose eminent knowledge and treatment
have brought so many ailing persons
the blessing of good health,
I gratefully dedicate this book

NOTE TO THE READER

1. The flour recommended for recipes in this book is Sterling Special Blend Flour. It can be purchased at your local health food store or ordered directly from:

    > Sterling Food Company
    > 5118 14th Avenue N.W.
    > Seattle, Washington 98107

2. The carob syrup referred to in the recipes is "light" not "white." It is Light Carob Syrup and can be purchased at your health food store or ordered directly from:

    > Balanced Foods, Inc.
    > 2500 83rd Street
    > North Bergen, New Jersey 07047

Contents

Foreword

It is fitting that *Sugarless Cookery for the Gourmet* should be published when we have already seen the price of refined sugar jump to well over fifty cents per pound. I hope that those of you who use sugar in your cooking will now consider using other natural sweeteners in place of refined sugar. From a health point of view, nothing could be more beneficial. Sugar has no nutritional value, no vitamins, no minerals, no protein, no fiber—nothing but calories. In addition, research has proven it to be a causative factor in dental caries, obesity, diabetes, hypoglycemia, and heart disease.

This book is a godsend to those people who have been requested by their doctors to refrain from eating refined sugar. Such patients usually handle complex carbohydrates much better in their body metabolism. The sweetener used in the recipes throughout this book is carob syrup, which has been around for thousands of years. It is derived from the long, fleshy seed pods which grow on an evergreen-type of tree in Mediterranean areas. It is actually a naturally sweet fruit with a flavor similar to chocolate. It is often called Saint-John's-bread—a name which came from the belief that carob fruit served as food for John the Baptist during his forty days and forty nights in the wilderness.

Mrs. Peckham has formulated, through trial and error, some delicious recipes. I highly recommend them to everyone for more nutritious, healthful eating, as well as for delectable taste treats.

JAMES R. HILL, M.D.
President,
International Academy of Metabology, Inc.

Preface

This cookbook evolved because of the old adage that the best defense is a strong offense. Upon learning that my husband and I were hypoglycemic and that we were, consequently, faced with eating a bland, tasteless, and sugarless diet, I began developing recipes using the several sugar and wheat-flour substitutes available. I wanted to develop tasty recipes that would especially tempt my husband, who had always demanded sweets and starches in his diet.

My many years' experience as a registered nurse had already brought home to me the importance of proper diet. Subsequent study and consultation with doctors who had enjoyed much success in treating hypoglycemia dictated my heavy reliance on such carob fruit derivatives as carob syrup and soya carob flour. Finally, trial and error, sweat and tears, and frequent tasting and sampling of my developing recipes by many patients suffering from hypoglycemia brought into being *Sugarless Cookery for the Gourmet.*

If properly used, the recipes in this book can satisfy the needs of most anyone—hypoglycemic or not. Many guests in my home who have enjoyed delicious meals have been amazed when later they found out they had partaken of a 100 percent dietetic meal. In fact, they always come back for more! Does this not prove that one can enjoy delicious food, yet still observe a carefully planned diet? I leave it to your judgment.

And many who have sampled my recipes have kept my telephone line busy, asking: "When will the cookbook be available?" Well, here it is!

ELSIE M. PECKHAM, R.N.

11

SUGARLESS COOKERY FOR THE GOURMET

Chips, Dips, and Snacks

ANCHOVY DIP

1 8-ounce package cream cheese
2 teaspoons grated onion
1½ tablespoons lemon juice

3 tablespoons heavy cream
½ teaspoon celery seed
2 teaspoons anchovy paste

Mix together all ingredients in a blender until fluffy.

AVOCADO DIP

2 large avocados, peeled and
   pitted
½ cup sour cream
3 tablespoons lemon juice

1 teaspoon onion, grated
1 teaspoon sea salt
4 slices bacon, cooked and
   crumbled

Mash avocados with a fork, or force through a sieve. Add sour cream, lemon juice, onion, and salt; chill. Just before serving, stir in bacon, reserving a few bits for garnish. Serve with corn chips.

AVOCADO-CREAM CHEESE DIP

1 8-ounce package softened
   cream cheese
1 cup mashed, peeled avocado

3 tablespoons lemon juice
1 teaspoon sea salt
½ teaspoon onion salt

Add avocado, lemon juice, salt and onion salt gradually to cream cheese, mixing well. Serve with corn chips.

15

GREEN GODDESS DIP

1 large ripe pitted, peeled avocado	½ teaspoon sea salt
1 cup sour cream	½ teaspoon seasoned salt
¼ cup Dietetic Mayonnaise (*see* Index)	⅓ cup parsley, finely chopped
	¼ cup green onions, finely chopped

Mash avocado well; add sour cream and mayonnaise; mix well. Add salt and seasoning salt, mixing well. Fold in parsley and green onions. Chill. Serve with corn chips.

BACON DIP

1 8-ounce package cream cheese	dash of garlic salt
3 tablespoons chives, finely cut	6 strips crisp, crumbled bacon
1 cup sour cream	dash of cayenne
1 teaspoon horseradish	

Soften cheese to room temperature. Blend together with chives, sour cream, horseradish, salt, and cayenne. Mix with crumbled bacon, reserving a few bits for garnish.

BACON-AVOCADO DIP

6 slices smoked bacon°	¼ teaspoon chili powder
2 large avocados	1 tablespoon lemon juice
1 tablespoon onion, minced	⅓ cup Green Goddess Dressing (*see* Index)
⅛ teaspoon garlic salt	
⅛ teaspoon pepper	

Mash avocados; blend in onion, garlic salt, pepper, chili powder, and lemon juice. Cover mixture with salad dressing (to seal out air; this keeps mixture from turning dark, so it can be made several hours before serving). Fry bacon until crisp; crumble it. When ready to serve, stir avocado mixture well and top with bacon.

°For all recipes calling for bacon, use smoked and not sugar cured.

CARROT DIP

3 medium carrots
3 medium kosher dill pickles
1 small jar pimentos
2 green peppers

1 small onion
sea salt and pepper to taste
3 hard-cooked eggs, chopped
Dietetic Mayonnaise (*see* Index)

Grind together carrots, pickles, pimentos, peppers, and onion. Drain mixture on paper towels or cheesecloth, then place in bowl. Add eggs, salt, pepper, and enough mayonnaise to hold mixture together.

CHEDDAR CHEESE DIP

1 cup finely shredded sharp
    Cheddar cheese
5 tablespoons Dietetic
    Mayonnaise (*see* Index)
2 teaspoons prepared
    horseradish

¼ teaspoon garlic salt
3 teaspoons finely cut-up onion
1 teaspoon finely cut-up parsley
paprika

Blend together cheese and mayonnaise. Add remaining ingredients. Heap into serving dish and dust with paprika.

CHEESE BALL I

¼ pound blue cheese
4 ounces Cheddar cheese
4 3-ounce packages cream
    cheese
2 tablespoons sour cream
¼ teaspoon sea salt
1 teaspoon cayenne

⅛ teaspoon white pepper
1 clove grated garlic
½ tablespoon lemon juice
1½ cup chopped pecans
1 tablespoon soy sauce
1 cup fresh, finely chopped
    parsley

Let cheeses reach room temperature. Mix together with sour cream, blending well. Add salt, cayenne and black pepper, garlic, soy sauce, lemon juice and ½ cup of the pecans. Spread remaining pecans and parsley on a large sheet of wax paper. Shape cheese into a ball; roll in the parsley-pecan mixture. Refrigerate overnight. Serve with crackers or corn chips.

CHEESE BALL II

2 8-ounce packages cream
  cheese
1 8-ounce can crushed,
  unsweetened pineapple,
  drained

2 cups chopped pecans, toasted
¼ cup finely chopped onion
1 tablespoon seasoned salt
¼ cup finely chopped green
  pepper

Combine cheese, pineapple, 1 cup of the pecans, onion, salt, and pepper. Form into 1 large ball or 2 small balls. Roll in the remaining pecans. Refrigerate overnight.

CHEESE BALL III

8 ounces blue cheese
8 ounces cream cheese
⅛ pound butter

⅜ cup chopped ripe olives
1 tablespoon dried chives
1 cup crushed nuts

Let cheese and butter soften at room temperature, then blend. Stir olives and dried chives into mixture; chill slightly. Form into ball, then chill well. Roll in crushed nuts before serving.

CHEESE OLIVES

½ cup soya carob flour
¼ teaspoon sea salt
⅛ teaspoon dry mustard
4 ounces sharp Cheddar cheese,
  shredded

3 tablespoons butter, melted and
  slightly cooled
1 tablespoon milk
1 or 2 drops hot sauce
1 bottle green olives

Blend together flour, salt, mustard, and cheese. Stir in butter, milk, and hot sauce to make a soft dough. Cover each green olive with 1 teaspoon of the dough. Bake in a preheated oven at 400° for 10 to 20 minutes. Makes 25 balls.

CHEESE PUFFS

1½ cups grated Swiss cheese
⅓ cup grated Parmesan cheese
½ cup butter at room
    temperature
¾ cup soya carob flour

¼ teaspoon sea salt
⅛ teaspoon cayenne
⅛ teaspoon nutmeg
1 egg

Knead together all ingredients except ½ cup of the Swiss cheese and the egg. Form into balls and chill for at least 15 minutes. Break off into tablespoonfuls and form into small balls; flatten each into a circle about ¼ inch thick. Arrange on cookie sheet. Brush tops with egg beaten with 1 teaspoon water. Sprinkle with the reserved ½ cup Swiss cheese. Refrigerate until ready to serve, then bake in a preheated oven at 425° for 10 minutes, until puffed and lightly browned. They may be kept in freezer until ready to serve.

PINEAPPLE-CHEESE TARTS

1 3-ounce package cream cheese
¼ pound butter

1 cup soya carob flour
Pineapple Preserves (*see* Index)

Thoroughly cream the cheese and butter together. Add flour; mix well to make a dough. Wrap in wax paper and chill 3½ hours. Roll out ⅛ inch thick on floured board; cut into 3-inch circles; put a teaspoon preserves on each piece of pastry; fold over and seal with prongs of fork. Bake in a preheated oven at 450° for about 12 minutes or until light brown. Yield: approximately 18 tarts.

CHEESE THINS

¼ pound Cheddar cheese, grated
    fine
½ cup sifted soya carob flour

½ cup ground nuts
¼ cup butter
¼ teaspoon cayenne

Mix all ingredients together well; roll up as for jelly roll. Freeze. Slice thinly and bake in a preheated oven at 375° for 10 to 12 minutes.

MEXICAN CHEESE DIP

1 8-ounce can tomatoes and
    green chili peppers,
    unsweetened

1 pound processed, spreadable
    cheese (that does not
    contain sugar), softened

Melt cheese in double boiler. Add tomatoes and chili peppers. Stir. Serve hot with corn chips.

TANGY CHEESE BALL

2 pounds cream cheese
2 teaspoons prepared mustard
3 tablespoons chopped chives
2 teaspoons lemon juice
½ cup paprika

½ teaspoon garlic powder
2 tablespoons caraway seed
1 tablespoon soy sauce
3 drops hot sauce

Let cream cheese stand at room temperature for 1 hour or longer, until softened. Place into a bowl all the ingredients except the paprika; blend until very creamy and smooth. Form into a ball. Spread paprika on wax paper, then roll the cheese ball in it, coating it completely with the paprika. Cover with the same wax paper; refrigerate overnight. Place on serving platter, and decorate with olives, tiny onions, and parsley.

FAVORITE DIP

1 8-ounce package softened
    cream cheese
1 tablespoon lemon juice
dash of paprika

¼ cup evaporated milk
1 tablespoon onion flakes or
    minced onion

Add milk to cream cheese; blend. Blend in lemon juice. **Add** onion and paprika.

VARIATIONS

1 can smoked clams or oysters
1 cup pimento cheese
¾ cup small shrimp

¼ cup carrots, grated
¼ cup green pepper, grated

Add any one of the above ingredients to the dip. Blend well.

HOT MUSHROOM DIP

¾ pound fresh mushrooms, sliced
1 clove garlic, crushed
1 small onion, grated
2 tablespoons butter
⅛ teaspoon dry mustard
1 teaspoon soy sauce

⅛ teaspoon paprika
1 tablespoon soya carob flour
⅛ teaspoon sea salt
⅛ teaspoon pepper
1 cup sour cream

Brown mushrooms, garlic, and onion in butter. Combine mustard, soy sauce, paprika, salt, pepper, and flour with a little of the sour cream to make a smooth paste; add to mushrooms. Blend in remaining sour cream. Stir over low heat, just until thickened —do not boil. Serve hot with corn chips.

SESAME CHIPS

1 cup soya carob flour	¼ cup corn meal
½ cup sesame seeds	1 tablespoon wheat germ
1 tablespoon dry grated	1½ teaspoons sea salt
Parmesan cheese	½ cup oil
pinch of baking powder	4 tablespoons cold milk

Mix together all dry ingredients. Measure milk and oil in same cup; do not stir. Add to dry ingredients and mix well until mixture forms a ball. Roll out, thinner than a pie crust, between two sheets of wax paper. Remove top sheet of paper; slice dough into strips, and cut into pieces. Place on greased cookie sheet and bake at 375° in a preheated oven for about 10 minutes, or until golden brown.

Note: The dough may be shaped into long rolls (as for refrigerator cookies) and sliced very thin, or sliced and pressed thin with the thumb before baking.

SHRIMP DIP

1 pound cooked shrimp	1 pint sour cream
1 large bunch dill, finely	sea salt to taste
chopped	1 tablespoon Dietetic
1 teaspoon dry mustard	Mayonnaise (*see* Index)
1 teaspoon white pepper	

Blend together all ingredients except cooked shrimp, then add that. Chill.

VEGETABLE MEDLEY CONFETTI DIP

1 green pepper, finely chopped	½ head cauliflower
1 tomato, finely chopped	½ bunch broccoli
1 bunch scallions, thinly sliced	4 stalks celery, cut into 2-inch
1 8-ounce package softened	pieces
cream cheese	2 green peppers, seeded and cut
½ pint sour cream	vertically into 5 slices each
1 teaspoon dry mustard	1 cucumber, cut into 10 slices
1 teaspoon sea salt	1 pint cherry tomatoes
½ teaspoon black pepper	

For dip, combine in a small bowl chopped green pepper, tomato, scallions, cream cheese, sour cream, mustard, salt, and black pepper. Blend well. Place in serving bowl and chill 1 to 2 hours in refrigerator. Cut off stems of cauliflower and broccoli; separate into 10 flowerets each. Arrange alternately with remaining vegetables on wooden skewers and serve with dip.

COLD BORSCHT

1 can whole beets (without sugar)
¼ cup white carob syrup
¾ teaspoon sea salt
5 tablespoons lemon juice
1 egg, well beaten

Drain beets, reserving liquid in a quart measuring cup. Grind or blend beets in a blender with about ½ cup of the reserved beet liquid. Turn into liquid in measuring cup and add enough cold water to make 1 quart. Combine with syrup, salt, and lemon juice in a saucepan; heat to boiling, stirring occasionally. Remove from heat. Stir ¾ cup of the hot mixture into the egg; return to saucepan. Heat until simmering (do not boil) Chill. Garnish each serving with a spoonful of sour cream.

HOT BORSCHT

1 cup tomato sauce (without sugar)
2 cups pared, coarsely shredded beets
4 cups water
1 small onion, chopped
½ pound lean beef, cut in small cubes
1 tablespoon lemon juice
¼ cup white carob syrup
½ teaspoon sea salt
4 eggs, beaten

Combine tomato sauce, beets, water, onion and beef; cover and bring to a boil; reduce heat and simmer 30 minutes. Add lemon juice, carob syrup and salt. Simmer 30 minutes. Add 2 cups of the hot soup, a small amount at a time, to the eggs, blending well after each addition. Return the egg-beet mixture to saucepan and heat to simmering, stirring constantly.

Serves 4.

CHEESE TUNA CHOWDER

¼ cup butter
1 medium-size onion, chopped
¼ cup chopped green pepper
½ cup chopped celery
2 tablespoons soya carob flour
1 teaspoon sea salt

¼ teaspoon pepper
3 cups milk
1 can (7-ounces) tuna, flaked
2 cups sharp Cheddar cheese, shredded

Melt butter in saucepan; add vegetables; simmer about 5 minutes. Blend in flour, salt, and pepper, and stir milk in gradually; cook, stirring constantly, until soup thickens. Add tuna and cheese, stirring until cheese melts.

Serve at once when soup reaches serving temperature.
Serves 6.

MUSHROOM SOUP

1 4-ounce can button mushrooms, drained and chopped (liquor reserved)
¼ cup butter or margarine
4 whole green onions, thinly sliced

4½ cups milk
1 cup beef bouillon
¼ cup soya carob flour
1 teaspoon sea salt

Sauté mushrooms and half of the onions in melted butter in heavy saucepan for 5 minutes, stirring occasionally. Stir in 4 cups of the milk, bouillon, and reserved liquor. Cook over low heat until mixture comes to a boil, stirring occasionally. In another pot, combine flour, salt and the ½ cup milk, blending until smooth. Add to mushroom mixture gradually, and bring to a boil, stirring constantly. Cook, stirring all the while, 3 or 4 minutes longer. Garnish with remaining onions. Serves about 8.

ONION SOUP WITH CHEESE TOAST

4 cups minced onions	3 10½-ounce cans condensed
3 tablespoons butter	beef broth
¼ teaspoon peppercorns,	1 bay leaf
coarsely chopped	¾ cup grated Swiss cheese
1 tablespoon soya carob flour	6 slices soya carob bread (*see*
3 cups water	Index), toasted

Heat butter in heavy saucepan over medium heat and add onions and peppercorns. Cook, stirring frequently, until onions are a light-golden color. Sprinkle flour over onions. Cook 1 minute, stirring constantly. Add water, beef broth, and bay leaf. Bring to a boil, then simmer for 30 minutes. Sprinkle toasted bread with cheese and place under broiler until cheese melts. Arrange 1 slice on each bowlful of soup and serve immediately.

OYSTER STEW

2 cups milk	1 teaspoon sea salt
1 can oysters, undrained	⅛ teaspoon pepper
2 tablespoons butter	

Scald milk in a 1-quart saucepan; add oysters, butter, salt, and pepper. Simmer over low heat until mixture is hot. Serve at once.

CREAM OF TOMATO SOUP

2 cups cooked tomatoes	2 tablespoons white carob syrup
1 teaspoon grated onion	2 tablespoons butter or
1 teaspoon sea salt	margarine
¼ teaspoon pepper	2 tablespoons soya carob flour
dash cayenne	1 quart milk, scalded

Cook tomatoes, onion, salt, pepper, cayenne and carob syrup together for 15 minutes, then blend in blender. Melt butter in

large saucepan; blend in flour. Add milk gradually, stirring constantly. Cook and stir mixture until it boils; cook 1 or 2 minutes longer. Add tomato mixture to milk mixture, stirring constantly.
Yield: 6 servings.

CREAM OF FRESH TOMATO SOUP

1 veal knuckle (about 3 pounds)	4 ripe tomatoes, quartered
¼ cup butter or margarine	1 1-pound can tomato puree
½ cup chopped onion	4 to 6 parsley sprigs
⅓ cup pared, chopped, carrot	2 teaspoons sea salt
2 cans (13¾ ounce size) chicken broth	10 whole black peppercorns
2 leeks, sliced	2 packets sugar substitute
1 stalk celery, sliced	1 tablespoon butter or margarine
	½ cup light cream

Wipe veal knuckle with damp paper towels. Heat butter in 6-quart Dutch oven or kettle and brown veal knuckle well, turning on all sides (this takes about 15 minutes). Lift out knuckle; set aside. To drippings, add onion and carrots; sauté, stirring, until onion is tender (about 5 minutes). Add chicken broth, leeks, celery, tomatoes, tomato purée, parsley, salt, peppercorns and sweetener; mix well. Bring to boiling; add veal knuckle; reduce heat and simmer, covered, 2½ hours, until veal is tender. At end of first half hour, skim foam from surface. Remove veal knuckle; set aside. Line a strainer or colander with double thickness of cheesecloth. Strain soup, pressing mixture through cheesecloth with wooden spoon. Pour soup back into kettle. Add cream and the 1 tablespoon butter. Stir over low heat until hot. Serve with French bread spread with marrow from the veal bone.
Makes about 1½ quarts (6 servings).

BAKED CELERY WITH CHEESE AND HAM

3 cups celery, cut into strips	½ cup butter or margarine
sea salt	¼ cup soya carob flour
3 cup chopped boiled or baked ham	1 cup chicken bouillon
	1 cup light cream
2 cups grated Cheddar cheese	¼ cup dry soya bread crumbs

Cover celery strips in salted water and cook until tender; drain. In a well-greased 2-quart casserole, place alternate layers of celery, ham, and grated cheese. Melt ¼ cup of the butter; stir in flour. Gradually add chicken bouillon and cream, stirring constantly. Cook over low heat, stirring all the while, until thick and smooth. Season to taste with salt. Pour sauce over casserole and sprinkle with dry bread crumbs, then drizzle remaining ¼ cup melted butter over top. Bake in preheated moderate oven (350°) for 25 to 30 minutes, or until top is browned and mixture is bubbly.

Yield: 6 servings.

HOT CHEESE CASSEROLE

2 4-ounce cans green chili peppers, drained	¾ cup canned evaporated milk
1 pound Monterey Jack cheese, coarsely grated	1 tablespoon soya carob flour
	½ teaspoon sea salt
4 egg whites	⅛ teaspoon pepper
4 egg yolks	2 medium tomatoes, sliced

Preheat oven to 325°. Remove seeds from chili peppers; dice. In a large bowl, combine grated cheese and chilis. Turn into a well-greased shallow 2-quart casserole (12" x 12" x 2"). In a large bowl, beat egg whites with electric mixer at high speed just until stiff peaks form when beater is raised slowly. In small bowl of electric mixer, combine egg yolks, milk, flour, salt, and pepper; beat until well blended. Using a rubber scraper, gently fold beaten egg whites into egg-yolk mixture, then pour over cheese mixture, "oozing" it into the cheese with a fork. Bake for 30 minutes. Remove casserole from oven and arrange sliced tomatoes over it, overlapping them around edges. Bake for 30 minutes longer, or until a silver knife inserted in center comes out clean. Garnish with a sprinkling of chopped green chilis, if desired.

Yield: 8 servings.

CHEESE SOUFFLÉ

1½ cups milk	cayenne
¼ cup butter or margarine	½ pound Cheddar cheese, finely
¼ cup soya carob flour	grated
sea salt	4 eggs, separated

Scald milk; remove from heat. In another saucepan, melt butter over low heat; stir in soya carob flour and blend until smooth. Add the milk all at once, and stir until smooth. Cook, stirring constantly, for 2 to 3 minutes. Add cheese; stir until melted. Beat in egg yolks, one at a time. Let mixture cool.

Beat egg whites until they stand in stiff peaks. Fold carefully and quickly into egg-yolk mixture. Turn into greased 2-quart baking dish. Bake in preheated moderate oven (375°) for 30 to 45 minutes (depending on whether a thin or firm soufflé is wanted). Serve immediately.

Serves 4-6.

CREAMED EGGS AND ASPARAGUS ON TOAST

1 pound cooked fresh or frozen
  asparagus, drained
3 tablespoons butter or bacon
  drippings
3 tablespoons soya carob flour
1½ cups milk

asparagus liquid (optional)
1 teaspoon sea salt
5 hard-boiled eggs, sliced
5 slices buttered soya-bread
  toast
pimento strips

Melt butter in top of double boiler over direct heat. Blend in flour and gradually add milk (liquid drained from asparagus may be substituted for part of milk), stirring constantly until sauce boils and thickens. Add salt, egg slices, and asparagus. Heat over boiling water (in bottom of double boiler). Serve on buttered toast garnished with pimento.

DEVILED EGGS

8 hard-cooked eggs
½ teaspoon sea salt
dash of onion salt
4 teaspoons prepared mustard

dash of cayenne
1 tablespoon vinegar
Dietetic Mayonnaise (*see* Index)

Cut eggs in half lengthwise. Scoop out yolks, and mash with all remaining ingredients, mixing well and using just enough mayonnaise to moisten. Fill egg whites with yolk mixture. Chill.

EGG FOO YONG

½ cup minced cooked ham
½ cup finely chopped onion
1 cup bean sprouts

¼ teaspoon sea salt
5 eggs, well beaten

Combine all ingredients and beat until thick. Drop from a large spoon into 1 inch of hot fat. Fry for about 10 minutes, turning once so it is brown on both sides. Drain on absorbent paper and serve hot.

Serves 6.

BAKED HAM AND EGGS

1 large onion, sliced
¼ pound ham, diced
3 tablespoons butter or
    margarine
1 clove garlic, minced
3 medium-sized tomatoes,
    peeled and chopped
1-1½ cups cooked peas, beans,
    carrots, or a combination of
    vegetables

1 tablespoon finely chopped
    parsley
¼ teaspoon sea salt
⅛ teaspoon pepper
½ cup sliced pimento-stuffed
    olives
8 eggs
½ cup shredded Cheddar cheese

In a frying pan, cook onion and ham in melted butter over medium heat, stirring constantly, until onion is tender (about 5 minutes). Add garlic and tomatoes; cook slowly for about 10 minutes longer. Add peas (or other vegetables), parsley, salt, pepper, and olives. Turn into 8 10-ounce baking cups and break an egg carefully into each. Sprinkle cheese on top and bake, uncovered, in a preheated moderate oven (350°) for about 20 minutes, or until eggs are set to your liking.

If you prefer, you can bake the eggs in a single 8-inch-square dish for about the same length of time.

Serve each egg on crisp toast with some of the sauce.

Serves 8.

SHREDDED ONION OMELET

3 eggs
½ teaspoon sea salt
dash of pepper

butter or margarine
¼ cup chopped onion

Beat the eggs in a bowl. Add salt and pepper. Melt butter in a frying pan and sauté onion for 2 minutes. Pour the eggs into the pan over the onion, spreading them to cover bottom of the pan. Turn. Remove from pan and slice very thin before serving.

SOFT SCRAMBLED EGGS

4 eggs
2 tablespoons heavy cream
sea salt

pepper
1 tablespoon butter

Beat eggs lightly with cream, salt, and pepper. Heat butter in a pan, pour in eggs, and scramble until lightly cooked.

SWISS-CHEESE PIE

2 cups (½ pound) Swiss cheese, grated
3 eggs, well beaten
1 cup light cream or milk

1 tablespoon soya carob flour
sea salt and pepper to taste
1 Soya Carob Pie Crust (*see* Index)

OPTIONAL

4 strips crisp bacon, crumbled
1 large onion, chopped and sautéed
½ cup finely chopped smoked or

boiled ham
½ cup finely minced cooked chicken

Line a deep pie pan with prepared pastry. Sprinkle cheese evenly over it. Mix eggs well with cream (or milk), seasonings, and flour, and pour over cheese. Bake for 15 minutes in a preheated hot (425°) oven, then reduce heat to 325° and bake for 30 minutes longer, or until a knife inserted in center of pie comes out clean.

Serve hot or warm—never cold.

Vary by adding any of the optional ingredients to the custard mixture. Serves 4.

TOMATOES AND EGGS ITALIAN

1 large can sliced mushrooms, drained
3 tablespoons butter or margarine
3 or 4 large tomatoes, peeled, cut in cubes, and drained

6 to 8 eggs
sea salt and pepper to taste
¾ cup shredded cheese

Sauté mushrooms in butter (or margarine), reserving a few mushroom slices for garnish. Add tomatoes; stir to heat through. With a spoon, make 6 to 8 nest spaces and break an egg into each space. Season with salt and pepper, top with shredded cheese, and garnish with mushroom slices. Cover pan; cook until eggs are set.

Makes 3 to 4 servings.

VEGETABLE-MACARONI-CHEESE CASSEROLE

1 8-ounce package artichoke
    macaroni
½ cup butter
2 6-ounce cans sliced
    mushrooms, drained
2 tablespoons chopped onion

4 tablespoons soya carob flour
3 cups hot milk
3 cups (about ¾ pound)
    American cheese, grated
1 teaspoon sea salt
⅛ teaspoon paprika

Cook macaroni according to directions on package; drain.

Melt half the butter in a large skillet and brown mushrooms and onions quickly in it. Lift out with slotted spoon and reserve. Add remaining butter to skillet and melt it; add flour, and blend in, cooking gently, without browning, for 3 minutes. Stir in hot milk; cook, stirring constantly, until sauce is smooth and thickened. Add seasonings and 2½ cups of the cheese, stirring over low heat until thoroughly blended.

Grease 2 1½-quart casseroles. In each, arrange a layer of macaroni, add part of the onions and mushrooms, and cover with a layer of sauce. Lay on second layers of the ingredients, and top the whole with ¼ cup of the cheese. Bake in a preheated oven at 400° for 15 to 20 minutes, or until lightly browned.

Serve hot. You may freeze one casserole (after cooling it) for use at a later time.

Note: Leftover chicken is delicious mixed in this casserole. And pimentos make a colorful substitute for the mushrooms.

Entrees
(Meat, Poultry, Fish and Seafood)

MEAT

Beef

BARBECUED HAMBURGERS

1 pound ground chuck	dash of cayenne
½ cup Chili Sauce (*see* Index)	½ clove garlic, finely chopped
1½ teaspoons soy sauce	1 tablespoon lemon juice
¼ teaspoon celery seed	¼ teaspoon chili powder
1½ teaspoons sea salt	1 packet sugar substitute
2 tablespoons chopped onions	chopped parsley (optional)
2 tablespoons vinegar	½ teaspoon pepper
1 tablespoon water	

Place chili sauce, soy sauce, celery seed, 1 teaspoon of the sea salt, chopped onions, vinegar, water, red pepper, garlic, lemon juice, chili powder and sugar substitute in a small saucepan over low heat and simmer for 5 minutes. Combine ground chuck, the teaspoon sea salt, and pepper, and shape into 4 patties. Broil lightly or pan broil. Carefully place browned patties in skillet, then pour in barbecue sauce; reduce heat, cover tightly, and simmer for about 10 minutes. Serve patties with sauce poured over them, and sprinkled with parsley.

BEEF-BACON PATTIES

1 pound ground beef
1½ teaspoons sea salt
⅛ teaspoon pepper

1 medium-size onion
4 slices bacon

Mix together beef, salt, and pepper; shape into 8 patties. Slice the onion into ¼-inch-thick slices, and place 1 slice between 2 patties, sandwich fashion. Wrap each "sandwich" in a slice of bacon, securing it in place with a toothpick. Pan fry or broil until browned and of desired doneness.

Serves 4.

CHEESE-BEEF PATTIES

1 pound ground beef
1½ teaspoons sea salt
⅛ teaspoon pepper

4 ounces smoked cheese (cut
  into 8 slices)

Mix together beef, salt, and pepper; shape into 8 patties. Put 2 slices of cheese between 2 patties, and press together, in sandwich fashion. Pan fry or broil on both sides until browned and of desired doneness.

Serves 4.

GRILLED BURGERS NAPOLI

1½ pounds lean ground beef
⅔ cup dietetic tomato sauce
1 teaspoon oregano
1 teaspoon sea salt

2 tablespoons garlic salt
⅛ teaspoon pepper
½ cup ricotta cheese

In a bowl, combine beef, tomato sauce, oregano, salt, garlic salt, and pepper. Form mixture into 12 flat thin patties. Spoon ricotta cheese onto 6 patties; top with remaining patties. Grease grill lightly. Place patties on grill. Cook 10-12 minutes, turning once.

Serves 6.

ITALIANO BURGERS

1½ pounds ground beef
½ cup tomato sauce
3 tablespoons garlic salt
1 teaspoon sea salt

6 anchovy fillets, minced
¼ teaspoon pepper
¼ cup chopped mushrooms
6 thin slices mozzarella cheese

In a bowl, combine beef, tomato sauce, garlic salt, salt, anchovies, pepper, and mushrooms. Shape mixture into 6 firm patties. Grease grill slightly. Cook 10 to 12 minutes, turning once, and top each hamburger with a slice of mozzarella cheese, then grill until done as desired.
Serves 6.

MIGNON IMITATIONS

1½ pounds finely ground sirloin
2 tablespoons garlic salt
1 teaspoon sea salt

3 crushed peppercorns
12 slices lean bacon
parsley sprigs

In a bowl, combine meat, garlic salt, salt, and peppercorns. Shape into 6 patties. Wrap 2 bacon slices around each pattie edge (use toothpicks to secure bacon). Lightly grease a grill. Cook patties 10-12 minutes. Garnish with parsley sprigs.
Serves 6.

TIJUANA BURGERS

1½ pounds lean ground beef
2½ teaspoons chili powder
½ cup dietetic catsup
¼ cup seeded, peeled, chopped
   red pepper

¼ teaspoon pepper
6 tablespoons hot mustard relish
3 tablespoons diced green onions

In a bowl, combine all ingredients except relish and onions and form into 6 patties. Grease grill lightly. Place patties on grill. Cook 10-12 minutes, until of desired doneness. Remove patties to platter. Top each patty with a tablespoon of relish. Spoon ½ tablespoon onion on each patty.
Serves 6.

BEEF AND OLIVE CASSEROLE

2 pounds beef chuck, cut into
  good-sized pieces
¼ cup soya carob flour
1 teaspoon sea salt
pepper
1 packet sugar substitute
½ teaspoon marjoram
2 tablespoons shortening

1 pound small whole white
  onions, peeled
8 to 10 tiny carrots, scraped
2 10½-ounce cans beef bouillon
1 cup pimento-stuffed green
  olives, drained
butter
flour

Dust beef with mixture of the flour, salt, pepper, sugar substitute, and marjoram. Brown meat on all sides in the shortening.
Place in a 2-quart casserole; add the onions and carrots. Add
bouillon. Cover, and bake in a moderate oven (350°) for about
1 ½ hours, or until meat and vegetables are almost tender. Add
olives and bake for another 20 minutes, or until very tender.
Pour off and measure juices. Thicken slightly with butter and
flour kneaded together (use 1 tablespoon of each for each cup
of sauce).

Makes about 6 servings.

BEEF POT PIE

2 pounds round steak, cut into
  1-inch cubes
salt and pepper to taste
flour as needed
4 tablespoons olive oil
2 tablespoons butter
4 cloves garlic, peeled
1 pound mushrooms, cut into
  halves
1 4-ounce can green chili

peppers, drained, seeded,
  and minced
¼ teaspoon marjoram
½ teaspoon dill weed
1 cup beef consommé or red
  table wine
1 tablespoon wine vinegar
2 cups cooked artichoke bottoms
Parmesan Biscuit Crust

Sprinkle meat with salt and pepper; roll in flour. In a large
heavy frying pan, heat oil and butter with garlic; brown meat.
Discard garlic and set meat aside. Add mushrooms to pan; cover
and simmer for about 7 minutes. Add chilis. Return meat to
pan; add marjoram, dill weed, consommé (or wine), and vinegar;
cover and simmer very slowly for 1½ hours, stirring occasionally.

Add artichokes. Pour into a deep 2½-quart casserole. Top with Parmesan biscuits and bake in a hot oven (400°) for 10 to 15 minutes, or until biscuits are well browned.

PARMESAN BISCUIT CRUST

Separate 1 8-ounce package of refrigerator biscuits; dip each biscuit in shredded Parmesan cheese. Place on top of meat and sprinkle lightly with dill weed.

PEPPER STEAK

1½ inch-thick round steak, cut into 1-inch cubes
¼ cup salad oil
3 egg-size onions, sliced
½ clove garlic
⅓ cup tomato sauce
⅓ cup white soya carob syrup

1 teaspoon sea salt
dash of pepper
pinch of thyme or basil
1½ cups water
3 medium-size green peppers, cut into ¾-inch squares

Heat oil in 10-inch heavy skillet. Add garlic and meat and brown slowly for about 15 minutes, stirring occasionally so meat browns on all sides. Add onions and let brown 5 minutes more. Now add tomato sauce, soya carob syrup, salt, pepper, thyme (or basil), and ½ cup of the water. Cover and simmer until meat is tender, from 50 to 60 minutes, stirring occasionally (add remaining water as liquid evaporates). Add cut-up green peppers. Cover and cook 15 to 20 minutes longer. This makes its own rich gravy. Serve hot with the meat.

EGGPLANT AND GROUND BEEF BAKE

1 medium-size eggplant, cut into ⅜-inch-thick slices
sea salt
2 tablespoons butter or margarine
½ pound ground beef

1 tablespoon parsley
½ small onion, chopped
¼ teaspoon pepper
2 tomatoes, peeled and sliced
⅓ cup water

Sprinkle eggplant lightly with salt and let stand a few minutes; then pat dry. Sauté in melted butter on both sides until golden brown. Remove from pan and set aside. Brown meat in the same pan, stirring until crumbly. Stir in parsley, onion, pepper, an additional ½ teaspoon salt, and tomatoes, and cook 10-15 minutes, until flavors are blended. Layer half the sautéed eggplant in a greased 9-inch square baking pan, pour the meat sauce over it, and then add the remaining eggplant. Stir water into the drippings in the pan and pour over the casserole. Bake, uncovered, in a preheated moderate oven (350°) for 35 minutes, or until eggplant is tender.

Serves 4.

HAMBURGER POT PIE

1 pound lean ground beef
1 tablespoon vegetable shortening
½ cup chopped onion
1 8-ounce can Spanish-style tomato sauce (without sugar)
1 20-ounce can green beans, drained

1 teaspoon sea salt
¼ teaspoon black pepper
⅛ teaspoon oregano
1 tablespoon white carob syrup
4 tablespoons heavy cream
2 Soya Carob Pie Crusts (*see* Index), sprinkled with onion salt

Prepare pie shells.

In a skillet, heat shortening; add ground beef, onion, cream, and syrup; stir, and cook until meat is browned. Stir in tomato sauce, green beans, seasonings. Pour into pastry-lined plate. Place top crust over pie filling. Fold top crust under edge of bottom crust. Seal and flute with fingers or fork. Cut slits in top crust and sprinkle with onion salt. Bake in a preheated oven at 400° for 25 minutes.

ITALIAN GREEN MACARONI AND MEAT SAUCE

1 pound can whole tomatoes
1 can tomato sauce (without sugar)
½ cup water
¼ teaspoon basil
1 teaspoon onion salt
¼ teaspoon oregano
¼ teaspoon garlic powder

1 teaspoon chili powder
¾ pound ground chuck or round, browned
1 8-ounce package of artichoke macaroni
3 quarts boiling water
2 teaspoons sea salt

Combine undrained tomatoes, tomato sauce, water, basil, onion salt, oregano, chili powder, and garlic powder. Heat to boiling point. Add beef. Cover and cook over low heat for 30 minutes, stirring occasionally.

Meanwhile, boil 3 quarts of water, add sea salt. When boiling rapidly, gradually add noodles so that the water continues to boil. Cook uncovered, stirring occasionally, until tender. Drain in colander. Serve with meat sauce.

ITALIAN SPAGHETTI AND MEAT SAUCE

2 pounds ground chuck
2 cans Spanish-style tomato sauce (without sugar)
½ teaspoon oregano
½ teaspoon sweet basil
¼ teaspoon garlic powder
1½ tablespoons hot sauce

salt and pepper to taste
4 ounces (½ package) artichoke macaroni
2 tablespoon butter (optional)
2 cups grated American or Cheddar cheese

Cook ground chuck in a heavy kettle with tight fitting cover at low temperature for 2 hours, stirring occasionally. Drain off excess fat. Add tomato sauce, oregano, sweet basil, garlic powder, hot sauce, salt and pepper. Mix well; cook for 10-15 minutes.

Bring to a boil 3 quarts of water. When boiling, gradually add macaroni while water continues to boil rapidly. Cook uncovered, stirring occasionally, until tender. Drain in colander. Add butter, salt, and pepper.

In a large greased casserole, place a layer of macaroni, a layer of cheese, and a layer of meat; add second layers of macaroni, cheese, meat. Cover and cook 30 minutes at 325°. Serve hot accompanied by tossed salad with vinegar-and-oil dressing.

MACARONI BEEF CASSEROLE

2 pounds ground beef
1 medium-size onion, chopped
½ cup butter or margarine
1 8-ounce package artichoke
    macaroni, cooked and
    drained
¼ cup dietetic catsup
¼ cup beef bouillon or water
1 cup shredded Cheddar cheese

⅓ cup chopped parsley
½ teaspoon pepper
½ teaspoon cinnamon
3 teaspoons sea salt
⅓ cup soya carob flour
2½ cups milk
1 teaspoon dry mustard
3 eggs, slightly beaten

Sauté ground beef and onion in 2 tablespoons of the butter until browned and crumbly. Combine with the cooked macaroni, catsup, bouillon, ½ cup of the cheese, parsley, pepper, cinnamon and 2 teaspoons of the salt. Turn into a greased 13-by-9-by-3-inch baking pan. Heat remaining 6 tablespoons butter; blend in flour, and cook until bubbly. Gradually stir in milk. Add remaining teaspoon salt and mustard, and cook, stirring constantly, until thickened. Gradually stir the hot mixture into the beaten eggs. Pour into casserole. Sprinkle with remaining ½ cup cheese. Bake, uncovered, in a preheated moderate oven (325°) for about 30 minutes; let stand for 15 minutes before serving.

Makes 8 to 10 servings.

TAMALE CASSEROLE

1 15-ounce can tamales in chili
    gravy
1 1-pound can whole tomatoes
3 tablespoons butter or
    margarine
1 small onion, sliced
2 teaspoons soya carob flour

½ teaspoon dried basil leaves
½ teaspoon dried tarragon
⅛ teaspoon dried red chili
    pepper
1 teaspoon sea salt
⅓ cup grated Parmesan cheese
chopped parsley

If tamales are in paper wrappers, remove and discard them. Place tamales in a 1½-quart shallow baking dish. Drain tomatoes, reserving ⅔ cup liquid. Arrange tomatoes over tamales. In a skillet, heat butter; sauté onion until tender (about 3 minutes). Combine flour and reserved tomato liquid; mix until smooth. Add to sautéed onion. Sprinkle basil, tarragon, chili pepper, and salt. Bring to a boil, stirring; pour over tamales. Sprinkle with Parmesan cheese. Bake in a preheated oven, uncovered, for 15 minutes, or until bubbly.

To serve, sprinkle with parsley.

Serves 4.

TAMALE PIE

3 cups water	¾ pound ground beef
2½ teaspoons sea salt	3 tablespoons fat or oil
1 cup cornmeal	1½ cups canned tomatoes
⅓ cup chopped onion	1½ teaspoons chili powder
½ cup chopped green pepper	

Add 1½ teaspoons of the salt to water and bring to a boil. Stir cornmeal slowly into rapidly boiling water, stirring occasionally until water is absorbed, then reduce heat and cook ½ minute longer. In a skillet, sauté onion, green pepper, and ground beef in fat (or oil), cooking until onion is tender and meat is brown. Add tomatoes, 1 teaspoon salt, and chili powder; cook until thoroughly heated. Stir in the cornmeal mixture. Pour into greased 9 by 9 baking pan and bake in a preheated oven at 400° for 1 hour.

Serves 6.

BEEF 'N BEAN PLATTER

3 pound boneless rolled pot roast	1 cup water
2 tablespoons shortening	¼ teaspoon garlic powder
1½ cups dried soy beans	½ cup sliced stuffed olives
1 cup tomato sauce (without sugar)	1 large bay leaf
	1 tablespoon soya carob flour (optional)

Soak soy beans 6 to 8 hours, then wash 6 times. Heat pressure cooker and add shortening. Brown roast on all sides. Turn heat selector to "off"; pour off fat. Add remaining ingredients. Close cooker securely; place pressure regulator on vent pipe. Cook at 15 pounds pressure for 1 hour. Turn off; let pressure drop to normal of its own accord. Remove bay leaf; place meat and beans on platter. To thicken sauce, add soya carob flour and bring to a boil, stirring constantly. Serve with meat.

Makes 6 servings and about 2 cups sauce.

BEEF BRISKET AND ONION SAUCE

3 pound beef brisket	1½ teaspoons sea salt
boiling water	3 whole cloves
1 small onion, diced	1 egg, slightly beaten
1 carrot, diced	½ cup dry soya-bread crumbs
3 whole black peppercorns	

Cover meat with boiling water; add vegetables and seasonings. Simmer until tender (about 3 hours). Remove meat from stock (reserving it); place in shallow baking dish. Spread egg over meat and sprinkle with bread crumbs. Bake in a preheated oven at 400° for 20 minutes or until brown.

Make an onion sauce with 1 cup of the reserved liquid; serve with the meat.

Yield: 6 servings.

ONION SAUCE

1½ tablespoons melted butter	1 cup of reserved liquid
½ cup finely chopped onion	1 teaspoon Worcestershire sauce
1½ tablespoons soya carob flour	¼ teaspoon sea salt

In a frying pan combine butter and onion, cook for 10 minutes. Blend flour gradually into mixture. Add liquid and Worcestershire sauce. Cook slowly, stirring constantly until thickened. Sprinkle with salt. Yields approximately 1 cup.

SMOKED BRISKET

1 ounce liquid smoke	barbecue spice to taste (without
1 4-pound brisket	sugar)
salt and pepper to taste	¼ cup water

Pour liquid smoke over brisket. Place in tightly covered container or wrap in plastic wrap or aluminum foil; store in refrigerator overnight. Place in roasting pan and sprinkle with salt and pepper. Add barbecue spice; then add water. Roast at 250° for 4 hours.

Serves 8.

BEEF POT ROAST WITH LEMON

3- to 4-pound beef pot roast	½ teaspoon pepper
2 tablespoons vegetable	½ small clove garlic
shortening	4 lemon slices
½ cup lemon juice	½ teaspoon sea salt
2 tablespoons chopped onion	pinch of thyme
½ teaspoon celery salt	

Combine all ingredients except roast and shortening for sauce. Cover and let stand overnight. Brown roast in shortening; then add sauce. Bake in preheated 250° oven for 3 hours.

CHINESE POT ROAST

3 to 4 pound chuck roast	1 medium onion, quartered
1 tablespoon soy sauce	1 large head cabbage, cut into
½ cup water	1-inch slices

In a heavy skillet or Dutch oven, brown roast on all sides. Add soy sauce, onion and water; cover. Simmer slowly until meat is tender (about 3 hours). Remove meat from pot. Add cabbage to liquid. Cook cabbage until just tender, about 10 minutes. Slice meat and surround the slices with cabbage.

Serves 6-8.

EYE ROUND ROAST

6-pound eye round roast
3-4 slices bacon, cut into small
    pieces
2-3 cloves garlic, slivered
1½ teaspoons sea salt
½ teaspoon black pepper
½ teaspoon basil

2-3 teaspoons olive oil
4 tablespoons butter
2 large onions, diced
2 tablespoons paprika
3 tomatoes, diced
2 green peppers, sliced
½ to 1 cup water

With a sharp knife, make 25 to 30 incisions in the meat. Place a piece of bacon and a sliver of garlic in each incision. Rub the roast on all sides with salt and pepper, basil, and the olive oil. Wrap in foil and refrigerate 4 or 5 hours or overnight.

In a Dutch oven, melt the butter; add the onions and cook just until limp. Add paprika, blending well. Place roast on plastic cooking wrap (or in casserole) and pour onion mixture over roast, then wrap (or cover) and put in preheated oven at 400° for 15 minutes. Reduce heat to 200° and cook for 4 or 5 hours (until well done). Then 20 minutes before serving, in another pan cook green peppers in water for 15 minutes; add tomatoes and cook until tender. Return roast and onions to Dutch oven and simmer for 20 minutes. Remove the roast and cut into thin slices. Serve on a heated platter, surrounded by the vegetables.

MARINATED POT ROAST

4 pound rump roast
½ teaspoon pepper
½ teaspoon ground cloves
½ teaspoon mace
½ teaspoon allspice
1 tablespoon sea salt

½ cup water
1 medium onion, chopped
1 or 2 cloves garlic, chopped
¼ cup salad oil
2 tablespoons lemon juice
3 tablespoons vinegar

Mix together pepper, cloves, mace, allspice, and salt; rub into meat. Place in covered roasting pan; add water. Cover meat with onion and garlic. Mix together salad oil, lemon juice, and vinegar, and drizzle over meat. Marinate meat for at least 4 hours, turning every hour. Bake in preheated oven at 250° for 5 hours.

PEKING ROAST

4 pound beef roast	2 cups strong black
1-2 cloves garlic	decaffeinated coffee
1 onion, cut up into chunks	2 cups water
1 cup vinegar	salt and pepper to taste
oil	

Cut deep slits in roast; insert garlic and onion in slits. Pour vinegar over roast. Refrigerate for 24 hours. Place small amount of oil in Dutch oven. Add roast and brown on all sides. Pour coffee over meat; add water. Cover; simmer on top of stove for 4 to 6 hours. Season with salt and pepper 15 minutes before serving.

RUMP ROAST I

1 4-pound boneless rump roast	black pepper
2 tablespoons vegetable	cayenne
shortening	2 tablespoons soya carob flour
meat tenderizer	8-10 ounces water

In a heavy skillet, melt shortening. Sprinkle all sides of roast well with tenderizer, black pepper, and cayenne. Brown meat on all sides in hot skillet, then lay on plastic cooking wrap (or in casserole) suet side up. Add flour to skillet; stir to brown well; add water, and cook until gravy is thickened, stirring constantly so it does not lump. Pour over roast. Seal wrap (or cover casserole). Cook in preheated oven at 300° for 30 minutes, then reduce temperature to 200° and continue to cook for 4 to 5 hours longer (slow temperature tenderizes the meat). Remove roast from oven and lay on a platter. Put gravy into a covered pan in freezer and chill until fat is firm and can be removed from the top. Pour gravy over roast and reheat before serving.

RUMP ROAST II

3- to 4-pound boneless rump roast	⅓ cup vinegar
½ teaspoon black pepper	water as needed
2 tablespoons vegetable shortening	3 small onions
	1 bay leaf
	1 tablespoon sea salt

Sprinkle meat with black pepper. Brown on all sides in shortening; add vinegar and enough water to cover meat. Add whole onions, bay leaf, and salt. Cover, and simmer for 3 hours, or until tender.

Yield: 6 to 8 servings.

BEEF TENDERLOIN PLUS

1 3-pound tenderloin	½ cup melted butter
½ teaspoon garlic salt	5 small onions, cut in rings
1 teaspoon sea salt	5 tablespoons butter
½ teaspoon pepper	

Let meat come to room temperature. Pierce holes in it with a fork. Combine garlic salt, salt, pepper, and the half-cup butter. Spread half the mixture on the roast. Brush a hot barbecue grill with oil. Place roast on grill, 4 to 5 inches from hot coals. Grill 20-30 minutes, then brush with remaining marinade and turn. Grill 1 to 1½ hours more. Place on a platter.

In a frying pan on the edge of the grill, cook the onion rings in remaining butter until tender. Slice meat in ½-inch-thick pieces; top with onions.

Serves 6.

BEEF AND ONIONS

1 pound round steak	½ pound large onions, cut into thick slices
1½ teaspoons sea salt	
dash of pepper	2 tablespoons soya carob flour
3 tablespoons shortening	1 teaspoon white carob syrup
1 cup water	

Season meat with salt and pepper, and brown on both sides in shortening heated in a heavy skillet or Dutch oven. Add ¼ cup water. Cover tightly and simmer gently 1 to 1½ hours (or until meat is almost tender). Add remaining water, ¼ cup at a time, as needed, to keep utensil from going dry. Push meat to one side and carefully place onions in the drippings. Cover and simmer 20 to 30 minutes longer, or until meat is tender and onions are transparent. Carefully transfer meat and onions to a platter; cover, and keep warm. Combine flour and carob syrup and stir into drippings. Heat to boiling and pour over meat and onions.

HORSERADISH STEAK

1 3-pound 2-inch-thick sirloin steak	3 tablespoons horseradish
1½ tablespoons lemon juice	¾ cup Chili Sauce (*see* Index)
1 teaspoon garlic salt	2 tablespoons melted butter
1 teaspoon onion salt	parsley sprigs

Let steak come to room temperature and slash fatty edge to keep meat from curling during cooking. Place on a deep platter. In a bowl, combine lemon juice, garlic salt, onion salt, horseradish, and chili sauce. Pierce holes in steak with a fork. Spread mixture evenly on steak. Let stand one hour. Brush hot grill with oil. Place steak on barbecue grill 6 inches from hot coals. Pour marinade into a cup. Grill steak 15-20 minutes; brush with marinade; turn. Grill until steak is done as desired. Place on platter; brush with melted butter.

Let stand for 5 minutes before slicing. Garnish with parsley sprigs.

Serves 6.

ITALIAN ROUND SPECIAL

1 3-pound 1-inch-thick round
steak
⅔ cup oil
⅓ cup vinegar
½ teaspoon sea salt
½ teaspoon white carob syrup

¼ teaspoon pepper
⅜ cup tomato juice
1 cup minced onion
2 garlic cloves, minced
2 tablespoons butter
1 teaspoon marjoram

Let steak come to room temperature and slash fatty edge of meat to prevent curling during cooking. Place on a deep platter. In a bowl, combine oil, vinegar, salt, carob syrup, pepper and tomato juice. Pierce holes in steak with a fork. Spread mixture over steak evenly. Let stand 1 hour. Pour marinade into cup. Brush hot barbecue grill with oil. Place steak on grill 6 inches from hot coals. Grill 10-15 minutes; brush with marinade; turn. Grill until steak is done as desired. Place on a platter.

While steak is grilling, cook onion and garlic in butter until tender in a frying pan on edge of grill. Add marjoram and balance of marinade; cook 10 minutes longer. Pour mixture over steak. Let stand 5 minutes before serving.

Serves 6.

LONDON MUSHROOM BROIL

1 3-pound 1½-inch-thick London
broil
2 tablespoons oil
2 tablespoons lemon juice
¼ teaspoon pepper
dash cayenne
1 tablespoon celery salt

½ teaspoon dry mustard
2 tablespoons vinegar
2 tablespoons butter
1 small onion, minced
1 pound chopped fresh
mushrooms

Place steak on a large platter and let come to room temperature. In a bowl, combine oil, lemon juice, pepper, cayenne, celery salt, dry mustard, and vinegar. Pierce holes in steak with a fork, and spread mixture evenly over steak. Let stand for 1 hour. Brush hot barbecue grill with oil. In a frying pan cook onion in butter on edge of grill until tender. Add mushrooms; cook for 5 minutes.

Pour marinade into a cup. Place steak on grill, 6 inches from hot coals. Grill 10-15 minutes; brush with marinade; turn. Grill until steak is done as desired.

Place on a platter. Let stand 5 minutes before slicing. Slice across the grain in 1-inch strips. Top with mushroom-onion mixture, and serve immediately.

Serves 6.

MEXICAN ROUND

1 3-pound 1½-inch-thick round steak	1 teaspoon sea salt
½ cup oil	2 teaspoons chili powder
⅓ cup vinegar	1 teaspoon oregano
1 packet sugar substitute	¼ teaspoon garlic powder
	⅛ teaspoon hot sauce

Let steak come to room temperature and slash fatty edge (to keep meat from curling during cooking). Place on a deep platter. In a bowl, combine oil, vinegar, sugar substitute, salt, chili powder, oregano, garlic powder, and hot sauce. Pierce holes in steak with a fork. Spread mixture evenly over steak. Let stand 1 hour.

Pour marinade into a cup. Brush hot barbecue grill with oil. Place steak on grill 6 inches from hot coals. Grill 20 to 30 minutes, then brush with marinade, and turn. Grill steak to desired doneness.

Place on a platter. Let stand 5 minutes before serving.

Serves 6.

GRILLED PEPPER STEAK

3 rib-steak eyes, each 2 inches thick	½ teaspoon onion salt
3 teaspoons dry mustard	4 large, trimmed, seeded red peppers, cut into rings
½ cup warm water	2 tablespoons butter
1 teaspoon garlic salt	

Let steak come to room temperature and slash fatty edge to prevent meat from curling during cooking. Place on a deep platter. In a bowl, combine mustard, water, garlic salt, and onion salt. Pierce holes in steak with a fork. Spread mixture on steak and let stand for 1 hour. Brush hot barbecue grill with oil. Place steak on grill, 6 inches above hot coals. Grill 15-20 minutes. Brush steak with marinade; turn. Grill until steak is done as desired. While steak is grilling, cook red pepper rings until tender in butter in a frying pan at edge of grill.

Place steak on a platter and top with sautéed pepper rings. Let stand for 5 minutes before serving.

Serves 6.

SIRLOIN BROIL

1 3-pound 1½-inch-thick sirloin steak	½ teaspoon garlic salt
⅔ cup oil	¼ teaspoon pepper
¼ cup vinegar	3 tablespoons butter
½ teaspoon sea salt	2 large onions, sliced into rings
½ packet sugar substitute	1 6-ounce can drained whole
½ teaspoon thyme	mushrooms

Let steak come to room temperature and slash fatty edge to keep meat from curling during cooking. Place steak on a deep platter; pierce with a fork. In a small bowl, combine oil, vinegar, sea salt, sugar substitute, thyme, garlic salt, and pepper. Pour mixture over steak; cover. Let stand for one hour. Brush hot barbecue grill with oil; place steak on it, 6 inches above coals. Pour marinade into a deep cup. Grill steak 15 to 20 minutes. Brush with marinade; turn. Grill until steak is done as desired.

While steak is grilling, melt butter in a frying pan on edge of grill; add mushrooms, onions, and leftover marinade. Cover and cook until vegetables are soft, then remove from grill; keep warm.

Place on a platter and pour mushroom mixture over it. Let stand for 5 minutes before slicing.

Serves 6.

SIRLOIN STEAK BARBECUE

1-inch-thick sirloin steak (3 or 4 pounds)	1 tablespoon prepared horseradish
seasoned meat tenderizer	½ teaspoon sea salt
½ cup minced onion	¼ teaspoon pepper
½ cup oil	1 garlic clove, minced or mashed
½ cup fresh lemon juice	2 bay leaves
1 tablespoon dietetic catsup	

Sprinkle steak with tenderizer. To make barbecue sauce, sauté onions in oil until limp, then stir in remaining ingredients. Cook 10 minutes; cool. Pour sauce over steak and let marinate at room temperature for 30 minutes. Charcoal broil, turning while cooking and basting with remaining marinade, to preferred doneness.

PEPPERCORN SIRLOIN BROIL

1 3-pound 2-inch-thick sirloin steak	1 teaspoon garlic salt
3 tablespoons oil	1 teaspoon onion salt
3 tablespoons vinegar	4 tablespoons crushed peppercorns
1 packet sugar substitute	2 tablespoons melted butter

Let steak come to room temperature and slash fatty edge to keep meat from curling during cooking. Place on a deep platter. In a bowl combine oil, vinegar, sugar substitute, garlic salt, and onion salt. With a sharp knife, cut 1-inch slits in meat and insert crushed peppercorns. Brush marinade evenly on steak, reserving balance. Let stand 1 hour. Brush hot barbecue grill with oil. Place steak on grill, 6 inches from hot coals. Grill 20 to 30 minutes. Brush with marinade; turn. Grill until steak is done as desired.

Place on a warm platter; brush with melted butter; let stand for 5 minutes before slicing.

Serves 6.

POPPY SEED SIRLOIN BROIL

1 3-pound ½-inch-thick sirloin steak	2 tablespoons carob flour
2 tablespoons poppy seeds	¼ cup hot water
⅓ cup white carob syrup	2 tablespoons butter
½ teaspoon ginger	2 green onions, cut into 1½-inch strips
1 cup soy sauce	1 clove garlic, minced

In a bowl, combine poppy seeds, carob syrup, ginger, and soy sauce. Blend flour and water together in a separate bowl, and add to sauce, mixing in well.

Place steak on a deep platter and pour prepared sauce mixture over it. Let stand 1 hour, turning steak once. Cook onions and garlic in butter in a frying pan on edge of grill until tender. Grease barbecue grill slightly. Place steak on grill; pour marinade sauce into a cup. Cook steak 8-10 minutes, basting with sauce and turning as needed. Remove to a heated platter; pour onion-garlic mixture over it; let stand for 5 minutes before serving.

Serves 6.

FRUIT FRANK* KABOBS

6 frankfurters	3 tablespoons lemon juice
½ cup dietetic catsup	2 ripe tomatoes, wedged
2 packets sugar substitute	1 8-ounce can drained unsweetened pineapple chunks
1 teaspoon ginger	
2 tablespoons soy sauce	

In a bowl, combine catsup, sugar substitute, ginger, soy sauce, and lemon juice. Cut each frankfurter into 4 pieces. Place frankfurters and tomatoes in a deep bowl and pour catsup mixture over them; let stand for 30 minutes. Remove tomatoes and frankfurters; pour sauce into a cup. Lightly grease 6 skewers. Thread frankfurter pieces, pineapple chunks, and tomatoes alternately on skewers. Brush with half the sauce. Grease barbecue grill lightly. Place skewers 5 inches from coals. Turning frequently, cook until frankfurters are brown. Remove to a platter, brush with remaining sauce.

Serves 6.

---

*Select frankfurters that do not have sugar added.

Liver

ITALIAN BAKED LIVER WITH
MUSHROOM-OLIVE SAUCE

2 pounds sliced beef liver
1 medium onion, chopped
1 clove garlic, minced or mashed
1 tablespoon soya carob flour
½ cup dietetic catsup
1 teaspoon minced parsley
½ cup chopped celery
½ cup chopped green pepper
1 8-ounce can mushrooms
    (stems and pieces)

1 4-ounce can pitted ripe olives
2 tablespoons oil
1 8-ounce can tomato sauce
    (without sugar)
1 cup water
1 teaspoon oregano
1 teaspoon sea salt
½ teaspoon pepper

Place liver slices in a greased baking pan or dish (about 9 by 13 inches). Combine all the other ingredients, mixing well until thoroughly blended, and pour over liver. Bake, uncovered, in a preheated moderate oven (350°) for 30 to 40 minutes, or until tender.

Makes 6 to 8 servings.

LEMONY SAUTÉED LIVER

1½ pounds beef liver, sliced in
    2 x ½ inch strips
¼ cup oil
½ cup sliced onion

¾ teaspoon sea salt
black pepper
1 ounce lemon juice
⅓ cup chopped parsley

Heat oil in large skillet; add onions and sauté until golden brown, then remove to paper towel and cover. Add liver to skillet and sauté quickly over medium heat, stirring frequently, until browned on both sides. Season with salt and pepper. Sprinkle with lemon juice and parsley, and toss. Arrange on serving platter. Top with onions.

LIVER LOAF

1 pound liver	½ pound pork sausage
1 medium-size onion, chopped	1 cup dry soya-bread crumbs
1 teaspoon soy sauce	1 teaspoon sea salt
1 teaspoon celery seed	dash of pepper
2 eggs, beaten	4 slices bacon

Cover liver with hot water; simmer for 5 minutes; drain, reserving ½ cup of the stock. Put liver and onion through food chopper, using medium blade. Blend with liver stock and all the remaining ingredients except bacon. Place in 10-by-5-by-2-inch loaf pan. Top with bacon slices. Bake in a preheated oven at 350° for 1 hour, or until brown.

Ham

HAM LOAF

1 pound ground ham	cloves
1 pound ground chuck	1 teaspoon ground mustard
1 cup soya bread crumbs	2 tablespoons cider vinegar
1 cup milk	2 tablespoons white carob syrup
1 egg, beaten	½ cup pineapple juice

Combine ground ham, beef, bread crumbs, milk, and egg. Press into loaf pan. Stick cloves in top. Combine carob syrup, pineapple juice, and mustard; mix well, and pour over meat mixture. Bake in a preheated oven at 350° for 45 minutes to 1 hour.

HAM-MACARONI CASSEROLE

1½ cups elbow-style artichoke
    macaroni
4 quarts boiling salted water
¼ cup butter or margarine
2 eggs, separated

1½ cups cooked ham, coarsely
    chopped
6 tablespoons grated Parmesan
    cheese

TOMATO-MUSHROOM SAUCE

1 8-ounce can tomato sauce
    (without sugar)
¼ cup water
1 tablespoon lemon juice

1½ teaspoons chopped chives or
    sliced green-onion tops
1 3- or 4-ounce can mushroom
    slices, drained

Cook the macaroni in the boiling water for about 15 minutes; drain and let cool.

Cream butter; add the egg yolks and ham; mix together, then mix thoroughly with the cooked macaroni. Beat the egg whites until they form stiff peaks, then quickly mix them into the macaroni. Turn into a buttered 2-quart casserole; sprinkle top with cheese. Bake, uncovered, in a preheated moderately hot oven (375°) for about 45 minutes or until nicely browned.

In a small pan, combine tomato sauce, the quarter-cup water, lemon juice, onions, and mushrooms; heat through thoroughly. Serve warm to spoon over casserole.

Makes 4 servings.

STUFFED BELL PEPPERS

8 bell peppers
2 small onions, chopped
2 tablespoons butter
2 cups cracker crumbs (or 1
    cup soya carob bread
    crumbs)

1 small can tomatoes
½ cup chopped ham
salt and pepper to taste

Chop up 2 of the peppers and with the onions sauté in butter until well done. Add tomatoes, cracker crumbs, and chopped ham. Scald peppers and stuff with mixture; sprinkle with cracker crumbs. Brush with butter. Bake in a greased casserole in a preheated, moderately hot (375°) oven for about 35 minutes.

Veal

GRILLED VEAL

3 pounds lean veal, cut into
  ½-inch-thick cubes
1 cup dietetic catsup
½ teaspoon grated lemon rind
3 tablespoons oil
3 tablespoons vinegar
1 teaspoon sea salt
⅛ teaspoon pepper
2 cored, seeded red peppers,
  cut into 2-inch strips

12 small white onions, peeled
⅛ cup minced green onions
½ cup minced celery
2 tablespoons mashed capers
2 cloves garlic, finely chopped
½ pound bacon
5 tablespoons butter

In a bowl, combine catsup, lemon rind, oil, vinegar, salt, and pepper. Place veal cubes, red peppers, and white onions on a deep platter. Pierce holes in cubes with a fork. Cover with catsup mixture and let stand for 1 hour. In a frying pan on edge of barbecue grill, cook green onion, celery, capers, and garlic in butter until tender. Remove cubes and vegetables from platter and pour sauce into a cup. Wrap cubes in bacon. Grease 6 skewers lightly and thread bacon-wrapped cubes alternately with red peppers and onions on skewers. Combine green-onion mixture with catsup sauce and brush over skewer combinations. Cook for 18 to 20 minutes, brushing with sauce frequently and turning. Remove to a platter.

Serves 6.

COLD ROAST VEAL LOAF

1½ pound ground veal
½ pound ground pork
2 eggs
½ cup soya carob bread crumbs
2 tablespoons prepared mustard
1 teaspoon dried basil
1½ teaspoons sea salt
½ teaspoon pepper

dash hot sauce
½ cup finely chopped onion
¼ cup finely chopped green
  pepper
1 tablespoon chopped parsley
1 lemon, thinly sliced
6 slices bacon

Preheat oven to 350°. In a large bowl, combine eggs, bread crumbs, mustard, basil, salt, pepper, hot sauce, onion, green pepper, and parsley; beat with fork until well blended. Let stand 5 minutes. Add veal and pork; mix well. Line a 13-by-9-by-1¾-inch pan with foil (use a piece long enough to hang over ends). Turn mixture into pan; shape with hands into a loaf 8 inches long and 4 inches wide. Lay lemon slices on top, overlapping them, and top with bacon slices, placed lengthwise. Bake, uncovered, 1 hour and 15 minutes. Let cool, in pan, on a wire rack for 30 minutes. Lift out meat loaf with foil to serving platter; refrigerate for several hours, covered, until well chilled.

Serve with mustard and garnish with salad greens and sliced tomatoes, if desired.

Makes 8 servings.

Lamb

LAMB RIB BARBECUE

6 pounds breast of lamb	¼ cup tupelo honey*
1 8-ounce can tomato sauce (without sugar)	1 teaspoon sea salt
	⅛ cup prepared mustard

Trim excess fat from riblets. Grease grill lightly. Cook riblets on grill 4 inches from heat for 6 to 8 minutes, or until browned. Remove to a platter. Cut riblets into 3-inch strips.

Combine tomato sauce, honey, salt, and mustard in a bowl, and pour over riblets. Let stand 30 minutes. Place strips on a large piece of aluminum foil. Close package securely. Place on grill 4 inches from heat. Cook for 30 to 45 minutes, or until done as desired. Remove meat to a platter. Top with its sauce.

Serves 6.

---

*Tupelo honey is produced only about 6 weeks each year from tupelo groves in Florida's Everglades. It has remarkable nutritional value, a deliciously distinctive flavor, and is the one honey that will not crystallize. Its high content of fruit sugars makes it the only honey some people on restricted diets can use.

LAMBCHOP-AND-GREEN-SOYBEAN CASSEROLE

6 rib or shoulder lamb chops (about ½ inch thick)	2 cans green soybeans, drained
sea salt	2 cans whole tomatoes
pepper	½ teaspoon dried basil leaves
	¼ teaspoon thyme

Wipe lamb chops with damp paper towels; sprinkle lightly with salt and pepper. Arrange on broiler rack; broil, 4 inches from heat, 5 minutes on each side, or until of desired doneness.

Meanwhile, in medium saucepan, combine soybeans, tomatoes (1 can undrained and 1 can drained), the herbs, 1 teaspoon salt and ⅛ teaspoon pepper; mix well, breaking up tomatoes slightly with spoon. Bring to boiling; reduce heat, and simmer for 15 minutes. Turn onto heated serving platter. Arrange chops on top. Sprinkle with chopped parsley.

Serves 4-6.

LAMB EGGPLANT CASSEROLE

1½ pounds lean lamb, cut into ½-inch cubes	⅛ teaspoon cinnamon
1 large onion, coarsely chopped	2 teaspoons sea salt
2 small tomatoes, peeled, diced and drained	1 medium-size eggplant, peeled and cut into ¾-inch wedges
¼ cup sliced almonds	butter as needed
½ teaspoon pepper	1 8-ounce can tomato sauce (without sugar)

Mix together lamb cubes, onion, tomatoes, almonds, pepper, cinnamon, and 1 teaspoon of the salt. Spoon into a buttered 2-quart casserole. Lightly brown eggplant on both sides in butter, then arrange over the meat mixture. Season tomato sauce with remaining teaspoon salt, and pour over casserole. Bake, uncovered, in a moderately slow oven (325°) for 2 hours.

Serves 4.

LAMB-STUFFED EGGPLANT WEDGES

1 large eggplant, unpeeled, cut
lengthwise into 4 wedges
3 tablespoons butter or
margarine
¾ pound ground lamb
1 small onion, chopped
5 tablespoons finely chopped
green pepper

2 tablespoons minced parsley
sea salt
¼ teaspoon garlic salt
1 8-ounce can tomato sauce
(without sugar)
thin tomato and onion wedges

Sprinkle eggplant with sea salt. Let stand for about 1 hour, then wipe wedges dry. Melt butter in frying pan and lightly brown cut surfaces of eggplant wedges. Place, skin side down, on a greased baking sheet and bake in a preheated hot oven (400°) for 10 minutes.

Meanwhile, make filling: Add to pan in which the eggplant was browned the lamb, chopped onion, 4 tablespoons of the green pepper, parsley, ½ teaspoon salt, and garlic salt. Cook, stirring, constantly, until lightly browned.

Split eggplant sections from end to end to make a pocket, running knife down through apex of the wedge. Press pocket open with a spoon and fill with meat mixture, pressing it in firmly. Pour tomato sauce into a shallow casserole (about 9 inches square). Set filled eggplant wedges, skin side down, in sauce. Top each wedge with alternating slices of tomato and onion, and sprinkle with remaining chopped green pepper. Bake, uncovered, in a preheated, moderately hot oven (375°) for 30 minutes.

Serves 4.

Deer or Venison

Deer meat is one of the most delicious of all big game animals. It is much like beef, except that the lean is sweeter and the fat is stronger. The scent glands should be removed as soon as the deer is skinned. There are four sets of glands or "kernels" on the legs; two are found under the forelegs, and there are two on each thigh. They are brownish, yellow or red in color, and oval or round in shape. Glands of this type are also found along the small of the back. Thorough removal of all fat will also assure removal of the scent glands and, consequently, assure more mild flavor in the cooked game.

BARBECUED VENISON TENDERLOIN

1 deer tenderloin	2 tablespoons butter
1 cup dietetic catsup	2 tablespoons grated onion
½ cup chopped celery	½ cup water
2 tablespoons water	1½ teaspoons sea salt

Cut tenderloin into 1¾-inch-thick slices. Trim off any fat or tough membrane. Heat butter in a skillet and brown slices of deer quickly on both sides. Meanwhile, in a small pan, combine remaining ingredients; pour over hot meat. Place, uncovered, in a moderate oven (250°) and bake for 1½ hours, basting meat occasionally with the sauce. Turn once during baking.

Serves 4.

BRAISED VENISON IN MUSHROOM GRAVY

4 good-sized loin chops	1 8-ounce can of mushroom
1¾ teaspoons sea salt	soup
pepper	1 teaspoon sherry extract (or ¼
3 tablespoons butter	cup sherry wine)
1 cup water	2 drops hot sauce

Wipe chops clean with a damp cloth and trim off any strong-smelling fat. Sprinkle with salt and pepper. Using a skillet with a tight-fitting lid, brown chops slowly—but uncovered—on both sides in hot butter. Add ¼ cup of the water; cover, and simmer for 15 minutes. Add the rest of the water and the soup. Cover, and continue cooking very slowly for half an hour (or until fork tender). Add sherry extract and hot sauce.

Serve at once.

Serves 4.

BROILED TENDERLOIN OF VENISON

2¼ pounds deer tenderloin   2 tablespoons butter
2½ teaspoons sea salt   ½ cup hot water
  pepper

Wipe tenderloin clean with a damp cloth and cut into 1½- to 1¾-inch slices. Remove any strong smelling fat or tough membrane; flatten slightly with rolling pin. Sprinkle with salt and pepper and place on a hot, greased broiler rack, 3 or 4 inches from heat. Broil for 8 minutes on each side for medium rare. Remove from broiler; add some of the butter to each slice.

To make gravy, pour water over broiler rack and scrape any residue into drip pan. Serve immediately.

Serves 8.

PAN-BROILED VENISON CHOPS

5 venison loin chops, cut ½-inch   dash of pepper
    thick (approx. 2 pounds)   ¼ cup butter
1½ teaspoons sea salt   ¼ cup hot water

Wipe chops clean with a damp cloth. Trim off any strong-smelling fat, then sprinkle with salt and pepper. Heat butter in skillet. Brown chops slowly on both sides, then lower heat and cook slowly for 6 minutes on one side. Turn, and cook on the other side 6 minutes longer. Remove to a hot platter and cover to keep warm. Add hot water to pan and thoroughly scrape loose all brown residue from bottom; heat liquid to boiling and pour over meat or into a heated gravy boat. Serve immediately.

Serves 5.

POULTRY

BAKED ALMOND CHICKEN

1 broiler-fryer (about 3½ pounds), cut up
¼ cup soya carob flour (approx.)
1 teaspoon celery salt
1 teaspoon paprika
1 teaspoon sea salt
½ teaspoon curry powder
½ teaspoon oregano

½ teaspoon pepper
7 tablespoons melted butter or margarine
¾ cup sliced almonds
1½ cups light cream
½ cup sour cream
3 tablespoons fine dry soya-bread crumbs

Coat chicken pieces with flour. Blend celery salt, paprika, sea salt, curry powder, oregano, and pepper with 6 tablespoons of the butter (or margarine); roll chicken pieces in seasoned butter, coating all sides; arrange in a baking dish (about 9 by 13 inches), and sprinkle evenly with almonds. Pour light cream between pieces. Bake, covered, in a preheated moderate oven (350°) for 45 minutes.

Spoon about ½ cup sauce (from pan) into the sour cream and mix together. Pour evenly over chicken; sprinkle with bread crumbs blended with remaining tablespoon butter. Bake, uncovered, about 15 minutes longer, or until chicken is tender.
Serves 6.

BARBECUED CHICKEN

2 2-pound halved broiler-fryers
2 tablespoons butter
¼ cup chopped green onions
¾ cup dietetic catsup
2 tablespoons lime juice
1 teaspoon sea salt

⅛ teaspoon pepper
¼ tablespoon red pepper flakes
2 tablespoons garlic salt
lime slices
parsley sprigs

Wash chicken; dry with paper toweling and place on a platter. In a frying pan on edge of barbecue grill, cook onion in butter until tender, then remove to a bowl and combine with catsup, lime juice, salt, pepper, red pepper flakes and garlic salt. Let stand for 15 minutes. Pour sauce over chicken and refrigerate.

Let stand 1 hour, turning once. Place chicken, skin side up, on a grill 5 inches from heat. Pour sauce into a cup. Let the chicken cook on this side 10 to 15 minutes. Brush with more sauce and turn. Watch carefully after turning to be sure skin does not become charred and black. Brush liberally with sauce and turn several times to get an even browning. Be sure not to overcook or your broiler will be dry and tasteless. Test for doneness with a sharp fork at the thigh joint. If the juice still runs pink the chicken needs a little more cooking. If it is colorless, the chicken is done. Remove from grill to a platter and garnish with lime slices and parsley.

Serves 6.

BUTTER-BAKED CHICKEN

1 large fryer, washed and cut up	3 tablespoons chopped chives
salt and pepper to taste	1 tablespoon dry parsley
paprika	½ stick butter

Salt and pepper chicken pieces well. Place fat side up in plastic cooking bags or in aluminum-foil-lined pan. Sprinkle with paprika, chopped chives, and parsley. Dot with butter. Close the foil or plastic securely. Bake in preheated 375° oven for about 1 hour. Remove chicken when done and cover to keep warm.

Add water to browned stock and liquid and fat parts that are loose in pan (around neck, back, etc.) Reserve for cooking noodles or dumplings made from soya carob flour. Also delicious when added to chicken soup.

BREAST OF CHICKEN PROVENCALE

4 halves chicken breasts, skinned and boned	1 can whole tomatoes
2 tablespoons salad or olive oil	½ teaspoon sea salt
1 small onion, sliced	¼ teaspoon pepper
½ teaspoon oregano	1 2-ounce can anchovy fillets
½ teapoon dried thyme leaves	4 slices soy bread
	6 black olives, halved

In hot oil in a large skillet, sauté onion, oregano, and thyme, stirring, for about 5 minutes. Wipe chicken breasts with damp cloth or paper towels; cut in half lengthwise. Add to skillet; sauté over high heat for 5 minutes, turning once. Add tomatoes (with their juice), salt, and pepper. Let cook, uncovered, over high heat for 25 minutes or until chicken is tender.

Meanwhile, drain anchovies, reserving oil. Brush one side of each bread slice with anchovy oil; toast under broiler. On each slice of toast, arrange anchovies and olives. Turn chicken and sauce into serving dish and surround with toast.

Serves 4.

CHICKEN-AND-ARTICHOKE CASSEROLE

2 broiler-fryers (about 3 pounds each) cut up
1-2 sprigs parsley
1 celery top
1 carrot, quartered
1 bay leaf
2 teaspoons thyme

1 tablespoon sea salt
¼ teaspoon pepper
2 cups water
2 10-ounce packages frozen artichokes
1 teaspoon savory

SAUCE

6 tablespoons butter or margarine
¼ cup soya carob flour
2 cups stock

3 cups shredded mild Cheddar cheese
½ teaspoon nutmeg

Set the artichokes aside to thaw. Make a bouquet garni by tying together in a piece of cheesecloth the parsley, celery top, carrot, bay leaf, and 1 teaspoon of the thyme (use a long string so bouquet can be easily retrieved from pan). Place chicken pieces, bouquet garni, salt, pepper, and water in a large pot. Cover, and simmer for about 1 hour, or until chicken is tender. Cool chicken in stock, then remove meat from bones in large-size pieces. Reserve stock. Arrange chicken pieces in 3-quart casserole along with thawed artichoke hearts.

To make cheese sauce, melt 4 tablespoons of the butter; blend in flour until smooth. Gradually add the chicken stock, and cook, stirring constantly, until sauce is thick and smooth. Stir in cheese and nutmeg. Pour sauce over chicken and artichoke hearts; sprinkle with savory, the rest of the thyme, and bread crumbs; dot with the remaining 2 tablespoons butter. Bake, uncovered, in a preheated moderate oven (350°) for 30 minutes or until golden brown.

Serves 8.

Note: If you prefer, you may refrigerate the casserole, covered, before baking it, as in the last part of the instructions.

CHICKEN MARENGO

2 broiler-fryers (about 3 pounds each), quartered, and including giblets
16 small white onions, peeled
1 clove garlic, mashed or minced
2 cups small whole (or large, sliced) fresh mushrooms
¼ cup olive (or other) oil
8 medium-size tomatoes, peeled and quartered

1 tablespoon sea salt
¼ teaspoon freshly ground pepper
1-2 sprigs parsley
1 celery top
1 carrot, quartered
1 bay leaf
1 sprig fresh (or 1 teaspoon dried) thyme
2 cups water

SAUCE

¼ cup lemon juice
½ cup water

½ cup soya carob flour

Sauté onions, garlic, and mushrooms in 2 tablespoons of the oil in a large frying pan or Dutch oven. Remove onions and mushrooms from pan with a slotted spoon and set aside. Add remaining 2 tablespoons oil to the pan and brown chicken well on all sides. Add tomatoes, sautéed onions and mushrooms, and salt and pepper. Cover, and bake in a preheated moderate oven (350°) for 1 hour, or until chicken is tender.

Meanwhile, make a bouquet garni by tying together in a piece of cheesecloth the parsley, celery top, carrot, bay leaf, and thyme (use a long string so bouquet can easily be removed), and place in a pot with the giblets, neck, and water. Simmer for about 25 minutes; reserve stock.

Place baked chicken parts and vegetables in a greased 3-quart casserole; keep warm while preparing sauce. Blend flour with lemon juice and the ¾ cup of water until smooth and creamy, then stir into pan drippings. Add 1 cup of the stock from giblets and cook over medium heat, stirring constantly, until sauce is thick and smooth.

Serve immediately; or refrigerate, and reheat, covered, in a moderate oven for about 1 hour before serving.

Serves 8.

GINGER CHICKEN

2 whole chicken breasts, split	1 teaspoon thyme
4 chicken thighs	¼ teaspoon pepper
6 tablespoons butter or margarine	1 lemon, cut in half
½ pound fresh mushrooms, sliced	1¼ teaspoons shredded fresh ginger (or ⅛ teaspoon ground ginger)
⅔ cup soya carob flour	
2 teaspoons sea salt	2 9-ounce packages frozen cut green beans
1 teaspoon sage	

Let green beans thaw. Wash chicken parts and dry well. Melt 2 tablespoons of the butter in a frying pan and sauté mushrooms about 5 minutes; remove from pan and reserve. Combine flour with salt, sage, thyme, and pepper. Rub chicken parts all over with lemon and dust lightly with seasoned flour. Melt remaining 4 tablespoons butter in the frying pan and brown chicken well; remove to a 2-quart casserole; sprinkle with ginger.

Dust green beans with some of the seasoned flour and brown lightly in the same pan, adding more butter if needed. Mix beans with mushrooms; spoon over chicken. Bake, covered, in a pre-heated hot oven (400°) about 40 minutes.

Makes 4 to 6 servings.

LEMON CHICKEN

6-8 broiler-fryer pieces (breasts, legs, thighs)
2 lemons
¼ cup soya carob flour
1½ teaspoon salt

¼ teaspoon paprika
4 tablespoons oil
2 tablespoons carob syrup
1 cup chicken broth
2 sprigs fresh mint

Wash chicken; drain on paper towels. Grate peel from 1 lemon and set aside; then cut the lemon in half and squeeze its juice over the chicken, rubbing well into each piece. Shake in paper bag with flour, salt and paprika. Brown chicken slowly in oil. Arrange in 2-quart casserole or baking pan. Sprinkle grated lemon peel over chicken; add carob syrup. Slice the second lemon thinly and lay the pieces over the chicken. Pour broth over chicken; place mint on top. Cover, and bake in preheated moderately hot oven (375°) until chicken is tender (40 to 45 minutes). Remove mint before serving.

Makes 6 to 8 servings.

OVEN-FRIED CHICKEN

6 large whole chicken breasts, skinned and boned
1 cup Lemon-Pepper Butter (*see* Index)
salt

1 egg
1 tablespoon water
soya carob flour
⅔ cup soya-bread crumbs

Shape ¾ of a cup of the Lemon-Pepper Butter into 6 sticks; freeze firm.

Place 1 chicken breast at a time between pieces of waxed paper; pound to flatten. Sprinkle lightly with a little salt. Place 1 stick Lemon-Pepper Butter on each breast; roll up; secure with wooden toothpicks. Beat together egg and water. Coat meat lightly with flour; dip in egg mixture, then coat with bread crumbs. Heat the remaining 4 tablespoons butter over medium heat and cook chicken in it 10 to 15 minutes, turning gently on all sides. Place chicken in shallow baking pan. Bake in preheated 400° oven for 20 minutes.

Serve hot.

Makes 6 servings.

SAVORY CHICKEN

2½ pound chicken, cut in serving pieces	1 medium-size onion, chopped
¼ cup fat	1 medium-size carrot, chopped
sea salt and pepper to taste	1½ cups tomatoes, strained
paprika to taste	1 cup canned mushrooms
	2 tablespoons chopped olives

Heat pressure cooker. Add fat. Add salt, pepper and paprika. Add onion, carrot, and tomatoes. Close cover securely; place pressure regulator on vent pipe, and cook for 15 minutes at 10 pounds pressure. Let pressure drop to normal of its own accord. Open lid, add mushrooms and chopped olives, and reheat in open cooker.

Serves 4 to 6.

TASTY BAKED CHICKEN

6 chicken thighs	½ cup tupelo honey
6 chicken legs	¼ cup soy sauce
oil	

Heat oil in large skillet. Brown chicken pieces well on all sides. Arrange in single layer in shallow, lightly greased baking dish. Combine honey and soy sauce and brush on chicken pieces. Bake at 200° for 1½ to 2 hours, or until tender, brushing frequently with honey-soy mixture.

ROASTED ROCK CORNISH HEN

1 Rock Cornish hen
2 tablespoons butter or
   margarine
juice of ½ lemon
sea salt
2 tablespoons butter or
   margarine (melted)
½ medium-size onion, chopped
1 cup chicken broth
⅓ cup tomato purée

⅛ teaspoon oregano
⅛ teaspoon thyme
⅛ teaspoon basil
⅛ teaspoon marjoram
⅛ teaspoon tarragon
¼ cup chopped pimento
½ bay leaf
2 tablespoons chopped ripe
   olives

Pat bird dry and skewer the neck opening closed. Fill cavity with giblets and butter; rub bird with lemon juice. Sprinkle bird with salt. Skewer shut abdominal opening. Brush bird with melted butter, and roast in preheated moderate oven (350°) for 30 minutes, basting with more butter as needed. Remove from oven; set aside.

Pour drippings (scrape free any residue) into saucepan. Simmer onion in drippings until transparent; add broth, tomato puree, seasonings, bay leaf, pimento, and olives. Bring to a boil and simmer for 5 minutes.

Cut bird in half along breastbone and backbone and place in a shallow casserole (about 9 inches square). Chop giblets, add to sauce; pour sauce over bird; cover. Bake in preheated moderate oven (350°) for 20 minutes; uncover and bake for 10 minutes longer, basting occasionally.

Makes 1 or 2 servings.

GRILLED ROCK CORNISH HENS

6 whole Rock Cornish hens
⅓ cup chopped green onion
3 tablespoons butter
1 10-ounce can unsweetened
   peach halves, drained
⅓ cup juice from peaches
2 tablespoons white carob syrup

6 cloves
3 tablespoons oil
1 teaspoon sea salt
⅛ teaspoon pepper
3 tablespoons lemon juice
parsley sprigs

Wash hens inside and out; dry with paper toweling. In a frying pan on edge of barbecue grill, cook green onions in butter until tender. Remove from heat. Cut peaches into ½-inch cubes; add to onions. Cook over heat for 5 minutes, until thoroughly warm. Remove from heat. Add peach syrup and carob syrup.

Place hens on deep platter. Combine onion-peach mixture, cloves, oil, lemon juice, salt, and pepper. Let stand 15 minutes, then pour over hens. Let stand 2 hours, turning birds twice. Remove hens; pour sauce into a cup. Remove cloves.

Grease skewers lightly. Balance hens on skewers. Cook, 5 inches from coals, for 45 to 50 minutes, basting during cooking with half the sauce. Remove hens to a platter. Baste with balance of the sauce. Let stand 5 to 10 minutes before serving. Garnish with parsley.

Serves 6.

SPANISH TURKEY LEGS

2 turkey drumsticks (about 3 pounds)
2 tablespoons cooking oil
1 cup chopped celery
½ cup chopped onion
1 small green pepper, slivered
1 cup chopped fresh or canned tomatoes
1 cup water
1 bay leaf
1 teaspoon sea salt
6 stuffed olives, sliced (optional)
1 cup uncooked artichoke macaroni

Wash drumsticks and pat dry with paper towel. Brown on all sides in hot oil in heavy skillet. Stir in celery, onion, and green pepper, and sauté lightly. Add tomatoes, water, bay leaf, and salt. Simmer, covered, for 2 hours or until turkey is tender. Add olives and macaroni, cover, and simmer for 20 minutes longer, or until macaroni is tender, adding more liquid if necessary. Separate meat from turkey legs, discarding the bones, and serve at once.

Makes 6 servings.

TURKEY AND OYSTER CASSEROLE

1 package artichoke macaroni	½ cup chopped pimentos
1½ cups sour cream	½ cup sliced ripe olives
5 tablespoons butter or margarine	1 3- or 4-ounce can sliced mushrooms, drained
5 tablespoons soya carob flour	1 teaspoon sea salt
2 cups turkey or chicken broth	¼ teaspoon pepper
3 cups diced cooked turkey	1 pint oysters, drained

Cook macaroni as directed on package; drain. Mix the cooked macaroni with ½ cup of the sour cream.

Melt butter in a small saucepan; blend in flour; gradually stir in chicken broth, and cook, stirring constantly, until thickened. Blend in the remaining sour cream. Stir into the noodles and add the turkey, pimentos, olives, mushrooms, salt, and pepper. Turn half of mixture into a greased 2-quart casserole, and arrange a layer of oysters over it; then cover with remaining macaroni mixture. Bake, uncovered, in a preheated moderate oven (350°) about 30 minutes.

Makes 6 to 8 servings.

FISH AND SEAFOOD

GRILLED STRIPED BASS

2 pounds fresh or frozen (thawed) striped bass steaks	3 tablespoons soy sauce
	⅛ cup lemon juice
	1 teaspoon sea salt
6 tablespoons melted butter	1 large clove garlic
2 tablespoons crushed dill	

Place fish on a deep platter. In a bowl, combine ½ cup of the butter, dill, soy sauce, lemon juice, salt, and garlic. Pour over fish. Let stand 30 minutes, turning once. Remove fish and pour sauce into a cup. Place fish in a greased, hinged-basket broiler. Cook 4 inches from coals for 8 minutes. Baste with sauce. Turn;

cook for 7 to 10 minutes longer, or until fish flakes with a fork. Remove fish to a platter. Spread with remaining 2 tablespoons melted butter. Garnish with parsley sprigs and lemon slices.

Serves 6.

CHARCOAL FISH

12 frozen flounder fillets
   (2½ to 3 ounces each),
   thawed
1 teaspoon sea salt

dash of pepper
grapefruit sections
tartar sauce

Place defrosted flounder fillets in a single layer in a greased, hinged-basket broiler. Season with salt and pepper. Cook 4 inches from coals 8 to 12 minutes. Turn. Cook until fish is heated through and flakes easily with a fork. Garnish with grapefruit sections; serve with tartar sauce.

Serves 6.

CHARCOAL-BROILED FISH

3 pounds fresh pan-dressed fish
¼ cup melted butter
¼ cup lemon juice
½ tablespoon garlic salt
1½ teaspoons sea salt

dash of pepper
parsley sprigs
orange sections
¾ teaspoon paprika

Clean, wash, and dry fish with paper toweling. Place in a greased, hinged-basket broiler. Combine butter, lemon juice, garlic salt, salt, and pepper in a bowl; blend, and brush fish with it. Cook 4 inches from coals 12 to 18 minutes, basting with sauce. Turn. Cook until fish flakes easily with a fork. Garnish with parsley sprigs and orange sections; sprinkle with paprika.

Serves 6.

FISH CUSTARD

1 pound fillets of flounder	⅓ cup light cream
1 small onion, sliced	6 egg yolks, beaten
2 carrot slices	dash of pepper
1 thick lemon slice	6 egg whites, stiffly beaten
1½ teaspoons sea salt	1 tablespoon melted butter,
water as needed	as needed
⅓ cup chopped green olives	minced parsley

Place onion, carrot, lemon and 1 teaspoon of the salt into frying pan ¾ full of water. Simmer until liquid is reduced by one-half, then add fish. Simmer, covered, for 10 minutes, or until fish has lost its transparent look. Drain; chop fine. Add olives, cream, butter, egg yolks, pepper, and remaining ½ teaspoon salt. Fold stiffly beaten egg whites into mixture. Pour mixture into a buttered 2-quart baking dish, set in a larger pan of hot water, and bake in preheated moderate oven (350°) for 30 minutes, or until set.

Garnish with parsley sprigs before serving.

Makes 6 servings.

HADDOCK CASSEROLE

2 pounds frozen haddock fillets	½ pound fresh mushrooms, sliced
water as needed	1 small onion, minced
¼ cup butter or margarine	2 tablespoons oil
4 tablespoons soya carob flour	1 10-ounce package frozen peas,
2 cups milk	cooked and drained
1 cup sharp Cheddar cheese,	1 cup sour cream
shredded	sea salt and pepper to taste

Barely cover haddock fillets with water and simmer gently for 15 minutes, or until fish flakes with a fork; drain, and break meat in large chunks.

While fish is cooking, melt butter; blend in flour. Add milk and, stirring constantly, cook over low heat until smooth and thick. Add cheese, continuing to cook until it melts. Remove sauce from heat.

Sauté mushrooms and onion in oil for 5 minutes. Add to cream sauce along with peas, sour cream, and fish. Mix lightly, add salt and pepper, and turn into a shallow 3-quart casserole or baking dish. Heat under the broiler until bubbly and lightly browned on top.

Makes 8 servings.

BARBECUED HALIBUT STEAKS

3 pounds fresh or frozen halibut steaks
6 tablespoons melted butter
3 tablespoons chopped green onion
1 minced garlic clove
1 8-ounce can tomato sauce (without sugar)

5 dashes hot sauce
¼ teaspoon oregano
1 teaspoon sea salt
dash of pepper
5 tablespoons grated Parmesan cheese

In a frying pan on edge of barbecue grill, cook onion and garlic in 2 tablespoons of the butter until tender. Add tomato sauce, hot sauce, oregano, salt, and pepper. Cook for 5 minutes, stirring occasionally. Chill.

Place fillets on a deep platter. Cover with sauce. Let stand 30 mintues, turning once. Pour sauce into a cup. Place fish in a greased, hinged-basket broiler, and cook 4 inches from coals for 15 to 20 minutes. Brush with sauce. Cook until fish flakes easily with a fork. Remove to a platter; sprinkle with cheese.

Serves 6.

GRILLED PERCH

2 pounds fresh or frozen perch fillets, cut into serving pieces
½ tablespoon onion salt
¼ cup milk
1½ teaspoon sea salt

dash pepper
½ cup carob flour
¼ cup yellow cornmeal
1 teaspoon paprika
2 tablespoons melted butter
lemon wedges

In a bowl, combine onion salt, milk, salt, and pepper. Combine flour, cornmeal and paprika. Dip fish in seasoned milk, then coat with flour mixture. Place in a greased, hinged-basket broiler, 4 inches from coals, for 4 minutes. Turn. Grill for 4 to 6 minutes longer, or until fish flakes easily with a fork. Remove from basket. Drain on paper towels. Place on a platter; brush with melted butter; garnish with lemon wedges.

Serves 6.

PERCH DRESSED WITH BACON

2 pounds fresh or frozen pan-dressed perch	2 tablespoons lemon juice
4 tablespoons melted butter	½ pound cooked, crumbled bacon
2 teaspoons sea salt	½ tablespoon chopped chives
¼ teaspoon pepper	

Place fish on a deep platter. In a bowl, combine butter, salt, pepper, and lemon juice. Pour over fish. Let stand for 30 minutes, turning once. Pour sauce into a cup with which to baste fish while cooking.

Grease grill lightly with oil. Place fish on grill. Cook 5 inches from coals until fish flakes easily with fork. Remove fish to a platter. Sprinkle with bacon and chives.

Serves 6.

GRILLED SALMON

2 pounds fresh or frozen salmon steaks	¼ teaspoon thyme
	1 teaspoon sea salt
¼ cup vinegar	¼ teaspoon pepper
¼ cup oil	paprika
¼ teaspoon tarragon	½ cup grated Parmesan cheese
¼ teaspoon garlic salt	parsley sprigs

Place fish on a deep platter. In a bowl, combine vinegar, oil, tarragon, garlic salt, thyme, sea salt and pepper, and pour over fish. Let stand for 30 minutes, turning once. Pour sauce into a cup.

Score fish on both sides and place in a greased, hinged-basket broiler. Sprinkle with paprika. Cook 4 inches from coals, basting with marinade. Sprinkle with half the cheese. Turn when brown on first side; cook until it flakes easily with a fork. Remove fish to a platter, sprinkle with remaining cheese, and garnish with parsley.

Serves 6.

SALMON CASSEROLE

1 1-pound can salmon, drained, skinned and flaked	¼ cup finely chopped parsley
2 eggs	¼ cup finely chopped onion
½ cup non-fat dry milk	½ cup finely sliced celery, leaves included
1 teaspoon sea salt	
¼ teaspoon pepper	1 teaspoon caraway seed
1 cup milk	1 cup Cheddar cheese, shredded

Mix together eggs and dry milk until smooth. Stir in salt, pepper, and liquid milk. Add salmon, parsley, onion, celery, and caraway seed, and mix thoroughly. Turn into a greased 1½-quart casserole. Sprinkle with shredded cheese. Bake, uncovered, in preheated moderate oven (350°) for 30 minutes, or until set.

Makes 6 servings.

SALMON-CHEESE CASSEROLE

1 1-pound can salmon, drained, skinned, and flaked	2 tablespoons minced parsley
1½ cups milk	2 tablespoons finely chopped onion
2 tablespoons butter or margarine	1½ cups sharp Cheddar cheese, shredded
1 cup soft soya bread crumbs	⅛ teaspoon pepper
3 eggs, well beaten	dash paprika

Heat milk and butter together until butter is melted. Stir bread crumbs into eggs; then stir in hot milk mixture. Add parsley, onion, cheese, pepper, and paprika, and mix until well blended.

Spread salmon in bottom of greased 1½-quart casserole. Pour custard mixture over salmon. Set casserole in larger pan of hot water and bake, uncovered, in preheated moderate oven (350°) for about 1 hour, or until custard is set.

Serve hot.

Serves 4-6.

SALMON-AND-GREEN-OLIVE CASSEROLE

1 1-pound can salmon	⅓ cup diced green olives
2 tablespoons chopped shallots or green onions	2 teaspoons dill weed
	sea salt to taste
¼ cup butter	¼ cup soft soya-bread crumbs mixed with 1 tablespoon melted butter
¼ cup soya carob flour	
freshly ground pepper	
1¾ cup light cream (approx.)	

Drain salmon, reserving liquid. Remove skin and bones, and break into large pieces.

Sauté shallots (or green onions) in butter until wilted. Stir in flour and about 2 grindings of pepper from a pepper mill. Add enough cream to salmon liquid to make 2 cups, and stir into flour. Cook, stirring constantly, until thick and smooth. Add olives, dill weed, and salt to sauce.

Place salmon in 1-quart buttered casserole. Pour in sauce, and turn gently with a fork 2 or 3 times to mix through. Sprinkle with buttered crumbs. Before serving, place in preheated oven at 400° for 15 minutes, or until thoroughly heated and brown on top.

Serves 6.

SALMON AND OYSTERS EN CASSEROLE

2 cans (1-pound each) red
    salmon, drained, skinned,
    boned, and broken into
    small pieces
2 12-ounce jars oysters
butter or margarine as needed
¾ cup soya carob flour
½ cup melted butter or
    margarine

4 cups milk
1 teaspoon sweet basil
2 teaspoons sea salt
1 teaspoon pepper
2 cups shredded Cheddar cheese
2 tablespoons lemon juice
thin tomato slices

Arrange salmon in bottom of buttered 3-quart casserole.

Poach oysters in their liquid (add butter if needed) until edges curl. Drain liquid and reserve. Place oysters on salmon.

Stir flour into the ½ cup melted butter to make a smooth paste. Gradually add milk, oyster liquid, sweet basil, salt, pepper, and lemon juice. Add the shredded cheese, stirring constantly, and heat until cheese is melted and sauce is thick and smooth. Pour into casserole. Bake, uncovered, in moderate preheated oven (350°) for about 30 minutes. Just before serving arrange tomato slices on top of casserole.

SOLE FILLETS AND OYSTERS THERMIDOR

4 large sole fillets
1 12-ounce jar Pacific oysters
¼ pound fresh mushrooms, sliced
2 tablespoons chopped green
    onions
¼ cup melted butter or
    margarine
1 cup milk or light cream

¼ cup grated Parmesan cheese
½ teaspoon dry mustard
2 tablespoons chopped green
    pepper
3 tablespoons soya carob flour
2 tablespoons lemon juice
sea salt and pepper to taste

Arrange fish fillets in a buttered baking dish about 9 inches square. Place 2 or 3 oysters on each fillet.

Sauté mushrooms, onion, and green pepper in butter; stir in flour until well blended. Gradually stir in milk or cream until well blended. Add lemon juice, salt and pepper, and mustard. Cook, stirring constantly, until smooth. Spoon sauce over fish. Bake, uncovered, in a preheated moderate oven (350°) for 20 minutes, or until fish flakes with a fork. If desired, slip under broiler to brown lightly.

Makes 4 generous servings.

FILLET OF SOLE CASSEROLE

1½-2 pounds thin fillets of sole
3 10-ounce packages frozen
    chopped spinach
2 cups sour cream
3 tablespoons soya carob flour
½ cup finely chopped green
    onions (including some
    tops)

juice of 1 lemon
2 teaspoons sea salt
2 tablespoons butter or
    margarine
paprika

Cook spinach according to directions on package; drain very thoroughly. Blend sour cream with flour, green onions, lemon juice and salt. Combine half this mixture with spinach, and spread evenly over bottom of a shallow, buttered baking dish (about 10 by 15 inches).

Arrange sole fillets on spinach, overlapping when necessary. Dot with butter. Spread remaining sour cream evenly over sole, leaving a border to show spinach if desired. Dust lightly with paprika. Bake in a preheated moderately hot oven (375°) for 25 minutes, or until fish flakes when broken with a fork.

Makes 6 to 8 servings.

GRILLED RAINBOW TROUT

6 fresh or frozen pan-dressed
    rainbow trout
¼ cup melted butter
2 tablespoons lemon juice

½ teaspoon sea salt
⅛ teaspoon pepper
¼ cup finely chopped almonds
lemon slices

Clean trout; dry with paper towels. Combine butter, lemon juice, salt, and pepper. Brush fish with half this mixture and place in a greased, hinged-basket broiler. Cook 4 inches from coals. Baste with remaining sauce. Turn. Cook until fish flakes easily with a fork. Remove fish to a platter. Garnish with almonds and lemon slices.

GRILLED TROUT

2 pounds fresh lake trout fillets, cut into serving pieces	1 tablespoon lemon juice
3 tablespoons vinegar	1 tablespoon grated onion
3 tablespoons oil	2 teaspoons sea salt
¼ teaspoon garlic salt	¼ teaspoon pepper
dash of thyme	lemon wedges
¼ teaspoon oregano	2 tablespoons chopped chives

Place fillets on a deep platter. In a bowl, combine all ingredients except chives and lemon wedges and pour over fish. Let stand for 30 minutes, turning once. Pour sauce into a cup.

Place fish in a greased, hinged-basket broiler. Cook 4 inches from coals. Baste with half the sauce. Turn. Cook until fillets flake easily with a fork. Remove to a platter and brush with remaining sauce. Garnish with chives and lemon wedges.

Serves 6.

GRILLED TUNA CAKES

2 7-ounce cans white meat tuna, drained, flaked	½ teaspoon sea salt
2 tablespoons butter	⅛ teaspoon pepper
½ cup green onion, chopped	1 cup Chili Sauce (*see* Index)
½ cup chopped celery	2 tablespoons vinegar
2 tablespoons white carob syrup	1 beaten egg
2 dashes hot sauce	½ cup grated Cheddar cheese
1 teaspoon dry mustard	½ cup bread crumbs
	6 pimento strips

In a frying pan on edge of barbecue grill, combine butter, green onion, celery, carob syrup, hot sauce, mustard, salt, pepper and chili sauce. Remove from heat. Blend in vinegar, egg, and bread crumbs.

Place fish on a deep platter; cover with hot mixture. Let stand for 30 minutes. Shape into 6 patties. Discard remaining liquid. Place patties in a greased, hinged-basket broiler. Cook 4 inches from coals for 3 to 5 minutes or until brown, then sprinkle with half the cheese. Turn; cook until brown.

Remove tuna patties. Sprinkle with remaining cheese. Garnish with pimento.

Serves 6.

TUNA CROQUETTES

2 6½-ounce cans tuna, drained	2 tablespoons chopped parsley
2 tablespoons butter	2 teaspoons lemon juice
¼ cup soya carob flour	fine, dry soya-bread crumbs
¾ teaspoon salt	1 egg, slightly beaten with
⅛ teaspoon pepper	2 tablespoons water
1 cup milk	fat for deep frying

Melt butter; add flour, salt, and pepper, and blend well. Gradually add milk and cook until thick, stirring constantly. Combine tuna, parsley and lemon juice with the white sauce; mix well. Chill.

Shape into 8 croquettes; roll in crumbs, dip into egg-and-water mixture, and roll again in crumbs. Fry in deep fat heated to 375° for about 5 minutes, or until golden brown.

Serves 4-5.

TUNA-MACARONI

8 ounces artichoke macaroni	2 tablespoons minced onion
2 tablespoons butter or	1 7-ounce can tuna, drained
margarine	and flaked
2 cups tomatoes, drained	¼ teaspoon sea salt
2 tablespoons chopped parsley	

Prepare macaroni; boil 3 quarts water. When boiling rapidly, gradually add 8 ounce package of macaroni, so that water continues to boil. Cook uncovered, stirring occasionally, until tender. Drain in colander. In a large oven-proof casserole, cook onion in butter or margarine until tender. Add macaroni, tuna, tomatoes, parsley, and salt. Heat in oven 20 minutes; serve immediately.

TUNA-OYSTER CASSEROLE

1 7-ounce can white meat
    tuna, drained and flaked
1 7¾-ounce can oysters (or 1
    cup Pacific oysters)
1 egg, slightly beaten
1 cup milk
1 cup soft artichoke- or soya-
    bread crumbs
½ teaspoon sea salt

pinch of cayenne pepper
½ green pepper, seeded and
    finely chopped
1 small onion, finely chopped
2 tablespoons melted butter or
    margarine
¼ cup fine dry artichoke- or
    soya-bread crumbs

Stir milk into egg; add soft bread crumbs, salt, and pepper. If oysters are large, cut into bite-sized pieces, then mix with milk mixture. Add tuna, green pepper, and onion, and mix together well. Turn into a greased round 8-inch casserole.

Toss together the dry bread crumbs and melted butter; sprinkle over oyster-tuna mixture. Bake in a preheated oven (350°) for 30 minutes.

Serves 4.

CHARCOAL-BROILED KING CRAB LEGS

3 12-ounce precooked frozen
    king crab legs
1 cup melted butter
1 garlic clove, minced

2 tablespoons lemon or lime
    juice
½ teaspoon onion salt
½ teaspoon paprika

Thaw crab. In a saucepan on edge of barbecue grill, combine ⅓ cup of the butter, with garlic, lemon or lime juice, onion salt, and paprika, and cook slowly for 5 minutes.

Place crab on deep platter and pour sauce over legs. Let stand for 30 minutes. Pour sauce into cup.

Place crab legs in a greased, hinged-basket broiler. Baste with
¼ cup of the butter. Cook 4 inches from coals for 5 minutes;
baste with marinade. Turn; cook 6 minutes longer. Remove to a
platter and spread with remaining butter.

Serve immediately.

Serves 6.

GRILLED SOFT-SHELL CRABS

12 fresh or frozen dressed and thawed soft-shell crabs
½ cup melted butter
¼ teaspoon grated lemon rind
1 teaspoon lemon juice
¾ cup chopped parsley
dash of hot sauce

1 clove garlic, minced
sea salt to taste
pepper
¼ teaspoon mace
lemon wedges
parsley sprigs

Clean (or thaw) and dry crabs with paper toweling. Place
in a greased, hinged-basket broiler. In a frying pan on edge of
barbecue grill, combine other ingredients except lemon wedges
and parsley sprigs. Cook 4 inches from coals for 5 minutes; baste
with one-half the sauce. Cook for 8 minutes and turn; baste with
remaining sauce and cook for 7 minutes longer. Garnish with
parsley and lemon wedges and serve immediately.

Serves 6.

CRAB-AND-MUSHROOM CASSEROLE

2-3 cups crab meat, cooked
2 cups chopped onions
½ pound fresh mushrooms, sliced
2 cups chopped onions mashed
½ cup butter or margarine
½ cup sliced stuffed green olives
½ pound sharp Cheddar cheese, shredded

1 large 1-pound-12-ounce can tomatoes, broken in pieces
1½ teaspoons sea salt
½ teaspoon basil
½ cup sour cream
1 8-ounce box artichoke spaghetti, cooked

In a large pan, slowly sauté the onions, mushrooms, and garlic
in butter until soft. Combine remaining ingredients, stirring until

well mixed. Pour mixture into greased 3-quart casserole and bake, uncovered, in a preheated moderate oven (350°) for 35 to 45 minutes, or until hot and bubbly.

Serves 8-10.

CRAB-AND-SPINACH CASSEROLE

1 pound crab meat chopped, cooked
2 pounds fresh or 2 10-ounce packages frozen spinach, thawed
¼ pound sharp Cheddar cheese shredded

1 tablespoon scraped onion
1 tablespoon lemon juice
dash of nutmeg
1 tablespoon soya carob flour
2 tablespoons melted butter
1 10½-ounce can tomato soup
1 cup sour cream

Cook spinach about 1 minute in small amount of water; drain thoroughly; chop. Arrange in bottom of greased 1½-quart casserole. Sprinkle with half the cheese, crab meat, and onion. Add lemon juice and nutmeg.

Blend flour in butter; add tomato soup; cook until slightly thickened. Remove from heat and stir in sour cream. Pour over spinach mixture; sprinkle with remaining cheese. Bake, uncovered, in preheated moderate oven (350°) for 30 minutes.

Serves 6.

PARTY LOBSTER

3 live lobsters, 1 pound each
¾ gallon water
¾ cup melted butter
½ tablespoon crushed capers
½ tablespoon garlic salt

1 tablespoon chopped pimento
1 tablespoon chopped parsley
¼ cup lemon juice
lemon wedges

Pour water into a large pot, add salt; cover and bring to a boil on edge of barbecue grill. Place lobsters in pot; cover; cook for 15 minutes; drain; crack claws. Place lobsters on a deep platter.

In a bowl, combine ¼ cup of the butter, capers, garlic salt, sea salt, pimento, parsley and half the lemon juice. Brush one-half of this mixture over inside of lobsters; let stand for 10 minutes.

Grease grill lightly. Place lobsters on grill. Cook 4 inches from coals for 5 to 10 minutes, or until white meat flakes easily with a fork. Remove to a platter. Brush with remaining sauce. Garnish with lemon wedges; serve with remaining melted butter. Serves 3.

BROILED LOBSTER TAILS

4 frozen lobster tails, 1½ pounds	¼ cup sea salt
2 quarts boiling water	¼ cup melted butter

Drop lobster tails into boiling water; add salt, and bring to a boil again. Reduce heat, cover, and simmer for 20 minutes. Drain. With a sharp knife or kitchen scissors, remove soft shell-like covering on underside of tail. Make a deep cut through center of flesh and remove dark vein.

Drizzle part of butter over lobster meat; place on rack and broil 6 minutes 4 to 6 inches from broiler. Serve in the shell with remaining butter. Serves 4.

GRILLED LOBSTER TAILS

3 fresh or frozen shelled lobster tails	1½ tablespoons lemon juice
1½ tablespoons oil	⅛ teaspoon oregano
dash of thyme	½ teaspoon garlic salt
½ teaspoon onion salt	½ cup melted butter
lemon slices	parsley sprigs

Place tails on a deep platter. In a bowl, combine all ingredients except lemon slices, butter, and parsley, and pour mixture over tails. Let stand 30 minutes, turning once. Remove tails; pour sauce into a cup.

Grease grill lightly. Place tails 4 inches from coals. Cook for 3 minutes. Brush with sauce; turn. Cook for 3 minutes longer. Remove to a platter. Garnish with parsley and lemon slices. Serve with melted butter.

Serves 6.

GRILLED OYSTERS

18 fresh oysters in the shell	½ cup melted butter
1 tablespoon garlic salt	tartar sauce
1 medium onion, cut into thin rings	lemon slices

Wash oysters. Place on grill. Cook 4 inches from coals for 5 minutes. Turn when shells open and sprinkle insides with garlic salt. Cook 5 minutes longer. On edge of grill, in a frying pan, cook onion rings in 2 tablespoons of the butter until tender. Remove from heat and place shells on a platter. Serve with remaining butter, onion rings, and tartar sauce.

Serves 3.

GRILLED SCALLOPS

2 pounds fresh or frozen scallops	2 teaspoons sea salt
2 ripe tomatoes, cut into quarters	¼ teaspoon pepper
¼ cup orange juice	3 tablespoons lemon juice
½ cup melted butter	lime slices
½ pound cooked, crumbled bacon	

Rinse scallops in water, dry on paper towels; place on a deep platter. In a bowl, combine quartered tomato slices, orange juice, butter, bacon, and seasonings; pour over scallops, and let stand for 30 minutes. Pour sauce into a cup. Place scallops in a greased, hinged-basket broiler. Cook 4 inches from coals for 5 minutes. Baste scallops with sauce. Turn; cook 5 minutes longer. Remove scallops to a platter. Sprinkle with lemon juice and garnish with lime slices.

Serves 6.

SWEET-AND-SOUR SCALLOP GRILL

2 pounds fresh or frozen (thawed) scallops	2 tablespoons soy sauce
¼ cup melted butter	2 tablespoons lemon juice
¼ cup grated onion	2 teaspoons dry mustard
¼ cup white carob syrup	½ teaspoon sea salt
	⅛ teaspoon pepper

Clean fresh scallops; dry with paper towels. Cut large scallops in half; place all on a deep platter. In a bowl, combine ⅛ cup of the butter, onion, carob syrup, soy sauce, lemon juice, mustard, salt and pepper. Pour over scallops and let stand for 30 minutes. Pour sauce into a cup. Place scallops in a greased, hinged-basket broiler. Cook 4 inches from coals for 5 minutes. Baste with sauce. Turn. Cook for 5 minutes longer. Place on a platter. Brush with remaining butter.

Serves 6.

AIOLI SUMMER FEAST

1 pound medium-size raw shrimp, shelled	6 medium-size carrots
3 zucchini	1 small cauliflower
3 summer squash	8 medium-size leeks
½ pound fresh green beans	salt and water as needed

AIOLI SAUCE

3 egg yolks	dash of white pepper
7 cloves garlic, crushed	1¼ cups oil
1 tablespoon prepared mustard	1 tablespoon warm water
1 tablespoon lemon juice	1 tablespoon capers, drained

GARNISH

3 tomatoes, sliced	2 gherkins, sliced
2 7-ounce cans tuna, drained	

In a saucepan, bring to a boil 2 cups of water and 2 teaspoons salt. Add shrimp, and cook, covered, for 3 minutes. Drain; devein; refrigerate.

Prepare vegetables. Wash zucchini; trim ends; cut into 1-inch pieces. Wash squash; trim ends; cut into 6 lengthwise pieces. Wash green beans; trim ends. Pare and wash carrots; cut on diagonal into ¼-inch-thick slices. Wash cauliflower; separate into flowerets. Trim root end and green tops from leeks so they are about 7 inches long; wash well. In a 2- or 3-quart saucepan, bring to a boil 4 cups of water and 1 teaspoon salt; add zucchini; cook, covered, for 5 minutes. Remove, and using slotted spoon, drain on paper towels. Cook remaining vegetables (in same saucepan, adding more water or salt as needed): 5 minutes each for squash, carrots, and cauliflower; 8 minutes for green beans; 15 minutes for leeks. Refrigerate all.

In a small bowl, prepare Aioli Sauce, using an electric mixer at medium speed. Beat together egg yolks, garlic, mustard, lemon juice, and pepper until thick and lemon colored. Add oil, 1 tablespoon at a time, beating constantly so mixture stays smooth and thick. Add warm water, beating in until mixture is smooth. Add capers. Refrigerate, tightly covered, until needed.

To serve, arrange salad greens on a large platter. Place cooked vegetables and sliced tomatoes on this in single rows. Arrange tuna on platter; decorate whole with gherkin slices. Place shrimp in a large bowl of crushed ice with Aioli Sauce in smaller bowl in center. Sauce can be spooned over vegetables or served as a dip.

Serves 8-10.

SHRIMP REMOULADE

2 pounds cooked, cleaned large shrimp	¼ cup minced celery
	¼ cup minced green onions
¼ cup tarragon vinegar	shredded lettuce
3 tablespoons dietetic catsup	½ cup salad oil
2 tablespoons horseradish mustard	½ teaspoon sea salt
	¼ teaspoon cayenne
1½ teaspoons paprika	

Place shrimp in a bowl.

In blender, blend together vinegar, catsup, horseradish mustard, paprika, salt, and cayenne. Stir in onions and celery; blend for 20 seconds. With cover ajar, gradually blend in oil. Pour sauce over shrimp and marinate in refrigerator for 5 hours.

To serve, arrange shrimp on shredded lettuce in cocktail or sherbet glass.

SHRIMP CUSTARD CASSEROLE

½ pound cooked, cleaned shrimp (or 2 5-ounce cans)	⅛ teaspoon pepper
	few grains cayenne
6 slices soya or artichoke bread, buttered and cubed	¼ teaspoon dry mustard
	3 eggs, slightly beaten
½ pound sharp Cheddar cheese, shredded	1 teaspoon sea salt
	⅛ teaspoon paprika
2 cups milk	

Arrange half the bread cubes in the bottom of a greased 9-inch round or square baking dish. Sprinkle with half the cheese, shrimp and mustard. Make a second layer of the remaining bread crumbs, shrimp and mustard, and top with remaining cheese. Combine eggs, milk, salt, pepper, paprika, and cayenne. Pour over bread and shrimp layers. Place baking dish in pan of hot water and bake, uncovered, in moderately slow oven (325°) for 40 minutes, or until firm.

Serves 6.

Breads, Muffins, Pancakes, Noodles

CORN BREAD

2 cups yellow cornmeal
½ teaspoon soda
2 teaspoons baking powder
1 teaspoon sea salt

2 eggs, beaten
2 cups buttermilk
2 tablespoons melted shortening
or oil

Sift together dry ingredients. Add eggs to buttermilk and stir into dry ingredients. Stir in shortening, mixing well.

Pour into a hot greased pan about 8 inches square, and bake in preheated oven at 425° for 20 to 30 minutes.

Serve hot with butter and tupelo honey.

CORNMEAL MUSH

1½ cups yellow cornmeal
(approx.)
1 cup cold water
1 teaspoon sea salt

4 cups boiling water
tupelo honey or white carob
syrup

Mix together 1 cup of the cornmeal, cold water, and salt. Pour boiling water into top of double boiler, and gradually stir in the cornmeal mixture. Cook over direct heat 2 to 3 minutes, stirring constantly. Pour into wet dish or pan; cover. Leave overnight in refrigerator.

Slice, dip in additional cornmeal, and fry until golden brown. Serve hot with honey or syrup.

Variation: Stir ½ pound grated Cheddar cheese into cooked mush before removing from heat.

CORN STICKS

1 egg	2 teaspoons baking powder
1 cup milk	2 cups white cornmeal
1 tablespoon melted shortening	1 teaspoon sea salt

Place dry ingredients in a bowl and mix well. In another bowl, beat egg; add milk and shortening. Add to dry ingredients and mix well. Spoon into well greased corn-stick pans and bake in preheated oven at 450° for about 15 minutes.

Serve hot.

Yield: 12-15 corn sticks.

MEXICAN CORN BREAD

1 cup soya carob flour	½ cup milk
1 cup yellow cornmeal	½ cup soft butter
4 teaspoons baking powder	¼ cup finely diced green pepper
1 teaspoon sea salt	¼ cup chopped onion
½ teaspoon chili powder	2 tablespoons chopped pimento
2 eggs	

Sift together dry ingredients into large bowl of electric mixer; stir in eggs, milk, butter, green pepper, onion, and pimento. Add syrup, if desired. Beat at high speed for about 1 minute. Turn into greased 8-by-8-by-2-inch pan and bake in preheated oven at 425° for about 20 minutes.

Makes 6 servings.

SPOON BREAD

¾ cup yellow cornmeal	3 tablespoons butter or
1 tablespoon soya carob flour	margarine
½ teaspoon sea salt	3 eggs, separated
2¾ cups milk	

Combine cornmeal, flour, salt, and milk in top of double boiler. Cook, stirring constantly, until mixture is consistency of mush. Stir in butter or margarine. Remove from heat and cool slightly.

Beat egg yolk and blend into cornmeal mixture. Fold in egg whites which have been beaten until stiff. Bake in a 9-by-9-inch pan in a preheated oven at 375° for 45 minutes.

Serve hot with butter.

CARROT-AND-PEANUT-BUTTER BREAD

1 cup white carob syrup
½ cup chunk-style peanut butter
¼ cup oil
1 teaspoon vanilla
2 eggs
2 cups finely shredded carrots
1¾ cups soya carob flour

1 teaspoon baking powder
1 teaspoon baking soda
½ teaspoon sea salt
¼ teaspoon ground allspice
¼ teaspoon nutmeg
½ cup milk
½ cup chopped prunes

In large bowl, and at high speed, with electric mixer, beat together syrup, peanut butter, oil, vanilla, and eggs until creamy. Beat in carrots at low speed.

Sift together flour, baking powder, soda, salt, allspice and nutmeg. Stir flour mixture and milk alternately into batter. Add prunes, mixing in at low speed. Turn batter into greased and floured 9-by-5-by-3-inch loaf pan. Bake for 1 hour in a preheated oven at 350°.

CROISSANTS

¼ cup warm water
3 envelopes active dry yeast
2 tablespoons white carob syrup
  or tupelo honey, or 4
  packets sugar substitute
4 cups soya carob flour

1½ tablespoons salt
1 cup warm milk
1 cup butter or margarine
1 egg yolk
1 tablespoon cold water

Measure water into small bowl and add yeast, stirring till it dissolves. Add 1 tablespoon of the syrup or honey (or 2 packets sugar substitute), and blend in well. Beat in ⅔ cup of the flour. Shape dough into a ball; cut a cross in the top. Place in greased bowl in warm place free from drafts; cover with clean cheese-cloth; let rise 10 to 15 minutes or until doubled in bulk.

Combine remaining flour, sweeteners, salt, and milk in large bowl, mixing with the hands or a rubber spatula; turn out onto lightly floured surface; top with yeast mixture. Knead together until smooth and elastic (about 10 minutes), then place in large greased bowl, turning dough until well greased. Cover with cheesecloth and let rise in warm place, free from drafts, for 1 to 2 hours or until doubled in size. Punch dough down. Let rise again for 25 to 30 minutes or until almost doubled in size.

While dough rises, knead butter with hands until of easy spreading consistency and free of lumps, but still cold. Turn dough onto lightly floured surface and pat or roll into a 10-by-18-inch rectangle. Spread softened butter evenly over upper two-thirds of the dough to within 2 inches of the edges. Moisten edges with cold water. Fold unbuttered third of dough up to middle of buttered section, then fold top of buttered section down so top edge is aligned with bottom fold. Pinch edges to-gether so butter is enclosed. Roll dough gently out again to 10-by-18-inch rectangle, dusting any tears that may occur in dough with flour to repair them, and again fold dough into thirds, fol-lowing the same procedure as above. Sprinkle folded dough lightly with flour; wrap in wax paper; chill for 2 hours. Remove from refrigerator and roll out and fold twice more, then wrap and refrigerate as before for another two hours.

Divide dough into thirds (work with one piece at a time, storing remainder in refrigerator until you are ready to use it). Roll each third out on lightly floured surface into a 12-inch cir-cle; cut into 6 wedges. Roll up wedges, starting at wide end, and place, 2½ inches apart, on lightly buttered cookie sheet; curve into crescent. Cover loosely with plastic wrap. Let rise in warm place for about 1 hour, or until dough is light and spongy. Brush with egg yolk beaten with water.

Bake in a preheated oven at 375° for 20 minutes or until golden brown. Transfer to wire rack to cool, or serve warm.

SOYA CAROB BREAD I

1 cake or 1 package active dry yeast	1½ teaspoons sea salt
1¾ cups lukewarm water	2 tablespoons melted shortening
1 tablespoon white carob syrup or tupelo honey	4 cups soya carob flour

Dissolve yeast in lukewarm water. Add syrup or honey, sea salt, and melted shortening. Mix together well. Stir in flour. Knead until smooth and satiny. Place in a large greased bowl and cover. Let rise in a warm place 30 to 45 minutes until double in size. Punch down and turn onto floured board; form into 2 loaves. Place in 1 large or 2 medium-size greased loaf pans; grease top of loaf with melted shortening or oil. Let rise until approximately double in volume. Bake in a preheated oven at 375° about 40 minutes or until done.

SOYA CAROB BREAD II

3 packages active dry yeast	2½ teaspoons sea salt
2½ cups water	2 tablespoons melted shortening
4 packets sugar substitute	5 cups soya carob flour

In a large mixing bowl, add yeast to warm water, mixing in well. Blend sugar substitute, shortening, and sea salt. Combine yeast mixture with flour. Turn onto floured board and knead until smooth and satiny. Shape into a ball. Place in a greased bowl with cover. Let stand in warm place until twice its size. Knead and shape into 2 loaves and place in greased loaf pans or shape into rolls and place in greased pans. Grease top of bread. Let stand in warm place until twice its size. Bake in a preheated oven at 400° about 40 minutes or until bread is golden brown.

SOURDOUGH BREAD

2 cups milk
2 tablespoons butter
⅓ cup tupelo honey
1 package active dry yeast
1 quart Sourdough Basic Starter
5½ cups (approx.) soya carob
flour

¼ cup wheat germ
5 packets sugar substitute
2 teaspoons sea salt
2 teaspoons baking soda

Scald milk; stir in butter and honey, then allow to cool until lukewarm. Add yeast and stir until dissolved. Mix with 1 quart Sourdough Basic Batter at room temperature. Add 2 cups of the flour and wheat germ, stirring until well mixed. Blend sugar substitute, salt, and soda, and sprinkle over top of dough, then stir in gently. Cover with cloth and set in warm place, free from drafts; let rise for 30 minutes (until double in bulk).

Stir dough down and gradually add 2½ cups more of the flour, until dough is too stiff to stir with a spoon. Turn onto floured board and begin to knead. The amount of flour used may vary from the quantity indicated; one must gauge the feel; too little is better than too much, for too much will make the sponge heavy and dry. Work in the remaining flour, a little at a time, kneading with the heels of the hands, until dough is light and satiny to touch. Shape dough into two loaves and place in greased loaf pans; pans should be half full. Grease tops of loaves, cover, and set in warm place, free from drafts, 1 to 2 hours, or until double in bulk again. Preheat oven 10 minutes. Bake the first 20 minutes in oven set at 400°, then reduce temperature to 325° and bake until bread shrinks from sides of pans. Remove from oven, turn out on rack, and butter tops.

SOURDOUGH STARTER

You may buy sourdough starter at a health food store and prepare as follows:

Mix contents of package with ¾ cup all-purpose flour and ½ cup of warm water. Place mixture in a covered jar; leave in a warm spot for 48 hours, then refrigerate.

Makes 1 cup.

BASIC BATTER

To make a basic batter, start the night before. In a large mixing bowl, add 2 cups warm water to each cup of starter. Blend in 2½ cups all-purpose flour; mix thoroughly. Mixture may appear lumpy or thick; fermentation will make it uniform. Cover and leave at room temperature for twelve hours. This makes 3 cups. After fermentation is complete, reserve 1 cup before adding other ingredients and return this to the refrigerator to use as the basis for the next batch of dough.

You can now proceed to follow your recipe.

LEMON-PEPPER SANDWICH LOAF

1-pound loaf unsliced soya carob
   bread
½ cup Lemon-Pepper Butter
   (*see* Index), softened
1 tablespoon prepared mustard

2 teaspoons poppy seed
8 slices (8 ounces) processed
   Swiss cheese
8 slices bacon, crisp-cooked,
   drained, and crumbled

Cut bread into 9 slices, cutting to but not through bottom crust. Combine Lemon-Pepper Butter, mustard, and poppy seed; mix well. Set aside 3 tablespoons of mixture. Spread remainder on all cut surfaces of bread. Place 1 slice cheese in each cut; sprinkle bacon over cheese. Spread reserved lemon-pepper butter mixture on top and sides of loaf. Bake on ungreased baking sheet in 350° preheated oven for 15 to 20 minutes.

Makes 9 servings.

REFRIGERATOR ROLLS

1 cake or 1 package active dry
   yeast
2 cups warm water
1½ sticks margarine

6 packets sugar substitute
1 egg
4 cups soya carob flour

Mix yeast in water. Melt butter; cream with sugar substitute in large bowl. Beat in egg. Add dissolved yeast to creamed mixture. Add flour and beat until well mixed. (You can use an electric mixer for this.) Place in a greased airtight bowl and refrigerate. Some rising takes place even in chilled dough but at a gently retarded rate. About 3 hours before serving, remove dough from refrigerator. Shape immediately; place in greased muffin tins, grease tops, and let rise in warm place about 1½ hours until double. Bake in a moderately hot, preheated 400° oven 10 to 12 minutes, or until brown. This dough keeps well for 5 or 6 days.

Note: Rolls may be used for biscuit topping in Beef Pot Pie (*see* Index).

CRUMBLED BACON MUFFINS

2 cups sifted soya carob flour
2 teaspoons baking powder
1 teaspoon sea salt
4 tablespoons oil
¾ cup crisp, crumbled, smoked
   bacon

1 cup cream
1 cup water
sesame seeds

In a bowl, combine flour, baking powder, and salt. Blend in oil and bacon. Beat until mixture is uniformly coarse. Blend in cream and water. Grease muffin tin liberally and pour in enough batter to fill half of each cup. Sprinkle with sesame seeds.

Bake in a preheated oven at 375° for 15 minutes, or until well browned.

Serve immediately with softened butter.

Yield: 18 muffins.

BREAKFAST MUFFINS

1 cup soya carob flour
1 teaspoon baking powder
1 teaspoon sea salt

½ cup heavy cream
½ cup water
2 tablespoons oil

Combine all ingredients in a bowl; mix well. Grease muffin tin and pour in batter. Bake in a preheated oven at 400° for 8 to 10 minutes, or until brown.

Serve warm.

Yield: 6-8 muffins.

CARROT MUFFINS

1 cup soya carob flour
1 teaspoon baking powder
½ cup heavy cream
½ cup milk or water
¼ cup white carob syrup
½ teaspoon sea salt

¼ teaspoon cinnamon
¼ teaspoon nutmeg
¾ cup grated carrots
3 tablespoons soft butter
1 beaten egg

In a bowl, combine flour, baking powder, cream, milk, syrup, salt and spices. Mix well. Add egg and mix well. Grease and lightly flour muffin tin and pour in batter, filling each cup half full. Bake in a preheated oven at 400° for 10 to 12 minutes, or until brown.

Serve warm.

Yield: 12 muffins.

SOYA CAROB PANCAKES

1 cup soya carob flour
½ teaspoon sea salt
1½ teaspoon baking powder
¼ teaspoon baking soda (if using buttermilk)

1½ tablespoons oil
2 eggs, beaten
1 tablespoon white carob or tupelo honey
¾ cup milk or buttermilk

Mix together flour, salt, baking powder (and baking soda if using buttermilk); add other ingredients and blend well. Bake on a greased, hot griddle, turning once after bubbles appear.

Yield: 9 4-inch pancakes.

Note: For thinner pancakes add more liquid. Serve with Elsie's Pancake Syrup (*see* below).

ELSIE'S PANCAKE SYRUP

⅔ cup white carob syrup
2 teaspoons maple extract
1 cup water

2 tablespoons butter or
    margarine

Heat 1 tablespoon of the syrup in saucepan over medium heat until caramelized; add the water, the rest of the syrup, the maple extract, and the butter. Boil for 1 minute. Serve hot over waffles or pancakes.

SOYA CAROB WAFFLES

Use above recipe, except increase oil to 2½ tablespoons.

SOYA CAROB DUMPLINGS

2¼ cups unsifted soya carob flour
2 teaspoons sea salt
pinch of sage

6 tablespoons margarine
1 cup milk

Mix flour, salt and sage well; cut in margarine. Use pastry blender or 2 knives. Add milk and beat well with fork. Chill in refrigerator 30 minutes. Drop by tablespoonfuls into hot broth. Cover tightly; return to boiling. Reduce heat; simmer 12 to 15 minutes, or until done.

SOYA CAROB NOODLES

2 cups soya carob flour
1 teaspoon sea salt
2 eggs, beaten slightly

1 eggshell of water
1 quart broth or salted water

Mix flour, salt, and eggs together well, until they adhere into a ball. Roll out on floured board until very thin, and let sit to dry out (about 30 minutes). Turn dough over so second side can dry out. Dough should be dry but not crackly. If edges become too dry, brush lightly with water and let sit again for a few minutes.

Cut dough into ¼-inch strips. Spread out and let dry 1½ hours. Drop into boiling broth or boiling, salted water and cook uncovered about 10 minutes. Drain. Serve hot.

Salads

APPLE-CARROT SALAD

3 medium apples, diced
2 carrots, grated
¼ cup chopped pecans

2 tablespoons white carob syrup
½ cup Dietetic Mayonnaise (*see* Index)

Combine apples, carrots, and nuts. Mix in syrup and mayonnaise. Refrigerate until ready to serve. Serve on a lettuce leaf. Serves 6-8.

APPLE-CRANBERRY SALAD

2 cups ground cranberries
1 orange, seeded and ground
¼ cup white carob syrup
2 envelopes low-calorie
   strawberry gelatin

3 cups hot water
2 cups chopped apples
1 cup chopped pecans
1 cup crushed pineapple
   (unsweetened), drained

Combine cranberries, orange, and syrup; let stand until juicy. Mix gelatin in water; cool; add apples, pecans, and pineapple. Refrigerate until firm. Use a 1½ quart mold.
Serves 6-8.

APPLE SURPRISE SALAD

1 envelope low-calorie raspberry
    gelatin
2 cups hot water
½ cup diced apples
½ cup crushed pineapple
    (unsweetened), drained

½ cup chopped celery
½ cup chopped nuts
½ cup whipped cream
2 tablespoons Dietetic
    Mayonnaise (*see* Index)

TOPPING

½ cup whipped cream
2 tablespoons Dietetic
    Mayonnaise (*see* Index)

Dissolve gelatin in water; chill until slightly thickened. Add fruit, celery, and nuts. Combine whipped cream and mayonnaise; fold into gelatin mixture. Pour into individual molds. Chill until firm. Serve on lettuce leaf. Serve plain or with topping of whipped cream blended with mayonnaise.

Serves 6.

MARINATED ARTICHOKES

2 cans artichoke hearts, drained
2 tablespoons wine vinegar
½ cup oil

⅛ teaspoon dry mustard
⅛ teaspoon sea salt
dash of pepper

Mix vinegar, oil, mustard, salt, and pepper in a jar, shaking vigorously. Pour over artichoke hearts and chill for 3 hours before serving.

Serves 6.

ARTICHOKE-AVOCADO SALAD

SALAD MIXTURE

1 large head of iceberg lettuce
1 14-ounce can artichoke hearts,
    drained

1 large avocado, sliced

DRESSING

1⅓ cups olive or other oil   ½ teaspoon sea salt
 3 tablespoons cider vinegar   dash of pepper

Tear lettuce into bite-size pieces and place in large salad bowl. Cut artichokes into thirds and add with avocado slices to lettuce.

In a small bowl, mix together ingredients for dressing; add to salad; toss gently to coat well. Chill for 20 minutes before serving.

Yield: 7 to 8 servings.

AVOCADO SALAD I

1 envelope low-calorie lime   ½ cup Dietetic Mayonnaise
   gelatin   (*see* Index)
1 cup boiling water   1 cup cold water
1 ripe avocado   few drops onion juice
1 3-ounce package cream cheese   ¼ teaspoon sea salt
¼ cup finely chopped celery
½ cup bell pepper, finely
   chopped

Dissolve gelatin in hot water; let set until almost firm. Peel and mash avocado and cream cheese; add to thickened gelatin. Add remaining ingredients; chill until firm.

Serves 6.

AVOCADO SALAD II

1 envelope low-calorie lime   1 3-ounce package cream cheese
   gelatin   1 avocado, peeled and cubed
1½ cups hot water   2 small stalks celery, chopped
½ cup Dietetic Mayonnaise   1 small onion, grated
   (*see* Index)   1 or 2 pimentos, chopped

Dissolve gelatin in hot water; chill until partially set. Mix mayonnaise and cream cheese together until smooth and well blended. Add avocado, celery, onion, and pimentos; blend well. Add to gelatin. Spoon into individual 4-ounce molds; chill until firm.

Serves 6.

AVOCADO SALAD III

1 envelope low-calorie lime gelatin	1 cup celery, finely chopped
2 cups boiling water	1½ teaspoon grated onion
1 8-ounce package cream cheese	1 teaspoon sea salt
2 large avocados, peeled and mashed	¼ teaspoon pepper
	½ teaspoon garlic powder
	stuffed olives, sliced

Dissolve gelatin in hot water; chill until syrupy. Beat cream cheese with electric mixer until creamy, then slowly add gelatin, beating constantly until mixture is thoroughly blended. Chill until partially thickened. Fold in remaining ingredients (except olives). Turn into 6-ounce molds. Chill until firm. Garnish with olives.

Serves 8-10.

AVOCADO SALAD IV

1 package low-calorie lime gelatin	½ cup Dietetic Mayonnaise (*see* Index)
1 cup water	1 lemon, juice only
2 cups mashed avocado	½ teaspoon sea salt
½ small onion, grated	¾ cup whipped cream

Dissolve gelatin in hot water; cool until syrupy. Add avocado, onion, mayonnaise, lemon, and salt. Fold in whipped cream. Mold and chill until firm in individual 6-ounce molds or 1 large mold.

Serves 6.

AVOCADO SALAD V

1 envelope unflavored gelatin
½ cup cold water
1 cup boiling water
¼ cup white carob syrup
½ teaspoon sea salt
juice of 1 lemon
¼ cup lime juice

1 drop green food coloring
3 average-size avocados, peeled
   and mashed
½ cup Dietetic Mayonnaise
   (*see* Index)
¾ cup whipped cream

Sprinkle gelatin onto cold water; add boiling water; stir until thoroughly blended. Add syrup, salt, lemon and lime juices, and coloring; mix well. Chill until syrupy, then add avocado, onion, and mayonnaise. Fold in whipped cream. Pour into mold and refrigerate until firm. Use individual 6-ounce molds.

Serves 6.

AVOCADO RING SALAD

1 envelope low-calorie lemon
   gelatin
1 cup boiling water
2 ripe avocados, peeled and
   mashed

¼ cup sour cream
⅛ teaspoon sea salt
1 cup whipped cream

Dissolve gelatin in water. Add avocado pulp, sour cream, and salt; beat until smooth and fluffy. Chill until mixture begins to set. Fold in whipped cream. Pour into a ring mold; chill until firm. To serve, unmold onto crisp dry salad greens.

Serves 6.

AVOCADO-LIME SALAD

1 envelope low-calorie lime
   gelatin
½ cup warm water
1 8-ounce can unsweetened
   crushed pineapple, drained
½ cup unsweetened pineapple
   juice

½ cup Dietetic Mayonnaise
   (*see* Index)
½ teaspoon sea salt
1 tablespoon lemon juice
¾ cup peeled and diced avocado
¾ cup whipped cream

Dissolve gelatin in water; stir in pineapple juice; cool until mixture begins to thicken. Add crushed pineapple, salt, and lemon juice, mixing in well. Fold in mayonnaise, whipped cream, and avocado. Chill until firm in individual 6-ounce molds or ring mold.

Serves 6.

AVOCADO-MUSHROOMS PIQUANT

½ cup oil
3 tablespoons tarragon vinegar
2 tablespoons lemon juice
2 tablespoons water
1 tablespoon chopped parsley
1 clove garlic, minced
¾ teaspoon sea salt

dash pepper
2 avocados, peeled, pitted, and sliced
8 ounces (about 3 cups) fresh mushrooms, halved lengthwise
parsley sprigs

Combine oil, vinegar, lemon juice, water, chopped parsley, garlic, sea salt, and pepper in a jar. Cover; shake to blend. Pour over avocados and mushrooms in a shallow dish. Chill for several hours, spooning marinade over occasionally.

To serve, drain avocados and mushrooms; arrange on platter; garnish with parsley sprigs.

Serves 8.

AVOCADO-ORANGE SALAD

1 8-ounce package cream cheese, softened
¼ cup milk
3 tablespoons fresh lemon juice
2 teaspoons white carob syrup or 2 packets sugar substitute

¾ teaspoon ginger
3 medium avocados, peeled and cut into bite size chunks
4 large oranges, peeled and sectioned
lettuce leaves

In blender, blend together cream cheese, milk, lemon juice, syrup (or sugar substitute), and ginger until just smooth; chill. In large bowl, toss avocado pieces and orange sections; turn into lettuce-lined bowl. Spoon dressing over salad and toss.

Serves 7-8.

AVOCADO-PECAN SALAD I

2 envelopes low-calorie lemon
   gelatin
2 cups boiling water
1 cup sour cream
1 cup Dietetic Mayonnaise
   (*see* Index)
2 cups broken pecans

2 tablespoons minced onions
1 cup chopped green pepper
1⅓ cups peeled and mashed
   avocado
2 teaspoons minced celery
1 teaspoon sea salt

Dissolve gelatin in boiling water. Refrigerate until gelatin reaches the consistency of egg whites, then whip until foamy. Beat in sour cream and mayonnaise, blending thoroughly. Fold in remaining ingredients. Refrigerate until firm.

Serves 8-10.

AVOCADO-PECAN SALAD II

1 envelope unflavored gelatin
½ cup cold water
1 cup boiling water
¼ cup white carob syrup
1 teaspoon sea salt
¼ cup lime juice
1 cup Dietetic Mayonnaise
   (*see* Index)

1 cup sour cream
1⅓ cups mashed avocado
2 teaspoons minced onion
2 teaspoons minced celery
1 medium-size green pepper,
   chopped
1 cup chopped pecans

Sprinkle gelatin onto cold water to soften; add boiling water and stir until thoroughly dissolved. Add syrup, salt, and lime juice. Mix well. Chill until firm, then whip until foamy. Beat in mayonnaise and sour cream, blending thoroughly. Fold in remaining ingredients. Refrigerate until firm.

Serves 6.

BANANA-COCONUT SALAD

4 bananas
lemon juice as needed
¼ cup Dietetic Mayonnaise
   (*see* Index)

½ cup whipped cream
1 teaspoon vanilla
1 cup toasted dietetic coconut
lettuce leaves

Cut bananas in half lengthwise, then in half crosswise. To prevent their discoloring, coat immediately with lemon juice.

Combine mayonnaise, whipped cream, and vanilla. Roll bananas in this mixture, and then roll in coconut. Serve on crisp lettuce leaves.

Serves 4.

Note: Finely chopped nuts may be substituted for the coconut.

TWO-BEAN SALAD

4 cups canned wax beans, drained
2 cups canned cut green beans, drained
1 medium-size Bermuda onion, thinly sliced

½ cup cider vinegar
1 teaspoon sea salt
¼ cup white carob syrup or 6 individual packets sugar substitute
lettuce

In large bowl, stir together vinegar, salt, and syrup (or sweetener) until blended. Add beans and onion; toss to mix well. Cover and refrigerate.

Using slotted spoon, place salad in lettuce-lined bowl. Serve immediately.

Serves 8-10.

PICKLED BEETS SALAD

¼ cup water
½ cup cider vinegar
2 teaspoons dry mustard
¾ teaspoon sea salt
¼ cup white carob syrup

2 cups sliced cooked beets
1 medium-size onion, sliced
½ teaspoon celery seed
2 tablespoons finely chopped parsley

Heat vinegar and water to boiling. Add mustard, salt, and syrup; blend well, and bring to a boil again. Meanwhile, combine beets, onion, and celery seed. Pour boiling mixture over vegetables and place in refrigerator. Let marinate overnight. Sprinkle with parsley before serving.

Yield: 4-5 servings.

BLUEBERRY MOLD

1 20-ounce can unsweetened
  blueberries, drained
blueberry juice from same can
pineapple juice, unsweetened
2 envelopes low-calorie lemon
  gelatin

1 large banana, mashed
2 tablespoons white carob syrup
1 cup whipped cream

Combine blueberry juice with enough pineapple juice to make 3 cups liquid. Bring juice to a boil and stir in gelatin, stirring until dissolved. Chill until thickened.

Fold in banana, syrup, whipped cream, and blueberries. Turn into 1½-quart mold; chill until firm.

Serves 6.

BLUEBERRY-HONEYDEW MOLD

¾ cup fresh blueberries
3 cups fresh honeydew melon
  balls
2 envelopes unflavored gelatin
½ cup cold water (approx.)
¾ cup hot water

⅓ cup white carob syrup
¼ teaspoon sea salt
1 cup fresh lime juice
2 drops green food coloring
mint leaves for garnish

Strain juice from melon rind and pulp. If necessary, add enough cold water to make ¾ cup liquid.

Soften gelatin in ½ cup cold water; add hot water, syrup, and salt. Add lime juice and melon juice. Arrange some of the melon balls and blueberries in bottom of an oiled 5-cup mold. Pour a third of the gelatin mixture over the fruit; chill until firm. Add food coloring to remaining gelatin mixture and chill until the consistency of egg whites. Fold remaining melon balls and berries into this soft gelatin mixture. Pour over firm gelatin layer. Chill until the whole is firm. Garnish with mint leaves and additional melon balls.

Serves 6.

BLUEBERRY-LIME MOLD

3 cups fresh blueberries
2 envelopes unflavored gelatin
1 cup cold water
1½ cups boiling water

½ cup white carob syrup
¼ teaspoon sea salt
¼ cup fresh lime juice

Soften gelatin in cold water; add boiling water and stir until dissolved. Add syrup, salt, and lime juice. Chill until mixture reaches the consistency of unbeaten egg whites, then fold in blueberries. Chill until set. Makes 6 individual 6-ounce molds.

BLUEBERRY-PINEAPPLE SALAD

1 #303 can blueberries, unsweetened
1 cup crushed unsweetened pineapple, drained
2 envelopes low-calorie raspberry gelatin

1 cup boiling water
¼ cup white carob syrup
1 cup whipped cream

Dissolve gelatin in boiling water; add syrup and fruit; mix well. Chill until partially set. Fold in whipped cream. Chill until firm. Use 1½-quart mold, or individual molds.

Serves 6-8.

BLUEBERRY SALAD I

1 20-ounce can unsweetened blueberries, drained
1 cup blueberry juice (from same can)
1 envelope low-calorie lemon gelatin

1 cup unsweetened pineapple juice
1 cup whipped cream
1 banana, mashed

Bring blueberry juice to a boil; dissolve gelatin in it. Stir in pineapple juice. Refrigerate until mixture is thick. Whip mixture with rotary beater until fluffy.

Fold in whipped cream, blueberries, and banana. Spoon into single 1½-quart mold or 6 individual 8-ounce molds. Chill until firm.

BLUEBERRY SALAD II

1 20-ounce can unsweetened
   blueberries
1 20-ounce can unsweetened
   crushed pineapple

2 envelopes low-calorie
   raspberry gelatin
1 cup chopped pecans

Drain blueberries and pineapple, reserving juices; bring juices to a boil. Add gelatin; stir until dissolved. Mix in blueberries, pineapple, and nuts. Pour into a 1½-quart mold or 6 individual molds.

BLUEBERRY-CREAM CHEESE SALAD

2 20-ounce cans unsweetened
   blueberries
1 envelope low-calorie lemon
   gelatin
2 envelopes low-calorie
   raspberry gelatin

1 8-ounce package cream cheese
1¼ cup hot water
3 tablespoons white carob syrup
1 teaspoon vanilla
½ pint heavy cream, whipped

Dissolve lemon gelatin in hot water; cool. In a large bowl, cream the cheese well and slowly mix in cooled gelatin mixture.

Add syrup and vanilla to whipped cream; fold into cheese mixture. Chill until firm.

Drain blueberries; reserve juice. Add enough water to blueberry juice to make 3 cups liquid; heat to boiling; pour over raspberry gelatin; stir to dissolve; chill until slightly thickened. Remove from refrigerator and add drained blueberries, stirring to distribute evenly. Pour over firm lemon-gelatin-cheese mixture; chill until firm.

Serves 8.

CABBAGE SALAD

1 small head cabbage
1 cup dietetic flaked coconut
⅓ cup sour cream
2 tablespoons vinegar
½ teaspoon sea salt
¼ teaspoon pepper

1 packet sugar substitute or 1 tablespoon white carob syrup
½ cup toasted coconut
paprika

Wash and finely shred cabbage. Add flaked coconut. Blend together sour cream, vinegar, salt, pepper, and sweetener, and add to cabbage and coconut. Toss lightly.

To toast coconut, spread a thin layer on a baking sheet and place in a preheated oven at 400° for 2 to 3 minutes, or until lightly browned. Sprinkle on salad and dust lightly with paprika.

Serves 6.

CABBAGE-CARROT-APPLE SALAD

2 cups shredded crisp tender cabbage
1 cup shredded carrots
1 cup diced tart apples
½ cup Dietetic Mayonnaise (*see* Index)

1 teaspoon sea salt
1 teaspoon white carob syrup
1 tablespoon fresh lemon juice

Combine cabbage, carrots, and apples. Blend mayonnaise well with salt, syrup, and lemon juice. Add to salad ingredients and toss lightly but thoroughly to mix. Heap on individual plates and serve at once.

Serves 4.

COLE SLAW

2 cups finely chopped cabbage
1 package low-calorie lemon gelatin
½ teaspoon sea salt
1 cup hot pineapple juice
½ cup cold water

½ cup Dietetic Mayonnaise (*see* Index)
½ cup sour cream
1 teaspoon grated onion
1 tablespoon prepared mustard
2 tablespoons vinegar

Dissolve gelatin and salt in pineapple juice; add water; chill until syrupy. Fold in all remaining ingredients except cabbage and chill until slightly thickened, then fold in cabbage. Chill until firm.

Serves 4-5.

DUTCH SALAD

½ medium-size head cabbage, chopped
1 medium-size green pepper, chopped
1 onion, chopped
1 medium-size cucumber, chopped

3 tomatoes, chopped
2 packets sugar substitute
½ cup cider vinegar
pepper to taste
salt to taste

Combine cabbage, green pepper, onion, cucumber and tomatoes; blend remaining ingredients and add, mixing well. Chill. *Note:* Salad will keep 24 to 48 hours in the refrigerator.
Serves 6.

CARROT AND PINEAPPLE SALAD

3 carrots, washed, peeled, and shredded
1 cup cut-up pitted prunes, uncooked
1 20-ounce can unsweetened pineapple chunks, drained

1 cup sliced celery
½ cup sour cream
crisp lettuce

Mix together carrots, prunes, pineapple chunks, and celery. Chill. To serve toss with sour cream and serve from lettuce-lined bowl.
Yield: 6 servings.

CAULIFLOWER-AVOCADO SALAD

4 cups cooked cauliflower pieces
4 avocados, peeled and cut into
   bite-size pieces
¼ cup olive oil or other salad oil
2 tablespoons vinegar
¾ cup Dietetic Mayonnaise
   (*see* Index)

1 teaspoon paprika
¼ teaspoon sea salt
⅛ teaspoon pepper
3 or 4 tomatoes, sliced

In a bowl, combine oil, vinegar, mayonnaise, paprika, salt, and pepper, mixing well. Add cauliflower and avocado, and mix thoroughly. Chill. Serve with tomato slices.

KRAUT SALAD

1 can sauerkraut, well drained
1 cup diced celery
1 cup chopped onion
1 cup chopped bell peppers

⅓ cup chopped pimento
¼ cup vinegar
½ cup white carob syrup

Combine vegetables and sauerkraut. Heat vinegar; add syrup. Pour over vegetables. Chill for at least 12 hours.

Note: This keeps for several days if stored well covered in refrigerator.

CAESAR SALAD

1 large head romaine lettuce
1½ cups soya- or artichoke-bread
   croutons
½ cup oil
1 garlic clove, minced
1 egg, beaten

3 tablespoons lemon juice
½ teaspoon sea salt
⅛ teaspoon black pepper
8 anchovy fillets, chopped
2 ounces blue cheese, crumbled
¼ cup grated Parmesan cheese

In a frying pan, combine half of the oil and garlic, and the croutons. Cook, stirring, until brown. Remove from pan and keep warm.

Rub inside of wooden salad bowl with remaining garlic. Tear lettuce into bite-size pieces and place in bowl. Pour remaining oil over lettuce; toss well.

In a small bowl, combine egg, lemon juice, salt, pepper, and anchovies. Add to lettuce; toss well. Sprinkle with cheese. Add croutons; toss again and serve immediately.

Serves 6.

CHERRY LAYER DELIGHT

2 envelopes low-calorie cherry gelatin
4 cups unsweetened pineapple juice
3 large carrots, peeled and finely grated
1 20-ounce can unsweetened crushed pineapple, drained

2 envelopes low-calorie lemon gelatin
3 cups hot water
1 8-ounce package cream chesee
1 cup milk

Dissolve cherry gelatin in 2 cups of the pineapple juice, heated, then add remaining juice; cool. Add carrots and pineapple. Chill until firm.

Mix lemon gelatin in hot water. Thoroughly dissolve cream cheese in milk, then pour into hot lemon gelatin. Cool to lukewarm. Pour over firm cherry gelatin and return to refrigerator to cool until firm.

Serves 12.

CITRUS SALAD WITH LEMON DRESSING

2 large grapefruits
3 oranges
1 avocado

1 persimmon
lettuce leaves

LEMON DRESSING

1 egg
¼ cup lemon juice
1 teaspoon dry mustard
1 teaspoon sea salt

1 teaspoon white carob syrup
¼ teaspoon paprika
1 pint oil

Peel grapefruits and oranges and separate into sections, removing membranes. Peel avocado and slice it lengthwise. Peel persimmon and cut into bite-size pieces. Arrange fruits attractively over bed of lettuce.

Combine all ingredients for Lemon Dressing except oil, then add that, slowly beating it in until dressing is thick. Serve with the salad.

Yield: 2½ cups.

CREAMY FROZEN SALAD

1 pint sour cream	unsweetened pineapple,
2 tablespoons lemon juice	drained
⅛ teaspoon sea salt	¼ cup chopped nuts
¾ cup carob syrup	2 diced bananas
1 8-ounce can crushed	lettuce leaves

Mix together sour cream, lemon juice, salt, and syrup. Add remaining ingredients and blend well. Pour into 2½ qt. mold and freeze for at least 12 hours. Unmold on lettuce leaves.

Note: This may also be poured into muffin tins lined with fluted paper cups and frozen until firm. The frozen cups may be stored in a plastic bag in freezer for use as salads or desserts.

Makes 10 servings.

CUCUMBER SALAD

3 medium-size cucumbers	1 tablespoon minced green
½ teaspoon sea salt	onion
1½ cups cottage cheese	⅛ teaspoon pepper
3 tablespoons vinegar	crisp lettuce
1 tablespoon minced parsley	crisp parsley for garnish

Wash, peel, and slice cucumbers; place in a salad bowl and sprinkle with salt; set aside. In electric blender, combine the cottage cheese, vinegar, minced parsley, onion, and pepper, blending well. Mix with cucumbers; chill. Serve on crisp lettuce leaves and garnish with parsley.

Yield: 6 servings.

COOL-AS-A-CUCUMBER-SALAD

1 package low-calorie lime
    gelatin
¾ cup boiling water
1 large cucumber, finely
    chopped
1 medium-size Bermuda onion,
    finely chopped

1 cup cottage cheese
1 tablespoon lemon juice
1 cup Dietetic Mayonnaise
    (*see* Index)
½ cup toasted, chopped pecans
    or English walnuts

Dissolve gelatin in boiling water; chill until set, then whip until fluffy. Gently add remaining ingredients. Chill until firm. Serves 4.

CUCUMBER ASPIC

2 tablespoons unflavored gelatin
¾ cup cold water
½ cup boiling water
¼ cup white carob syrup
¼ cup vinegar
1 cup cucumber, peeled and
    grated

1 cup crushed unsweetened
    pineapple, drained
⅛ teaspoon sea salt
few drops green food coloring

Soften gelatin in cold water; dissolve in boiling water. Add syrup, vinegar, cucumber, pineapple, and salt; stir until blended. Blend in food coloring. Chill until firm using 1½-quart mold. Serves 6.

CUCUMBER-BEET-ONION SALAD

2 medium cucumbers, peeled
    and diced
½ Bermuda onion, chopped
1 teaspoon dry mustard
1 teaspoon sea salt

½ cup cider vinegar
2 tablespoons white carob syrup
1 1-pound can unsweetened
    small whole beets, drained

In a pot, combine mustard, salt, vinegar, and syrup, and cook until mixture boils. Dice beets; cover with mixture; cool. Add cucumbers and onion to beet mixture. Place in a jar and chill for 3½ hours, shaking jar occasionally so that cucumber becomes tinted with beet color.

Makes 6 servings.

COOL CUCUMBER MOLD

1 envelope low-calorie lemon gelatin	2 tablespoons lemon juice
	¼ teaspoon sea salt
1 cup boiling water	1 large unpared cucumber
1 cup cold water	¼ cup green onions, chopped

Dissolve gelatin in boiling water. Add cold water, lemon juice, salt; chill until partially set. Meanwhile, halve cucumber, scrape out seeds, and shred (there should be about 1½ cups shredded cucumber). Stir shredded cucumber and onions into gelatin. Mold until firm in 6 individual 4-ounce molds.

CUCUMBER-ONION SALAD

2 large cucumbers	½ cup tarragon vinegar
2 mild onions	1 teaspoon white carob syrup
salted water	salt and pepper to taste
¼ cup water	

Peel cucumbers and onions and cut into wafer-thin slices. Cover with salted water and let stand in refrigerator for several hours. Drain. Combine ¼ cup cold water, vinegar, syrup, salt, and pepper, and add to vegetables. Serve chilled.

Yield: 4-5 servings.

CUCUMBERS AND ONIONS IN SOUR CREAM

2 medium-size cucumbers	2 tablespoons vinegar
1 large Bermuda onion	2 tablespoons lemon juice
1 cup sour cream	

Wash, peel, and finely slice cucumbers. Peel onion, slice finely and separate into rings. Arrange cucumbers and onion in a shallow dish with overlapping onion rings on top. Combine sour cream, lemon juice, and vinegar, and blend well. Pour over vegetables.

Yield: 6 servings.

MINTED CUCUMBERS IN SOUR CREAM

4 medium cucumbers
½ cup sour cream
1 teaspoon garlic salt

1 teaspoon minced fresh mint
   or ½ teaspoon dried mint

Wash, peel, and thinly slice cucumbers. Mix sour cream with garlic salt and mint. Mix gently but thoroughly with cucumber slices. Chill in refrigerator for 1 hour.

Yield: 6-8 servings.

CUCUMBER-SOUR-CREAM MOLD

2 medium-size cucumbers,
   peeled and grated (about
   1½ cups)
1 envelope low-calorie lemon
   gelatin
1 teaspoon sea salt
1 cup boiling water

¾ cup cold water
2 teaspoons vinegar
½ cup sour cream
1 tablespoon chopped onion
1 tablespoon chopped parsley
freshly ground black pepper to
   taste

Wrap grated cucumber in a clean cloth and squeeze tightly to remove juice; let drain completely. Meanwhile, dissolve gelatin and salt in boiling water; add cold water and vinegar. Blend sour cream into mixture. Chill until thickened, then fold in drained cucumbers and remaining ingredients. Pour into 6-ounce individual molds or a 1½ quart mold. Chill until firm (at least 3 hours). Unmold and serve with meat or seafood.

Serves 6.

STUFFED CUCUMBER SALAD

6 medium-size cucumbers
1 pound Longhorn cheese
4-ounce can pimentos, drained

lettuce
French dressing

Grate the cheese. Chop pimentos and add to cheese; mix well. Wash and peel cucumbers. Cut in half lengthwise and scoop out center portion containing large seeds; discard. Fill centers with pimento-cheese mix and press two halves of each cucumber together. Chill in refrigerator for 2 to 3 hours.

To serve, slice cucumbers crosswise and arrange on lettuce leaves on large platter on individual salad plates. Serve with french dressing.

Serves 8.

CRANBERRY CUPS

1 cup fresh ground cranberries
1 small unpeeled orange, seeded and ground
1 envelope low-calorie cherry gelatin
½ cup white carob syrup
1 cup drained crushed unsweetened pineapple
1 20-ounce can sliced unsweetened pineapple, drained

1 tablespoon lemon juice
1 unpeeled cored, chopped apple (optional)
1 cup chopped celery (optional)
½ cup broken walnuts or pecans
lettuce leaves
Dietetic Mayonnaise (*see* Index)

When draining the cans of pineapple, reserve the juices and add enough water to make 2 cups. Combine with gelatin and syrup and heat, stirring constantly, until these dissolve. Add lemon juice. Chill until partially set, then add crushed pineapple, cranberries, orange, apple, celery, and nuts. Pour into individual 6-ounce molds.

To serve, unmold on pineapple slices, top with mayonnaise, and garnish with tiny lettuce leaves standing upright.

Note: If less orange flavor is desired, peel orange before grinding it. If a firmer salad is desired, add 1 envelope unflavored gelatin to the hot juice mixture.

Serves 10.

CRANBERRY SALAD

2 cups cranberries, ground
2 envelopes low-calorie cherry
  gelatin
2 cups hot water
1 cup cold water
1 cup unsweetened pineapple
  juice
2 tablespoons lemon juice
½ teaspoon sea salt

½ cup white carob syrup
1 orange, finely ground
1 9-ounce can unsweetened
  pineapple tidbits, juice
  pack, drained
1 cup orange sections
¼ cup sliced celery
½ cup chopped walnuts

Dissolve gelatin in hot water. Add cold water, pineapple juice, lemon juice, and salt. Chill until partially set.

Add syrup to ground fruits, and add with pineapple tidbits, orange sections, and nuts to gelatin, mixing in well. Pour into 2½-quart mold. Chill until firm.

Serves 10.

CRANBERRY SALAD SUPREME

2 cups fresh cranberries
1 small orange, quartered and
  seeded
1 envelope low-calorie lemon
  gelatin
1 envelope low-calorie cherry
  gelatin
3 cups hot unsweetened
  pineapple juice
3 ounces cream cheese

1 tablespoon lemon juice
4 packets sugar substitute
1 cup diced celery
1 cup drained crushed
  pineapple, unsweetened,
  juice pack
½ cup toasted chopped pecans
  or walnuts
fresh cranberries for garnish
lettuce leaves

Dissolve gelatins in hot pineapple juice; add cream cheese and let melt, stirring in well. Chill until set, then whip with rotary beater until fluffy.

Grind the 2 cups cranberries and orange; mix lemon juice and sweetener into ground mixture. Fold into gelatin along with celery and nuts. Pour into 2½-quart mold and chill until firm. Unmold on crisp green lettuce to serve, garnished with fresh cranberries.

Serves 10.

EGGPLANT SALAD

1 large eggplant	¼ teaspoon sea salt
1 small onion, chopped	chopped parsley
½ cup oil	tomato wedges
1½ tablespoons apple cider vinegar	black olives (optional)

Bake eggplant in its skin in moderate (350°) oven for one hour or until soft. Remove skin. Chop flesh in a bowl with onion, oil, salt, and vinegar, mix well. To serve, garnish with chopped parsley, tomato wedges and olives.

Serves 4.

FRUIT SALAD SUPREME

1 envelope low-calorie lemon gelatin	1 cup crushed unsweetened pineapple, drained
1 cup hot unsweetened pineapple juice	½ cup chopped pecans
1 3-ounce package cream cheese	1 packet sugar substitute
1 cup dietetic fruit cocktail (drained)	½ pint whipped cream

Dissolve gelatin in pineapple juice. Add cream cheese; beat with rotary beater. Chill until firm. Again beat with a rotary beater; chill.

Fold fruit cocktail, pineapple, sweetener, and nuts into the whipped cream. Pour cream mixture over the firm gelatin mixture. Use 1½-quart mold. Chill.

Serves 6.

FRUIT-CHEESE-LOAF SALAD

1 envelope low-calorie cherry
   gelatin
1 pint hot water
1 #303 can dietetic fruit
   cocktail
1 envelope unflavored gelatin

¾ cup juice from fruit cocktail
1 3-ounce package cream cheese
¼ cup cold water
½ cup Dietetic Mayonnaise
   (*see* Index)

Dissolve cherry gelatin in hot water; cool. Drain fruit cocktail, reserving juice, and add to gelatin. Pour half of mixture into ice tray; chill until firm. Heat fruit-cocktail juice. Dissolve unflavored gelatin in cold water and hot fruit juice. Blend together mayonnaise, cheese, and fruit juice, and spread mixture on firm gelatin layer. Chill until partially set. Add remaining half of gelatin and fruit, then mixture, then another layer of gelatin.

Serves 8.

SUMMER FRUIT SALAD WITH LEMON SAUCE

2 pints washed fresh
   strawberries, sliced
4 bananas, sliced diagonally

1 can unsweetened pineapple
   chunks
3 peaches, peeled and sliced

LEMON SAUCE

2 tablespoons soya carob flour
¾ cup white carob syrup
½ cup unsweetened pineapple
   juice
2 tablespoons lemon juice

¼ cup water
1 tablespoon grated lemon rind
2 tablespoons butter
1 tablespoon poppy seeds
¼ teaspoon sea salt

Drain pineapple, reserving juice. Mix together flour, syrup, juices, and water in saucepan; bring to a boil over medium heat. Remove from heat and add other ingredients. Cool. Pour over salad.

Note: This sauce is also good on other fruit combinations. Makes enough sauce for large bowl of fruit.

GARDEN SALAD MOLD

1 tablespoon or 1 envelope
  unflavored gelatin
½ cup tomato juice
1 packet sugar substitute
¾ teaspoon sea salt
¼ teaspoon hot pepper sauce
1 cup buttermilk
1 cup cottage cheese
½ cup shredded carrot

2 tablespoons chopped green
  pepper
2 tablespoons chopped red
  pepper
1 tomato, chopped
¼ cup chopped celery
¼ cup chopped cucumber
salad greens

In a saucepan, sprinkle gelatin over tomato juice to soften; dissolve over low heat. Stir in sweetener, salt, and pepper sauce; remove from heat. Add buttermilk. Cool to jellylike consistency, then whip until fluffy. Beat in cottage cheese. Fold in carrots, green and red pepper, tomato, celery, and cucumber. Turn into a 4- to 5-cup salad mold. Chill until firm. Turn out onto salad greens.

Serves 5-6.

GREEK SALAD I

3 large cucumbers
24 radishes, sliced
1 cup pitted ripe olives
1 bunch green onions, chopped

¾ cup vinegar-and-oil dressing
½ pound feta cheese, cubed
½ teaspoon oregano
1 small head romaine lettuce

Peel and cut cucumbers in half lengthwise; remove seeds and cut into chunks. In large salad bowl, gently toss cucumbers and all remaining ingredients except romaine. Cover and refrigerate 45 minutes. Meanwhile, chill romaine. Tear into bite-size pieces; add to cucumber mixture, season, and toss gently. Serve immediately.

Serves 4.

GREEK SALAD II

5 or 6 lettuce leaves, torn into
   small pieces
1 tomato, quartered
1 small onion, sliced
10 black pitted ripe olives

1½ tablespoons olive oil
sea salt and pepper to taste
2 tablespoons vinegar or lemon
   juice

Combine lettuce, tomato, and onion. Add olives, salt, and pepper; toss. Just before serving, add olive oil and vinegar or lemon juice; toss well.

Serves 2.

GREEN SALAD BOWL

1 avocado, peeled and sliced
½ head romaine lettuce
5 ounces fresh spinach, torn into
   bite-size pieces
½ cup olive or other oil

⅛ cup cider vinegar
sea salt to taste
½ teaspoon dry mustard
¼ teaspoon basil
dash paprika

In a bowl, combine oil, vinegar, salt, mustard, basil, and paprika. Mix well; chill. Line a salad bowl with romaine lettuce. Pile spinach in center; surround with avocado slices. Drizzle dressing over all.

Serves 6.

INDIA SALAD

1 cucumber, peeled and sliced
½ green pepper, sliced
1 cauliflower, sliced
3 green onions, chopped

1 tomato, sliced
buttermilk
sea salt and pepper to taste

Arrange vegetables attractively in serving dish; cover with buttermilk. Season to taste.

Serves 2.

ITALIAN SALAD

½ head lettuce, torn into small
    pieces
½ head endive, torn in small
    pieces
2 cups dandelion greens, torn
    into small pieces
¾ cup celery, chopped
2 tomatoes, diced

4 pickled artichoke hearts,
    quartered
1 medium-size onion, diced
6 sprigs parsley
1 garlic clove, crushed
sea salt and pepper to taste
⅛ cup vinegar
⅛ cup olive oil

Combine and toss vegetables; add remaining ingredients.
Chill.

Serves 4.

ITALIAN GREEN SALAD

½ head escarole or endive torn
    into small pieces
½ head Boston lettuce torn into
    small pieces
1 pared, sliced cucumber
6 peeled, halved white onions
¼ cup olive oil

⅛ cup lemon juice
⅛ cup vinegar
¼ teaspoon sea salt
¼ teaspoon pepper
⅛ teaspoon garlic powder
¼ teaspoon oregano
½ teaspoon chopped parsley

Fill salad bowl with escarole and Boston lettuce leaves. In
another bowl or a jar, combine remaining ingredients. Mix thoroughly; chill for 2 hours. Pour over salad.

Serves 6.

KOREAN SALAD

2 cups canned bean sprouts, drained
2 green onions, finely chopped
1 clove garlic, crushed
2 teaspoons toasted sesame seeds
1 red sweet pepper or pimento, chopped

2 tablespoons soy sauce
1 tablespoon vinegar
2 tablespoons oil
½ teaspoon sea salt
¼ teaspoon pepper
1 hard-cooked egg, thinly sliced

Combine onions, garlic, sesame seeds, sweet pepper, and soy sauce; pour over bean sprouts. Combine vinegar, oil, salt, and pepper; add to bean-sprout mixture; toss lightly. Chill. Garnish with egg slices.

Serves 6.

LETTUCE SALAD WITH CHOPPED WALNUTS

1 head lettuce
1 clove garlic, finely chopped
dash sea salt
dash black pepper

1 tablespoon wine vinegar
½ cup oil
¼ cup chopped walnuts

Tear lettuce into bite-size pieces. Combine garlic, salt, pepper, and oil well; chill. Before serving, pour dressing over lettuce and toss. Top with chopped walnuts and toss again.

Number of servings: 6

WILTED LETTUCE SALAD

2 heads romaine lettuce, shredded
2 slices hickory-smoked bacon
2 tablespoons vinegar

¼ teaspoon sea salt
⅛ teaspoon pepper
1 hard-boiled egg, sliced

Place lettuce in salad bowl. In a hot frying pan, cook bacon until crisp; drain on paper towels; cut into bite-size pieces. Add vinegar, salt, and pepper to bacon fat left in frying pan; bring to a boil, and immediately pour over lettuce. Garnish with bacon pieces and egg slices.

Serves 6.

LETTUCE-RADISH SALAD

12 brilliantly colored radishes	1 teaspoon paprika
1 large head iceberg lettuce	½ teaspoon sea salt
⅓ cup oil	⅛ teaspoon pepper
2 tablespoons white vinegar	

About 25 to 30 minutes before salad will be served, make roses from 6 of the radishes as follows (use a sharp paring knife and a grapefruit knife): Slice just enough of the top of the radish off to leave a white dot (about ¼ inch in diameter). Remove a thin slice of radish at 5 points around its circumference so there are 5 round or oval white spots visible around it. At these points make a thin downward slice, parallel to the first cuts of the slices that were removed, but leave these attached at the bottom of the radish to simulate 5 petals. Drop the radishes into ice water, and the "petals" will curl back like realistic roses.

Another kind of rose can be made by cutting off the top of the radish, then marking it down from the cut-off top into 5 or 6 equal sections. For this, use a sharp knife, cutting just through the skin and down about three-fourths of the way toward the root end. Use the grapefruit knife to cut through each of the sections so as to loosen the skin from the flesh to make the "rose" petals. Scissors may be used to trim the petals uniformly. Drop the radish roses into ice water to encourage the petals to curve.

Thinly slice the remaining 6 radishes; set aside.

Remove 6 outer leaves from the lettuce to use as cups for the salad; arrange in individual salad bowls. Finely shred remaining lettuce. In a large bowl, combine oil, vinegar, paprika, salt, pepper, and mustard; beat well with a fork to blend. Add shredded lettuce and sliced radishes to dressing; toss until well mixed. Spoon into lettuce cups; top each salad with a radish rose.

Serves 6.

MELON SALAD

30 watermelon balls
20 cantaloupe balls
20 honeydew melon balls

4 bananas, sliced crosswise
10 fresh pineapple slices, cut up
½ lengthwise watermelon shell

Dressing

½ cup salad oil
2 tablespoons vinegar
2 tablespoons lemon juice
¼ teaspoon dry mustard

3 tablespoons carob syrup
½ teaspoon salt
¼ teaspoon paprika

Put all ingredients for dressing into a jar and shake well. Pour over salad. Mix lightly.

Serves 6.

MEXICAN SALAD I

1 pound ground beef
2 teaspoons chili powder
1 teaspoon garlic salt
1 cup cooked soybeans
1 cup chopped sweet peppers
1 cup chopped celery
1 cup green onions, chopped
1½ cups chopped tomatoes

1 hot pepper, finely chopped
¼ to ½ head lettuce, chopped
2 cups crushed corn chips
2 cups grated Cheddar cheese
whole corn chips for garnish
red and green pepper (raw)
    strips for garnish

Cook ground meat, chili powder, and garlic salt together until meat is browned. While this is cooking, mix together all vegetables and crushed corn chips. After the meat is sufficiently cooled, add vegetable mixture and 1 cup of the cheese. Mix well, then sprinkle rest of cheese over top. Decorate salad with whole corn chips and red and green pepper strips.

Serves 6.

MEXICAN SALAD II

1 head lettuce
1 peeled, sliced avocado
4 peeled tomatoes, diced
1 seeded green pepper, chopped
1 onion, chopped

4 slices hickory-smoked bacon
1½ teaspoons chili powder
½ teaspoon sea salt
½ cup cider vinegar

Line a salad bowl with broken lettuce leaves and avocado slices. Place tomatoes in the center. Top with pepper and onion. Cook bacon until crisp, then crumble over salad. Add chili powder, salt, and vinegar to bacon drippings; mix well. Pour over salad.

Serves 6.

FLUFFY ORANGE SALAD

2 envelopes unflavored gelatin
½ cup cold water
1 cup boiling water
¼ teaspoon sea salt
1 3-ounce package cream cheese
4 tablespoons lemon juice

1 6-ounce can frozen
   unsweetened orange juice
½ cup unsweetened crushed
   pineapple, drained
½ cup chopped pecans, toasted

In a large bowl, soften gelatin in cold water. Add boiling water and salt; stir until gelatin is dissolved. Add cream cheese; stir until dissolved. Add lemon juice and orange juice, blending in well. Chill until set. Remove from refrigerator and whip until fluffy, then fold in pineapple and nuts. Turn into 6-ounce individual molds. Chill again until set.

Serves 6.

MANDARIN ORANGE SALAD

1 cup canned dietetic pack
   mandarin oranges, drained
1 cup unsweetened crushed
   pineapple, drained
½ cup dietetic coconut

½ cup toasted pecans
¾ cup whipped cream
1 teaspoon vanilla
2 packets sugar substitute

Mix together oranges, pineapple, vanilla, and coconut. Toast pecans in preheated oven at 400° for a few minutes; cool. Add, with whipped cream. Chill before serving.

Serves 4-6.

PEACH SURPRISE SALAD

1 envelope low-calorie lemon
   gelatin
6 peach halves (canned,
   unsweetened, and drained,
   or peeled fresh)
2 cups unsweetened orange
   juice

6 canned unsweetened
   pineapple slices, drained
1 3-ounce package cream cheese
¼ cup chopped pecans

Heat 1 cup of the orange juice and dissolve gelatin in it; add remaining cold orange juice. Let set until thickened. Rinse 6 individual molds with cold water; spoon approximately 2 tablespoons of the gelatin mixture into each. Place a peach half, cut side up, in each mold.

Combine cream cheese and nuts; spoon some into each peach half and cover with a pineapple slice. Pour remaining gelatin mixture into molds and chill until firm.

Serves 6.

STUFFED PEAR SALAD

6 canned unsweetened pear
   halves, drained (reserve
   juice)
1¾ cups pear juice
1 envelope low-calorie
   raspberry gelatin

1 cup fresh raspberries
lettuce leaves
⅓ cup Dietetic Mayonnaise
   (*see* Index)
½ pint heavy cream, whipped

Heat juice; add gelatin; stir until gelatin is completely dissolved, then pour liquid, to a depth of about ¼ inch, into a glass baking dish that has been rinsed with cold water. Chill until gelatin layer is firm.

Place pears evenly, hollow sides up, on gelatin; fill centers with washed raspberries. Carefully pour remaining liquid gelatin over berries. Chill until firm. Cut into squares, each with a pear in center. Serve on lettuce leaf with mayonnaise and whipped cream.

PERFECTION SALAD

1 envelope low-calorie lemon
    gelatin
2 tablespoons lemon juice
1 teaspoon sea salt
1 cup finely shredded cabbage

1 cup diced celery
1 pimento, chopped
6 hot dill pickles, chopped
lettuce leaves
Dietetic Mayonnaise (*see* Index)

Prepare gelatin according to package direction; add lemon juice; chill until partially set. Add salt, cabbage, celery, pimentos, and pickles, mixing in well. Pour into a 1-quart mold; chill until set. Unmold on lettuce leaves; serve with mayonnaise.

Serves 6.

PINEAPPLE-CHEESE SALAD

1 envelope low-calorie gelatin
1 cup boiling water
1 3-ounce package cream cheese
1 cup unsweetened crushed
    pineapple

1 cup chopped nuts
1 small can pimentos, drained
    and chopped
½ cup finely cut celery
1 cup whipped cream

Dissolve gelatin in water; cool slightly; pour over cheese; stir until well blended. Cool. Fold in pineapple, nuts, pimentos, celery, and whipped cream. Pour into 1½-quart mold. Refrigerate for 24 hours to improve flavor.

Serves 8.

PINEAPPLE FLUFF SALAD WITH WHIPPED CREAM

1 envelope low-calorie lemon
   gelatin
2 cups unsweetened pineapple
   juice
½ cup whipped cream

½ cup chopped pecans
⅔ cup crushed unsweetened
   pineapple, drained
1 cup dietetic fruit cocktail
   drained

Heat 1 cup of the pineapple juice to boiling; add gelatin; stir until dissolved. Add balance of unheated pineapple juice. Chill until set, then whip until fluffy. Beat in whipped cream. Mix in pecans and fruits. Use 2-quart mold and chill until set.

Serves 8.

POLISH SALAD

6 medium-size cooked beets,
   thinly sliced
⅓ cup ground or crushed
   walnuts
1 green onion, chopped

1 tablespoon minced parsley
½ lemon, juice only
½ teaspoon sea salt
1 tablespoon white carob syrup
   or 2 packets sugar substitute

Combine all ingredients; toss lightly.
Serves 4.

RASPBERRY SNOW

1 envelope low-calorie
   raspberry gelatin
1 cup boiling water

1 cup cold water
1 tablespoon lemon juice
2 egg whites, beaten until stiff

Place bowl containing gelatin in a larger bowl of ice; whip until light and fluffy. Add beaten egg whites and continue to beat until mixture is thoroughly blended and light. Chill until thickened.

Serves 8.

RASPBERRY TANG GELATIN

1 envelope low-calorie raspberry gelatin
2 cups hot water
1 8-ounce package cream cheese
¼ cup Dietetic Mayonnaise (*see* Index)

1 banana, mashed
1 small can unsweetened crushed pineapple, drained
¼ cup shredded fresh coconut

Dissolve gelatin in water; chill until thickened, then whip until light. Mix cream cheese with mayonnaise; add to gelatin. Add banana, pineapple, coconut and walnuts; mix in well. Chill until firm.

Serves 8.

SHRIMP SALAD

3 cups small cooked shrimp
1 head iceberg lettuce
2 avocados
1 teaspoon prepared horseradish

2 tablespoons cider vinegar
6 tablespoons oil
2 tomatoes, quartered

Core, rinse, and thoroughly drain lettuce; refrigerate in plastic crisper. Peel and mash 1 avocado with vinegar, oil, and horseradish, and set aside until needed. Place lettuce, torn into bite-size pieces, in a chilled salad bowl. Add shrimp, tomato, and remaining avocado, sliced. Top with the avocado dressing and toss lightly.

Serves 4.

WILTED SPINACH SALAD

1½ quarts washed, torn-up spinach
3 tomatoes, sliced
¼ teaspoon sea salt

⅛ teaspoon pepper
3 sliced green onions
5 tablespoons melted butter
1 tablespoon sesame seeds

Line a salad bowl with the spinach and lay tomato slices on top. Sprinkle with salt and pepper; cover with onion slices.

In a pot, combine butter and sesame seeds, and cook slowly until melted. Pour over salad.

Serves 6.

STRAWBERRY BAVARIAN

1 envelope low-calorie
   strawberry gelatin
1 cup hot water
1 cup cold water

1 package low-calorie whipped
   topping
1 pint fresh strawberries

Dissolve gelatin in hot water, then add cold water; chill until partially set. Prepare whipped topping according to package directions; beat into gelatin. Fold in washed and hulled strawberries. Pour into salad bowl. Chill until firm.

Serves 4.

STRAWBERRY-COTTAGE-CHEESE SALAD

1 cup unsweetened crushed
   pineapple, undrained
1 envelope low-calorie
   strawberry gelatin
1 8-ounce container cottage
   cheese

1 cup chopped pecans or
   walnuts
1 cup whipped cream
1 tablespoon white carob syrup

Boil pineapple and gelatin together for three minutes; chill. Mix in cottage cheese and nuts. Fold in whipped cream sweetened with syrup. Chill until firm.

Serves 6.

OLD-FASHIONED SLICED TOMATOES

4 large tomatoes (about 2 pounds)	1 teaspoon sea salt
	⅛ teaspoon pepper
2 packets sugar substitute	¼ cup tarragon vinegar

Wash and core tomatoes and cut into ¼-inch-thick slices. Arrange half the slices in a large shallow serving dish; sprinkle with the sweetener, salt, and pepper. Top with remaining slices; sprinkle with rest of the sweetener, salt, and pepper, and drizzle vinegar over all. Refrigerate, covered, for at least 1 hour before serving.

Serves 6-8.

STUFFED TOMATOES FORESTIÈRE

6 large tomatoes (about 3 pounds)

FILLING

1 tablespoon oil	1 teaspoon sea salt
1 small onion, sliced	2 eggs
1 6-ounce can chopped mushrooms, drained	½ cup sour cream
1 teaspoon dried tarragon leaves	¼ teaspoon black pepper

Preheat oven to 400°. Wash tomatoes; cut a thin, horizontal slice from stem end of each. Carefully hollow out tomatoes (reserving pulp for another use) and place in shallow baking dish.

In hot oil in medium-size skillet, sauté onion until tender (about 4 minutes). Add mushrooms, tarragon, and salt; cook, stirring, for 5 minutes.

In small bowl with fork, beat together eggs, sour cream, and pepper, just until combined. Stir in mushrooms and fill tomatoes with mixture. Bake for 20 minutes. Serve hot.

Serves 6. Nice for brunch or supper.

TANGY TOMATOES

4 medium-size tomatoes
½ clove garlic
⅜ cup oil
¼ cup tarragon vinegar
⅛ teaspoon dry mustard
¼ teaspoon cayenne

½ medium-size onion, finely
    diced
1 tablespoon white carob syrup
    or 2 packets sugar substitute
1 tablespoon parsley
boiling water

Skin tomatoes (pour boiling water over tomatoes, let stand briefly so skins will slip off easily). Peel garlic. Measure oil and vinegar into bottle. Add mustard, cayenne, onion, garlic, and sweetener. Shake well. Place tomatoes in a bowl, top with chopped parsley, and pour dressing over all. Place in refrigerator and leave overnight.

STRAWBERRY SALAD

1 envelope-low-calorie
    strawberry gelatin
1 cup unsweetened fruit
    cocktail juice
1 cup juice pack fruit cocktail
    (drained)
½ cup pecans (optional)

1 cup unsweetened pineapple
    juice
3-ounce package cream cheese
½ cup juice pack pineapple
    (drained)
1 cup whipped cream
    (optional)

Dissolve gelatin in hot pineapple juice. Add cream cheese; melt over heat. Add cold fruit cocktail juice. Chill until firm. Whip until light and fluffy, then fold in fruit. Mix well, pour into salad bowl. Top with pecans and whipped cream.

Serves 8.

SUNSET SALAD

1 envelope low-calorie
 strawberry gelatin
1 envelope low-calorie orange
 gelatin
2 cups hot water
1 cup cold water
½ cup unsweetened pineapple
 juice
3 tablespoons lemon juice

1 cup cream cheese, softened
1 cup carrots, grated
1 cup unsweetened pineapple,
 drained
1 cup whipped cream
1 tablespoon white carob syrup
salad greens
strawberries or other fresh fruit

Dissolve both gelatins together in hot water; add cold water, pineapple juice, and lemon juice. Pour about ¼ of this mixture into bottom of 1½-quart salad mold and chill until firm. Cool remainder until it thickens, then beat until light and fluffy.

Work cream cheese until smooth and creamy. Blend into whipped gelatin. Fold carrots, pineapple, and whipped cream, sweetened with syrup, into gelatin mixture. Pour over the firm gelatin layer. Chill for several hours. Garnish with greens and fresh fruit.

Serves 12.

MARINATED TOMATO SLICES

4 large tomatoes (about 1½
 pounds)
¼ cup oil
1 tablespoon lemon juice

½ teaspoon minced garlic
½ teaspoon sea salt
½ teaspoon oregano

Peel and slice tomatoes, and arrange in a shallow dish. Combine oil, lemon juice, garlic, salt, and oregano; mix well. Pour over tomatoes. Refrigerate, covered, for several hours, or until very chilled.

Serves 6.

TOMATO ANCHOVY SALAD

4 large tomatoes
½ head lettuce, shredded
¼ cup french dressing
2 tablespoons anchovy paste

2 hard-boiled eggs
Dietetic Mayonnaise (*see* Index)
parsley sprigs

Peel tomatoes and cut each in half. Dip in french dressing, place on bed of lettuce. Spread tomato halves with the anchovy paste and top with slices of egg. Drop a dollop of mayonnaise on each egg slice, then garnish with sprig of parsley.

Serves 8.

TOMATO ASPIC

1 envelope low-calorie lemon
   gelatin
2 cups tomato juice

1 cup chopped celery
¼ cup chopped onion

Bring tomato juice to a boil; dissolve gelatin in it; cool until syrupy. Mix in celery and onion. Chill until firm.

Serves 6.

TRIPLE TREAT MOLDED SALAD

1 envelope each low-calorie
   lime, lemon, and raspberry
   gelatin
4 cups hot water
1 cup unsweetened pineapple
   juice
2 tablespoons lemon juice
1 9-ounce can sliced

unsweetened pineapple,
   drained
2 3-ounce packages cream
   cheese
¼ cup Dietetic Mayonnaise
   (*see* Index)
2 cups sliced bananas

Dissolve the lime gelatin in 1 cup of the water; then, in another bowl, dissolve the lemon gelatin in another cup of the water; in still another bowl, dissolve the raspberry gelatin in the final 2 cups water. Mix the lemon juice into the pineapple juice; add to lime gelatin; chill until partially set. Cut pineapple slices into thirds; arrange in an *S* design in bottom of 10-by-5-by-3-inch loaf pan and pour just enough lime gelatin over this to cover; chill until set. Pour in remaining lime gelatin and chill until firm.

Chill lemon gelatin until set, then whip until light and fluffy. Blend cream cheese and mayonnaise and fold into lemon gelatin; pour mixture over firm lime gelatin. Spread sliced bananas onto lemon gelatin; top with unchilled raspberry gelatin; chill until firm.

Serves 10.

TWENTY-FOUR HOUR SALAD I

½ cup unsweetened pineapple juice, reserved from
1 cup drained pineapple tidbits
2 eggs, slightly beaten
¼ cup white carob syrup
3 tablespoons soya carob flour
dash of salt

¼ cup lemon juice
1 cup whipped cream
1 cup drained mandarin oranges
1 teaspoon grated orange rind (optional)
½ cup chopped pecans
¼ cup nut halves

Mix together pineapple juice, eggs, syrup, flour, and salt in a saucepan. Cook over low heat, stirring constantly, until thick and smooth. Stir in lemon juice. Refrigerate until cool.

Fold in whipped cream, then lightly mix in pineapple tidbits, oranges, orange peel (if you are using it), and chopped nuts. Cover and refrigerate for 24 hours. Garnish with nut halves before serving.

Serves 8-10.

TWENTY-FOUR HOUR SALAD II

2 eggs, slightly beaten
2 tablespoons lemon juice
2 tablespoons butter
1 cup whipped cream sweetened with 1 tablespoon white carob syrup

2 cups unsweetened crushed drained pineapple
3 oranges, peeled and sectioned
2 cups peeled and sliced fresh peaches
1 cup cottage cheese

Cook eggs, lemon juice, and butter together over water in a double boiler until thick. Cool. Fold in whipped cream. Lightly mix in pineapple, oranges, and peaches, then fold in cottage cheese. Chill for 24 hours.

Serves 8.

MARINATED VEGETABLE SALAD

½ pound carrots, peeled and cut into sticks	6 hard-boiled eggs, halved
12 cherry tomatoes, halved	2 tablespoons wine vinegar
½ cup cauliflower sections	⅛ teaspoon sea salt
1 can artichoke hearts, drained	8 tablespoons oil
1 onion, sliced	¼ teaspoon dry mustard
	dash of pepper

Arrange washed and prepared vegetables, together with eggs, attractively on a platter. In a jar, mix together well vinegar, salt, oil, mustard, and pepper; pour over vegetables and eggs. Chill for 1½ hours before serving.

Serves 6.

MIXED VEGETABLE SALAD

1 medium-size cucumber	sea salt as needed
3 green onions, thinly sliced	vinegar and water, as needed
2 medium-size tomatoes	Dietetic Mayonnaise (*see* Index)
8 radishes, sliced	crisp lettuce (optional)

Wash, peel, and slice cucumbers, onions, and tomatoes. Wash and slice radishes. Combine vegetables in a salad bowl; sprinkle with salt; barely cover with vinegar diluted with water (use 2 parts vinegar to 1 part water). Chill for 1 to 2 hours. Serve as is, or serve on crisp lettuce with mayonnaise.

Serves 4.

WALDORF SALAD

2 cups diced tart apples
2 cups diced celery

1 cup broken pecans or walnuts

COOKED DRESSING

2 tablespoon soya carob flour
3 tablespoons carob syrup
¼ teaspoon salt
3 cups milk

1 egg, unbeaten
½ cup vinegar
1 tablespoon butter

To prepare dressing, make a paste of the flour, syrup, and salt. Add ½ cup of the milk; stir until smooth. Add the egg, beating in thoroughly. Beat in remaining milk.

In a saucepan, bring vinegar and butter to a boil, then add milk-flour mixture. Lower the heat and continue to cook slowly, stirring constantly, until thickened. (Because this mixture will curdle easily, constant stirring during cooking is important.) Cool.

Note: This recipe makes a very thin dressing, but any that is left over keeps well in the refrigerator.

WATERMELON BASKET

1 short plump well-chilled
    watermelon
1½ cups cantaloupe or honeydew
    melon balls
1½ cup whole fresh washed and
    hulled strawberries

1 small can unsweetened
    pineapple juice
few mint leaves

Cut watermelon lengthwise. Reserve larger section to hold the prepared fruit salad, but first scoop out the flesh, using a melon baller. Scallop cut edge of "basket," and fill with the prepared melon balls, mixing very gently. Add strawberries. Pour pineapple juice over all, then tuck in mint.

Serves 6.

Salad Dressings and Sauces

CATALINA DRESSING

¼ teaspoon black pepper
¼ cup vinegar
½ cup dietetic catsup
1 small onion, grated

½ teaspoon sea salt
½ cup white carob syrup
1 cup oil

Using a rotary beater, mix all ingredients except oil, adding them in the order listed. Add oil gradually, beating all the while. Refrigerate until ready to use.

FRENCH DRESSING

1 small grated onion
2 teaspoons white carob syrup
   or tupelo honey
2 teaspoons sea salt
2 teaspoons paprika

½ cup fresh lemon juice
½ cup apple cider vinegar
1 cup oil
1 clove garlic (optional),
   crushed

Mix onion with syrup or honey, salt, and paprika; add lemon juice and vinegar; then beat in the oil slowly. Put in a jar and let stand, with the garlic, for several hours. Stir the dressing before using. Chill. Keeps indefinitely.

Yield: 1 pint.

TOMATO-FRENCH DRESSING

3 tablespoons tupelo honey
1 tablespoon dietetic catsup
½ teaspoon dry mustard
1 teaspoon prepared horseradish
1½ teaspoons sea salt
½ teaspoon celery seed

2 tablespoons vinegar
2½ tablespoons lemon juice
½ cup salad oil
1 clove garlic, cut in half
1 teaspoon beaten egg yolk

Combine all ingredients in a pint jar with tight-fitting lid. Shake well and chill in refrigerator. Shake again before using. Remove garlic after 12 hours.

Yield: 2¼ cups.

GREEN GODDESS DRESSING

½ pint sour cream
½ cup anchovy fillets
2 tablespoons chopped parsley

½ medium-size peeled avocado
½ teaspoon black pepper
1 teaspoon sea salt

Mash anchovies and avocado; add remaining ingredients and mix well. Refrigerate until needed.

ITALIAN DRESSING

¼ cup olive oil
2 tablespoons lemon juice
1 teaspoon grated lemon rind
1 teaspoon sea salt
½ teaspoon oregano or thyme

1 clove garlic, minced
1 tablespoon grated Parmesan
cheese
½ teaspoon black pepper

Combine all ingredients; mix well. Chill until needed. Mix again before using.

PINEAPPLE DRESSING

2⅔ tablespoons butter
2 tablespoons soya carob flour
⅛ teaspoon sea salt
½ cup white carob syrup
2 eggs, separated

1 cup unsweetened pineapple
   juice
2 teaspoons lemon juice
½ cup whipped cream
   (optional)

Melt butter in top of double boiler over hot water. Add flour, salt, ½ of syrup, and egg yolks, stirring vigorously to blend. In a bowl, beat egg whites to a stiff foam, then add remaining syrup to them and beat to a shiny meringue. Fold carefully into yolk mixture, then slowly stir in the pineapple juice. This mixture should be thick. Remove from heat, stir in lemon juice; chill. Use as is for cole slaw, but fold in whipped cream if this is to be served with fruit salad. Refrigerate. Keeps well for 5 days.

Note: This is excellent for cole slaw and delicious on fruit.

POPPY-SEED DRESSING I

1 teaspoon dry mustard
¼ teaspoon sea salt
½ cup white carob syrup
¼ cup tupelo honey
2 tablespoons lemon juice

5 tablespoons tarragon vinegar
1 tablespoon onion juice
1 cup vegetable oil
1 heaping teaspoon poppy seed

Mix together mustard and salt, add syrup, honey, lemon juice, vinegar and onion juice; mix well. Slowly drop oil from a spoon into the mixture, beating constantly so it will not separate. Add poppy seed and chill. Yield: 1 pint.

POPPY-SEED DRESSING II

⅔ cup white carob syrup
⅓ cup white vinegar
1 teaspoon sea salt
⅛ medium-size onion, finely
   chopped

1 teaspoon prepared mustard
1 cup oil
¼ of an ounce of poppy seeds

Mix syrup with vinegar; add salt, onion, and mustard. Add small amount of oil at a time, beating until mixture is thick, like honey. Blend in poppy seed and refrigerate until needed. **Yield:** 1 pint.

POPPY-SEED DRESSING III

½ cup white carob syrup
1 teaspoon dry mustard
1 teaspoon sea salt
1 tablespoon grated onion

5 tablespoons vinegar
1 cup oil
1½ tablespoons lemon juice
1½ tablespoons poppy seeds

Mix syrup, mustard, salt, onion and 2 tablespoons of the vinegar. Add oil slowly, beating constantly. Add remaining vinegar and lemon juice and continue beating until dressing is thick. Stir in the poppy seeds. Serve with fruit salads, fruit gelatin molds, a grapefruit-avocado combination, or cole slaw.

RUSSIAN DRESSING

1 cup tomato sauce
1 cup oil
½ cup apple cider vinegar
1 teaspoon sea salt

1 teaspoon black pepper
1 teaspoon paprika
¼ teaspoon cayenne
1 medium-size onion, chopped

Mix well in blender at high speed; chill.
Yield: 1 quart.

SOUR CREAM DRESSING

1 teaspoon dry mustard
1 teaspoon flour
¼ teaspoon cayenne
½ teaspoon sea salt
1 egg yolk

2 tablespoons white carob syrup
2 tablespoons cider vinegar
1 tablespoon salad oil
½ cup sour cream

Mix dry ingredients in top of double boiler. In a bowl, beat egg yolk well; stir in syrup and vinegar until well blended, then add to double boiler, **stirring** thoroughly. **Place over boiling wa**-ter and cook for about 5 minutes, stirring constantly, until thick and smooth. Remove from heat; cool. Beat in oil and sour cream until dressing is velvety smooth. Scrape out immediately into a small container with cover and refrigerate.

Yield: about ⅔ cup.

Note: This is excellent over sliced tomatoes and cucumbers.

QUICK SOUR CREAM DRESSING

1 cup sour cream
4 teaspoons white carob syrup
    or 10 drops liquid sweetener
¼ teaspoon prepared mustard

3-4 dashes of black pepper
1 teaspoon sea salt
2 teaspoons cider vinegar

Put all ingredients into 1-quart mixing bowl and stir until well blended.

Delicious on sliced cucumbers, with sliced tomatoes and onions, or for cole slaw.

SOUR CREAM-OLIVE DRESSING

1 cup sour cream
1 cup finely chopped ripe olives
3 teaspoons white carob syrup

2 teaspoons lemon juice
¼ teaspoon celery salt
dash of sea salt

Combine all ingredients; chill.

Serve with any fresh- or cooked-fruit salad. Yield: approximately 1½ cups.

TOASTED-SESAME-SEED DRESSING

1 tablespoon sesame seeds
2 tablespoons water
2 tablespoons vinegar
1½ teaspoons lemon juice
½ cup oil
1 teaspoon white carob syrup
  or 2 drops liquid sweetener

1¼ teaspoons sea salt
½ teaspoon black pepper
1 medium-size clove garlic,
  peeled and sliced
2 teaspoons finely cut parsley

Spread sesame seeds on a shallow pan and toast in a pre-heated moderate (350°) oven to a light tan color. Combine rest of ingredients in a pint jar; add sesame seeds. Close jar; shake vigorously. Let stand for 30 minutes; remove garlic. Refrigerate. Yield: about 1 cup.

THOUSAND ISLAND DRESSING

1 cup Dietetic Mayonnaise
  (*see* Index)
½ cup Chili Sauce (*see* Index)
  or dietetic catsup
1 tablespoon chopped green
  onion

2 tablespoons chopped green
  pepper
2 tablespoons chopped stuffed
  olives
1 pimento, minced

Put all ingredients in jar and shake well. Chill.
Yield: about 2 cups.

COOKED MAYONNAISE

1 teaspoon butter or margarine
1½ tablespoons soya carob flour
½ cup water
½ teaspoon dry mustard
½ teaspoon sea salt

½ teaspoon paprika
1 egg yolk, well beaten
2 tablespoons lemon juice or
  vinegar
½ cup oil

Melt butter; stir in flour; add water, and cook, stirring constantly, until mixture is thick and clear. In a blender, combine remaining ingredients, blending well. Add flour-water mixture, blending in thoroughly.

Yield: approximately 1 cup.

DIETETIC MAYONNAISE

1 teaspoon dry mustard	2 egg yolks
1 teaspoon sea salt	¼ cup chilled cider vinegar
¼ teaspoon cayenne	or lemon juice
1 tablespoon carob syrup or	1½ cups chilled oil
6 drops liquid sweetener	

Blend mustard, sea salt, and cayenne together in a bowl. Add sweetener and unbeaten egg yolks, and beat well, then add 1 teaspoon of the vinegar or lemon juice. Add a few drops of the oil, beating them in with a rotary beater or electric mixer. Continue adding the oil, a few drops at a time, beating thoroughly after each addition, until about 2 tablespoons in all have been added and the mixture has thickened. Beat in a little more vinegar and continue to add the oil by teaspoonfuls until 2 more tablespoons have been used. When the mixture becomes fairly thick, oil may be added in larger quantities, but it must be beaten in well after each addition. Add enough vinegar to thin the mixture when it is too stiff. Continue adding oil and vinegar alternately, beating each addition in vigorously, until they have been incorporated completely.

Note: If the oil is added too rapidly at first, mayonnaise will not thicken.

Yield: 1 pint.

JIFFY MAYONNAISE

1 cup oil	¼ teaspoon cayenne
½ teaspoon sea salt	1 tablespoon lemon juice
¼ teaspoon paprika	1 tablespoon vinegar
¼ teaspoon dry mustard	1 egg

Pour ¼ cup of the oil into blender. Add seasonings, lemon juice, vinegar, and egg. Cover; blend for 15 seconds. While blender is still running, remove cover and pour in remaining oil; blend for 5 seconds longer.

Yield: 10 ounces.

BÉCHAMEL SAUCE
(RICH WHITE SAUCE)

2 tablespoons butter	1 cup chicken bouillon
2 tablespoons soya carob flour	2 tablespoons heavy cream
1 tablespoon finely chopped onion	sea salt and pepper to taste

Melt butter; combine with flour, and mix until smooth. Stir in onion. Add bouillon slowly, stirring constantly, until sauce is thickened. Add cream, mixing in well; season with salt and pepper. Simmer for about 15 minutes.

Yield: 1 cup.

LOW-CALORIE BÉCHAMEL SAUCE

2 tablespoons liquid skim milk	1 teaspoon butter
1 cup low-fat cottage cheese	dash of nutmeg
⅛ teaspoon onion powder	pinch of thyme
¼ teaspoon sea salt	

Blend skim milk and cottage cheese in electric blender at high speed until mixture is thick, smooth, and creamy. Turn into a small heavy saucepan and cook over very low heat, stirring constantly, until mixture is hot. Stir in onion powder, sea salt, butter, nutmeg and thyme. Use at once. Yield: 1 cup.

Note: Do not let sauce approach boiling point, as it will curdle.

CAPER SAUCE FOR COLD LOBSTER

¼ cup Dietetic Mayonnaise
  (*see* Index)
⅛ teaspoon paprika
3 tablespoons capers, liquid
½ cup small curd cottage cheese

whole capers
sea salt
⅛ teaspoon dry mustard
1 tablespoon anchovy paste
⅓ cup milk

Blend cottage cheese and milk in electric blender until consistency of whipped cream. Add all the remaining ingredients except capers and blend 2 minutes longer on high speed. Pour into a bowl and chill. Before serving, garnish with whole capers. Cut lobster into bite-size pieces and insert a toothpick in each. Serve on chipped ice centered about the sauce bowl.

CHILI SAUCE

12 medium-size ripe tomatoes
 2 medium-size onions, chopped
     fine
 2 green peppers, chopped fine
 2 cups cider vinegar

2 teaspoons sea salt
2 teaspoons whole cloves
¾ teaspoon cayenne
2 teaspoons ground cinnamon
¾ cup white carob syrup

Dip tomatoes into boiling water. Core, remove skins, and cut into eighths. Add remaining ingredients. Cook at low temperature until sauce is thick and vegetables are tender. Pour into hot, sterilized jars; seal, cool, and store.

Yield: about 2½ pints.

MEXICAN TOMATO SAUCE

1 tablespoon shortening
1 small onion, chopped
1 garlic clove, minced

2 or 3 tablespoons chili powder
3 cups tomato juice
sea salt to taste

Melt shortening in large saucepan. Add onion and garlic, and cook slowly until slightly browned. Add chili powder, tomato juice and sea salt, mixing well. Cook for 10 minutes.

Yield: about 3 cups.

TOMATO CHUTNEY

2 pounds ripe tomatoes
1 cup white carob syrup
1 cup cold vinegar
1 teaspoon instant minced garlic

1 teaspoon sea salt
¼ teaspoon crushed red pepper
1 teaspoon ginger

Wash and peel tomatoes and cut into eighths. Combine with syrup, vinegar, garlic, salt, and red pepper in saucepan; cook, uncovered, until syrup thickens and tomatoes are soft (about 45 minutes). Add ginger and cook 5 minutes longer.
Yield: 1 pint.

CLASSIC HOLLANDAISE SAUCE

3 egg yolks
1 tablespoon cold water
1½ cups butter or margarine
1 tablespoon lemon juice

sea salt to taste
white pepper or cayenne pepper
   to taste

Add water to egg yolks in enamel or stainless steel saucepan or top of double boiler; place pan over very low heat or over hot water. Beat egg yolks with wire whisk until the consistency of a cream sauce. Remove from heat; continue to beat for 1 minute longer.

Melt butter or margarine at the same temperature as the egg yolks. (This is essential to achieving a smooth sauce.) Pour slowly into egg yolks, a little at a time, beating constantly. Be sure each addition has been incorporated into the mixture before adding more butter. Do not incorporate the milky white residue left by the butter. Stir in lemon juice; taste, and correct the seasoning.

Use on fish or vegetables. Yield: 2 cups.

EASY HOLLANDAISE SAUCE

2 egg yolks
3 tablespoons lemon juice

½ cup butter or margarine
dash of cayenne

Beat together egg yolks and lemon juice in a saucepan until well blended. Divide the butter or margarine in half, and to one half add half the egg-yolk mixture. Place over low heat; stir briskly with wire whisk until butter is melted. Add balance of egg-yolk mixture, then add remaining butter and cayenne. Continue to stir briskly until butter is melted and sauce is thick. Serve at once.

Yield: approximately ⅔ cup.

THREE-MINUTE HOLLANDAISE SAUCE

¼ cup Dietetic Mayonnaise (*see* Index) or salad dressing

¼ cup sour cream
1 teaspoon lemon juice
½ teaspoon prepared mustard

Combine all ingredients in a saucepan and heat slowly. Serve with broccoli.

Yield: ½ cup.

QUICK HOLLANDAISE SAUCE

3 egg yolks
2 tablespoons lemon juice
¼ teaspoon sea salt

dash of cayenne
½ cup butter or margarine

Put egg yolks, lemon juice, salt, and cayenne into a blender jar. In a small saucepan, heat butter or margarine until bubbly, but be careful not to let it burn. Cover blender and run at high speed for 2 or 3 seconds. Remove center section of blender cover and pour in hot butter or margarine in a steady stream, operating blender at high speed. This should take about 30 seconds. Do not use milky white residue left by butter in saucepan.

Yield: ¾ cup.

LEMON-PEPPER BUTTER

1 cup butter
⅛ cup chives (fresh or freeze dried), snipped
¾ teaspoon grated lemon peel

1 tablespoon lemon juice
¼ teaspoon freshly ground black pepper

In a small mixer bowl, cream butter until light and fluffy. Add chives, lemon peel, lemon juice, and pepper. Mix thoroughly to blend all ingredients well. Store in refrigerator in tightly covered container til needed. Yield: 1 cup.

Note: Use this seasoned butter to add flavor to vegetables and to brush over broiled fish, beefsteaks, and pork cutlets. Melt it to use as a dip for shrimp, lobster, artichokes.

PEPPER BUTTER

½ cup soft butter or margarine
1 tablespoon each of minced raw red and green pepper
1 teaspoon grated onion

1 tablespoon minced parsley
1 teaspoon garlic salt
½ teaspoon cayenne
2 tablespoons lemon juice

Cream butter; add remaining ingredients, mixing well. Store in a covered jar in refrigerator. Spread on hot cooked fish or chops. Yield: 1 cup.

BASIC BARBECUE SAUCE FOR PORK

3 tablespoons butter
2 garlic cloves, minced
4 tablespoons minced onion
¼ cup soy sauce
2 tablespoons oil

2 teaspoons lemon juice
1 tablespoon poppy seeds
1 teaspoon sea salt
⅛ teaspoon pepper
dash of cinnamon

In a frying pan on edge of grill, cook onion and garlic in butter until brown. Add remaining ingredients. Cook 10 to 15 minutes or until bubbly hot. Remove from heat and use immediately.

Yield: ½-¾ cup.

BASIC BARBECUE SAUCE FOR VEAL

¼ cup butter
¾ cup chopped celery
1 cup dietetic catsup
1 cup unsweetened crushed
    pineapple, drained

3 tablespoons pineapple juice
1 teaspoon onion salt
2 teaspoons garlic salt
dash of cayenne pepper

In a frying pan on edge of grill, cook celery in butter until tender. Add remaining ingredients. Cook for 10 minutes, or until bubbly. Remove from heat; cover.

Yield: 1½ cups.

ELSIE'S BARBECUE SPICE

2 teaspoons paprika
1 teaspoon chili powder
1 teaspoon onion salt
1 teaspoon white pepper
1 teaspoon celery salt
1 teaspoon garlic salt
1 teaspoon nutmeg

1 teaspoon allspice
½ teaspoon oregano
1 teaspoon dry mustard
¼ teaspoon ground sage
½ teaspoon cloves
½ teaspoon cardamom

Mix well. Pour into shaker. Makes 12 teaspoons.

RHUBARB SAUCE

1 20-ounce package frozen
    rhubarb, unsweetened
¼ cup water

⅛ teaspoon sea salt
½ cup white carob syrup
dash of cinnamon

In a saucepan, combine all ingredients; simmer, covered, until tender, stirring occasionally. Refrigerate until ready to use.

Serve with Rhubarb Cake (*see* Index).

SEAFOOD SAUCE

Combine ½ cup dietetic catsup with 1 tablespoon lemon juice, dash of sea salt, and 2 teaspoons prepared white horse-radish.

SWEET AND SOUR MEAT SAUCE

1 8-ounce can undrained,
    unsweetened pineapple
¼ cup white carob syrup
¼ cup coarsely chopped onion
¼ cup coarsely chopped green
    pepper

dash of sea salt
1 packet sugar substitute
1 tablespoon vinegar
2 tablespoons soya carob flour
¼ cup water
1 pimento, sliced

Place pineapple, syrup, onion, green pepper, sugar substitute, salt, and vinegar in a saucepan. Cook, stirring constantly, over moderate heat until onion is clear. Thicken with flour mixed with water—add just enough to make a thin sauce. Add pimento for color.

Note: This is good on baked ham or may be used as sauce for pork.

SWISS CHEESE SAUCE

½ cup shredded process Swiss
    cheese
¼ cup Dietetic Mayonnaise
    (*see* Index)

½ cup sour cream
paprika

In a saucepan, combine cheese and mayonnaise and cook over low heat, stirring constantly until cheese melts. (If necessary, beat smooth with rotary beater.) Mix in sour cream and let heat through. Sprinkle with paprika. Serve with hot cauliflower or asparagus.

Yield: 1 cup.

VEGETABLE DRESSING

1 cup oil
½ cup dietetic catsup
½ cup apple cider vinegar
1 clove garlic, cut in half

1 teaspoon grated onion
1 teaspoon sea salt
1 teaspoon paprika

Measure all ingredients into bottle or jar; close, and shake well. Let stand 20 minutes, then remove garlic. Keeps indefinitely.

Yield: 1 pint.

Vegetables

ARTICHOKES ITALIAN STYLE

2 9-ounce packages frozen
   artichoke hearts
½ cup drained and cut up
   canned tomatoes
1 teaspoon sea salt
¼ teaspoon pepper

¼ teaspoon garlic salt
2 teaspoons chopped parsley
½ cup grated Parmesan cheese
¾ cup water
¼ cup olive oil
6 eggs

Arrange unthawed artichoke hearts in bottom of a greased 2-quart casserole and lay tomatoes on top. Sprinkle with salt, pepper, garlic salt, chopped parsley, and cheese. Pour water and olive oil over all. Cover and bake in preheated moderate oven (350°) for 1 hour, or until artichokes are tender.

Beat eggs with rotary beater until light and fluffy and pour over cooked artichokes. Continue to bake, uncovered, until eggs are set, about 15 to 20 mintues longer.

Serves 8.

ASPARAGUS CUSTARD

1 1-pound can cut asparagus,
   drained
3 eggs, well beaten
1 teaspoon sea salt
¼ teaspoon pepper
¾ cup cracker crumbs

1 pimento cut into small pieces
1 cup ¼-inch cubes Cheddar
   cheese
1 cup milk
3 tablespoons butter or
   margarine, melted

158

Add to the eggs the salt, pepper, cracker crumbs, pimento, cheese, and milk. Stir in the asparagus, and pour into a greased 1½-quart casserole. Pour butter over the top. Set into a preheated moderate oven (350°) and bake, uncovered, for about 30 minutes or until the custard is set.

Serves 6.

ASPARAGUS WITH CHEESE SAUCE

1 9-ounce can asparagus
1 tablespoon butter

2 slices American cheese
sea salt and pepper to taste

Drain liquor from asparagus into small saucepan; add butter and cheese; heat until cheese is melted. Season with salt and pepper. Add asparagus and bring to a boil. Serve immediately.

CURRY-CREAMED ASPARAGUS

2 1-pound cans of asparagus
   spears
¼ cup butter or margarine
3 tablespoons chopped green
   onion

¼ teaspoon curry powder
½ teaspoon sea salt
2 cups milk
⅓ cup soya carob flour
⅓ cup grated Romano cheese

Melt butter in a saucepan and stir in onion, curry powder, and salt; cook for a few minutes. Stir in flour, blending well, and gradually add milk. Cook and stir over medium heat until mixture boils and thickens (about 10 minutes). Add drained asparagus spears and turn into greased shallow baking dish (about 1½-quart size). Place 3 spears on top for garnish; sprinkle with cheese; bake uncovered, in preheated hot oven (425°) for 15 minutes.

Serves 4-6.

BABY BEETS IN SOUR CREAM

2½ cups drained halved cooked
    beets
¼ cup dairy sour cream
1 tablespoon vinegar

1 teaspoon minced green onion
1 teaspoon white carob syrup
½ teaspoon sea salt
dash of cayenne

Combine all ingredients, except beets, until blended. Add beets and heat slowly, stirring to coat.

Serves 4.

BROCCOLI PUDDING

1 10-ounce package frozen
    chopped broccoli
1 cup salted water
2 tablespoons butter or
    margarine, melted
2 tablespoons soya carob flour
¼ teaspoon sea salt

dash of pepper
1 cup milk
1 tablespoon scraped onion
¾ cup Dietetic Mayonnaise
    (*see* Index)
3 eggs, well beaten

Cook frozen broccoli in boiling salted water just until thawed and still bright green; drain. In another pan, blend melted butter and flour, salt, and pepper, and cook until bubbly. Gradually stir in milk, and cook, stirring constantly, until thickened and smooth. Remove from heat and stir in onion, mayonnaise, and beaten eggs. Carefully mix in the broccoli. Turn into a 2-quart casserole and set it, uncovered, in a pan of hot water. Bake in preheated moderate oven (350°) for about 30 minutes, or until the custard is set.

Serves 6.

BROCCOLI PIQUANT I

2 pounds broccoli
½ cup water
½ teaspoon sea salt
pepper to taste

garlic powder to taste
1 bay leaf
2 thin lemon slices
1 tablespoon butter

Remove large leaves and tough part of broccoli stalks. Score ends. Place on rack with water in pressure cooker. Sprinkle lightly with seasonings; add bay leaf, lemon slices, and butter. Close cover securely. Cook for 3 minutes at 5 pounds of pressure, and let stand until pressure drops of its own accord.

Serves 6.

BROCCOLI PIQUANT II

2 pounds broccoli	⅛ teaspoon garlic powder
1 cup water	1 bay leaf
½ teaspoon sea salt	2 thin lemon slices
¼ teaspoon black pepper	1 tablespoon butter

Remove large leaves and tough part of broccoli stalks. Score ends. Place in an uncovered saucepan. Add water, salt, pepper, garlic, bay leaf, lemon, and butter. Bring to boil, then reduce heat. Cook from 10 to 15 minutes, until tender. Serve immediately.

Serves 6.

GRILLED RED CABBAGE

1 medium-size head red cabbage	1 teaspoon sea salt
½ cup finely chopped onion	1 teaspoon paprika
1 teaspoon red pepper flakes	1 tablespoon garlic salt
3 tablespoons lemon juice	2 tablespoons water
3 tablespoons oil	¼ cup melted butter

Wash cabbage, cut into 6 pieces, and place on individual pieces of aluminum foil, turning ends up slightly. Place 1 tablespoon of the water on each piece of cabbage. Combine all the remaining ingredients except butter and mix well; let stand for 15 minutes. Using approximately half of this mixture, drizzle it equally over cabbage pieces; then close aluminum foil into secure packages. Place on hot barbecue grill 6 inches from coals;

cook for 20 minutes. Open packages, drizzle with remaining sauce and melted butter; reclose foil and cook cabbage for another 10 minutes, or until tender.

BAKED CARROTS WITH TOASTED SESAME SEEDS

12 medium-size carrots
  butter as needed
3 tablespoons sesame seeds

⅛ teaspoon sea salt
dash of pepper

Wash and peel carrots; cut in half lengthwise. Arrange in a greased shallow baking dish; dot with butter and cover; bake in a preheated moderate oven for 1 hour or until tender.

Place sesame seeds in a small shallow baking dish in the oven (toward the end of the cooking period for the carrots) for about 5 minutes or until they are golden brown, stirring occasionally. Sprinkle warm seeds, salt, and pepper over carrots just before serving.

Serves 6.

CARROTS WITH FRUIT SAUCE I

4 cups peeled sliced carrots
¾ cup unsweetened pineapple
  juice
1 tablespoon soya carob flour
2 packets sugar substitute

¼ teaspoon sea salt
¼ cup water plus 1 tablespoon
  water
1 tablespoon butter

Place carrots and pineapple juice in pressure cooker. Cover and cook at 15 pounds pressure for 3 minutes, then reduce pressure instantly. Mix together flour, sweetener, salt, and water, and add to carrots. Cook, uncovered, stirring constantly, until thickened, then stir in butter. Serve hot.

Serves 6.

CARROTS WITH FRUIT SAUCE II

4 cups peeled, sliced carrots
water
¾ teaspoon sea salt
1 tablespoon soya carob flour

2 packages sugar substitute
¾ cup unsweetened pineapple
    juice
1 tablespoon butter

Place carrots in a pot with water to cover. Add ½ teaspoon of the salt. Cover. Cook 10 to 15 minutes, or until tender. Drain. In another pan mix together flour, sweetener, remaining salt, and pineapple juice and add to carrots. Cook uncovered, stirring constantly, until thickened, then stir in butter. Serve hot.
Serves 6.

COMPANY CARROTS

2 bunches (about 2½ pounds)
    whole young carrots
boiling salted water, to cover
½ cup Dietetic Mayonnaise
    (*see* Index)
1 tablespoon minced onion
1 tablespoon prepared
    horseradish

sea salt and pepper to taste
¼ cup fine cracker crumbs
2 tablespoons butter or
    margarine
dash of paprika
chopped parsley

Scrub carrots thoroughly and scrape lightly to remove only the thin outer layer of skin. Cook the carrots in the water for about 15 minutes until tender; reserve ¼ cup of the cooking liquor. Cut carrots lengthwise into narrow strips and arrange in greased shallow baking pan 8 or 9 inches square.

In a saucepan, combine carrot liquor with mayonnaise, onion, horseradish, salt, and pepper. Just before mealtime, pour over the carrots, sprinkle with cracker crumbs, dot with butter, and sprinkle paprika and parsley over all. Bake, uncovered, in a preheated moderately hot oven (375°) for 15 to 20 minutes.
Serves 6.

DEEP-FRIED CARROTS

Wash and peel carrots; quarter them lengthwise, and lightly sprinkle with salt. Deep-fry in oil; drain on paper towels. Serve hot.

TROPICAL CARROTS

6 carrots, thinly sliced	½ cup water
½ teaspoon sea salt	2 teaspoons soya carob flour
2 tablespoons white carob syrup	½ cup orange juice
2 tablespoons dietetic coconut	2 tablespoons butter

Peel carrots.

Combine carrots, water, and salt in a saucepan. Cover and bring to a boil, then cook at low temperature for 6 minutes or until tender. Blend flour, syrup and orange juice until smooth; stir in carrots; continue to cook and stir until sauce is thickened, then add coconut and butter. Serve hot.

Serves 3.

CAULIFLOWER WITH ALMOND BUTTER

1 small head cauliflower	¼ cup butter
boiling salted water, to cover	¼ cup sliced blanched almonds

Trim cauliflower and break into flowerets. Cook in boiling salted water until tender. Drain; keep hot. Heat butter; sauté almonds until golden brown. Place cauliflower in hot serving dish and pour almond butter over it.

Serves 3-4.

CAULIFLOWER WITH WHITE SAUCE

1 large head cauliflower
    (approx. 2 pounds)
boiling salted water, to cover
3 tablespoons butter
1 medium-size onion, chopped
1 small green pepper, chopped

1 2-ounce can mushrooms
    (stems and pieces)
1 cup (¼ pound) shredded
    sharp Cheddar cheese
2 tablespoons sesame seeds

WHITE SAUCE

4 tablespoons butter
2 tablespoons soya carob flour
½ teaspoon sea salt

dash of pepper
1 cup milk

Prepare White Sauce as follows: Melt butter, mix in flour to make a smooth paste; gradually add milk, stirring all the while, and cook, continuing to stir constantly, until mixture thickens. Remove from heat.

Separate cauliflower into flowerets and cook in the water for about 10 minutes (until barely tender); drain and set aside. In another pan, heat butter to melting and sauté onion, green pepper, and mushrooms until onion is transparent.

Grease a 2-quart casserole and in it arrange alternate layers of cauliflower, the sautéed vegetables, cheese, and white sauce. Put the sesame seeds into a shallow pan and place in a preheated moderate oven (350°) for about 10 minutes, stirring occasionally, until seeds are toasted, then sprinkle them over casserole. Bake, uncovered, at 350° for 30 minutes or until bubbly.

Serves 8.

SWISS CHARD WITH CHEESE SAUCE

2 pounds Swiss chard
boiling salted water
2 tablespoons butter
2 tablespoons soya carob flour

2 teaspoons sea salt
½ cup milk
¼ pound process American
    cheese, diced

Wash chard, cut out heavy ribs, and cut them into 1-inch pieces. Cook them in ¾ inch boiling water, covered, for 5 minutes. Meantime, shred chard leaves; add to ribs, and cook 5 minutes longer. Drain well, pressing out extra liquid.

Melt butter in saucepan; add flour. Stir to moisten flour. Mix in and gradually add milk, stirring constantly. Cook over medium heat until sauce thickens. Add cheese; stir until it melts.

Combine chard and sauce in a greased 1½-quart casserole and bake, uncovered, in preheated 325° oven for about 45 minutes.

Serves 4.

SWISS CHARD AND GREEN ONIONS

2 pounds Swiss chard	1 bunch green onions, cut into
4 slices smoked bacon	1-inch lengths
½ teaspoon sea salt	1 hard-boiled egg, sieved

Fry bacon in skillet; drain and keep warm. Wash chard; cut away heavy ribs, shred leaves, and put into skillet with bacon fat. Add salt and onions. Cover, and cook slowly until tender. Put in serving dish; crumble bacon over top and add egg.

Serves 6.

BRAISED CUCUMBERS

3 medium-size cucumbers	1 beef or chicken bouillon cube
2 tablespoons butter or	1 tablespoon boiling water
margarine	salt and pepper

Peel cucumbers; cut once lengthwise and once crosswise. Brown slightly in butter. Add bouillon cube dissolved in water. Cook covered, over low heat for about 5 minutes. Season to taste.

Serves 4.

BAKED EGGPLANT I

1 large eggplant
salted water
¼ cup butter or margarine
salt and pepper to taste
½ pound fresh mushrooms, sliced

2 8-ounce cans tomato sauce
  (without sugar)
½ cup fine dry artichoke-bread
  crumbs, mixed with ½ cup
  grated Parmesan cheese

Place the whole unpeeled eggplant in enough salted water to
cover completely; bring to a boil, reduce heat; simmer for 10
minutes. Drain and cool enough to handle. Cut into quarters
lengthwise; peel each quarter, then cut crosswise into 1-inch
pieces. Arrange as follows in buttered 2-quart casserole, repeat-
ing layers once: a layer of eggplant pieces dotted with butter
and sprinkled with salt and pepper, uncooked mushrooms, tomato sauce, and bread-crumb-cheese mixture. Place, uncovered,
in a preheated moderate oven (350°) and bake for ½ hour.
Serve hot.

Serves 6.

BAKED EGGPLANT II

1 medium-size eggplant
oil for frying
1 pound ground chuck
1 teaspoon olive oil
salt and pepper

½ cup freshly grated Parmesan
  cheese
1 cup Béchamel Sauce
  (*see* Index)

Slice eggplant about ½ inch thick; do not peel.* Fry over
brisk heat until lightly browned on both sides. Meantime, in
another pan, cook beef in the olive oil until it loses its red color,
stirring often to keep it broken up. Season to taste with salt and
pepper.

Place a layer of eggplant slices in bottom of a greased shallow

---

*To cut down on absorption of oil, allow eggplant slices to "sweat" by
salting and letting stand ½-1 hour before frying.

1½-quart casserole. Add a layer of beef, then another layer of eggplant. Pour on a layer of white sauce. Sprinkle cheese on top. Bake in preheated hot (400°) oven for 15 minutes, or until top is golden brown and crisp.

FRIED EGGPLANT

1 medium-size eggplant	onion salt
1 egg, slightly beaten	cooking oil
1 tablespoon cold water	black pepper
½ cup scya carob flour	

Pare eggplant, cut in half lengthwise, then cut crosswise into half-inch-thick slices. Combine egg with water. Dip eggplant slices first in egg mixture, then flour; sprinkle with onion salt and pepper. Fry for 2-3 minutes on each side, or until tender and brown. Drain on paper towels.

Serves 6-8.

BEEF-EGGPLANT SKILLET

1 small eggplant, cut in ½-inch slices (pared or unpared)	¾ cup water
	¼ cup chopped green pepper
1 pound ground lean chuck	½ teaspoon chili powder
fat as needed	1 teaspoon oregano
¼ cup chopped onion	½ teaspoon sea salt
1 tablespoon soya carob flour	1 cup shredded sharp process cheese
1 8-ounce can Spanish-style tomato sauce (without sugar)	

Preheat electric skillet to 375° and brown beef and onion in small amount of hot fat, spooning off excess. Sprinkle flour over meat; stir it in. Add tomato sauce, water, green pepper. Arrange slices of eggplant over all; cover; simmer at about 230° for 10 to 15 minutes, until eggplant is tender. Top with shredded cheese.

Serves 6-8.

SWISS EGGPLANT

1 large eggplant, cut into
    ¼-inch-thick slices
½ cup chopped onion
2 tablespoons oil
1 6-ounce can tomato paste
1¾ cups water
2 teaspoons oregano

½ cup chopped fresh parsley
1 teaspoon sea salt
¾ pound Swiss cheese, sliced
2¾ cups day-old artichoke bread
    cut into ½-inch cubes
1 cup shredded Parmesan
    cheese

Combine the onion and oil in a saucepan; cook until onion is soft. Add tomato paste, water, oregano, parsley, and salt; simmer for 5 to 10 minutes.

Coat eggplant slices with the onion-tomato sauce. Arrange half the slices in a greased 13-inch-by-9-inch pan; cover with cheese slices. Spoon half the sauce over all, then top with remaining eggplant. Mix remainder of sauce with bread, stirring to coat well, and spoon over eggplant. Sprinkle with Parmesan cheese. Cover loosely with foil and bake in preheated moderately hot oven (350°) for 45 minutes; remove foil and bake 30 minutes more. Slip casserole under broiler for a few seconds to brown, if you like.

Serves 6-8.

TURKISH EGGPLANT

2 medium-size eggplants, sliced
    (but not necessarily peeled)
1 small head garlic
2 medium-size onions, chopped
3 cups chopped green peppers

6 tomatoes sliced, or 1 #3-can
    tomatoes
salt to taste
½ cup olive oil

Preheat oven to 300°. Blanch garlic cloves by placing in boiling water and boiling for 2 minutes, then peel and chop. Lightly oil a large heavy casserole; cover with a solid layer of eggplant slices and sprinkle some of the garlic over them. Add a layer of chopped onion, then one of green pepper, and then one of tomatoes. Sprinkle lightly with salt. Repeat until all vegetables are used. (If you are using canned tomatoes, pour juice from can over mixture.) Sprinkle oil over the top. Bake at 300° for 3 hours or at 250° for 5 hours. This should have a custardy texture.

Serves 6.

GREEN BEANS WITH BELL PEPPERS

1 16-ounce can green beans
2 tablespoons butter or
    margarine, or 1 slice bacon

⅓ cup chopped green and red
    bell peppers
sea salt and pepper to taste

In a saucepan, bring beans, butter (or bacon), bell peppers, salt, and pepper to a boil; cook until liquid is absorbed but vegetables are not dry. Serve hot.

Serves 4.

CREAM-STYLE GREEN BEANS

1 10-ounce package frozen
    green beans
1 3-ounce package cream
    cheese, softened

1 tablespoon milk
¼ teaspoon celery seed
¼ teaspoon sea salt

Cook beans according to package directions; drain. Combine remaining ingredients; blend thoroughly. Add to beans and heat through.

Serves 4.

DEVILED GREEN BEANS

1 1-pound can cut green beans,
    drained
1 medium-size onion, chopped
1 clove garlic, minced
½ green pepper, chopped
2 canned pimentos, sliced
3 tablespoons butter or
    margarine

2 teaspoons prepared mustard
1 8-ounce can tomato sauce
    (without sugar)
1 cup shredded Cheddar
    cheese

Sauté onion, garlic, green pepper, and pimentos in butter or margarine until onions are limp. Stir in mustard, tomato sauce, and cheese. Combine beans and sauce; turn into greased 1-quart casserole. Bake, uncovered, in preheated moderate oven (350°) for 25 minutes, or until cheese is melted.

Serves 4.

GREEN BEANS AND ONION

2 10-ounce packages frozen green beans	½ teaspoon basil
1 medium onion, sliced	1 teaspoon white carob syrup or 1 packet sugar substitute
1 teaspoon sea salt	3 tablespoons butter
¼ teaspoon pepper	

Place beans on a large square of heavy-duty aluminum foil; add onion. Sprinkle with salt, pepper and basil. Add syrup or sweetener; dot with butter. Fold foil into compact, tight bundle. Cook over glowing coals on barbecue grill for 25 to 35 minutes, turning occasionally. Fold back the foil to serve.

BUTTERED MUSHROOMS

1 6-ounce can mushrooms, drained	sea salt to taste
1 tablespoon butter	pepper to taste

Combine all ingredients in small saucepan; heat. Serve hot over meats or as a side dish.

MUSHROOMS IN CHEESE SAUCE

1 6-ounce can mushrooms	1 slice American cheese
1 tablespoon butter	sea salt and pepper to taste

Drain liquid from mushrooms into small saucepan; add butter and cheese, season with salt and pepper. Heat until cheese melts. Add mushrooms and bring to a boil. Serve immediately.

STEAMED OKRA

Wash young okra pods leaving the stems on. Place in colander over boiling water. Cover and steam for 15 minutes, or
until okra is tender. Serve hot, accompanied by individual con-
tainers of hot melted butter into which each person can dip the
pod. Salt to taste.

ROSEMARY PARSNIPS

10 parsnips (about 2 pounds)
boiling salted water
2 tablespoons butter (approx.)
2 tablespoons soya carob flour
¼ teaspoon chopped fresh or
    dried rosemary

¼ cup grated Parmesan cheese
2 cups light cream
½ cup crumbs (from salted
    round butter crackers)
    mixed with ¼ cup melted
    butter

Peel parsnips; cook in the water until tender (about 30 minutes). Drain. Cut each parsnip in half lengthwise, and arrange
half the pieces in a greased 2-quart baking dish; dot with butter.
Blend together flour, rosemary, and cheese; sprinkle half the
mixture over the layer of parsnips. Place the rest of the parsnips
in the casserole and cover with butter seasonings, and cream, as
before. Sprinkle buttered crumbs over casserole and bake, uncovered, in a preheated hot oven (400°) for 20 minutes.
Serves 6.

CANNED SOYBEANS

Pick over and wash 6 cups soybeans. Soak 6 to 8 hours. Rinse
2 times. Pack into quart jars; cover with hot water. Add 1 teaspoon sea salt to each jar. Seal. Place in a pressure cooker and
cook for 1 hour at 15 pounds pressure. Let pressure drop of its
own accord.
Yield: 6 quarts.

OVEN-BAKED SOYBEANS

1 quart Canned Soybeans
(*see* above), undrained
3 slices crisp fried and crumbled
bacon
1 cup dietetic catsup
1 teaspoon sea salt

¾ cup mixed red and green
peppers, chopped
1 medium-size onion, chopped
3 teaspoons hot sauce
(optional)
2 tablespoons bacon drippings

Fry bacon until crisp; crumble it. Mix with above ingredients in greased large casserole. Bake in preheated oven for 1 hour at 400°. Serve hot or cold.

SPINACH BAKE

2 cups chopped uncooked
spinach or 2 10-ounce
packages frozen chopped
spinach
3 slices bacon
1 small onion, minced

2 eggs
½ teaspoon sea salt
dash of pepper
3 tablespoon fine dry artichoke-
bread crumbs
1 cup shredded Cheddar cheese

Cook bacon until lightly browned; drain on paper towels. Pour off all but 2 tablespoons bacon drippings; add onion and cook until limp. Combine with onion, spinach, and cheese. Beat eggs well with the salt and pepper and stir into spinach. Turn into shallow greased 1-quart baking dish. Sprinkle with bread crumbs and bacon cut into small pieces. Bake, uncovered, in preheated moderate oven for 40 minutes, or until set.
Serves 6.

SPINACH CUSTARD

2 10-ounce packages frozen
chopped spinach
2 medium-sized onions, chopped
1 clove garlic, minced
¼ cup oil
6 eggs
1 teaspoon sea salt

¼ teaspoon pepper
2 cups shredded medium-soft
Monterey Jack cheese
½ cup cottage cheese
1 cup shredded sharp Cheddar
cheese

Cook onions with garlic in oil until soft. Add spinach and cook over low heat, breaking spinach block apart to hasten process until thawed. Meanwhile, beat eggs until foamy; season with salt and pepper. Stir cheeses into eggs, blending well. Combine with spinach mixture. Turn into a greased 2-quart casserole and bake, uncovered, in hot preheated oven (400°) for 40 minutes, or until softly set (stir 4 or 5 times during baking).

Serves 8.

SPINACH AND MACARONI ITALIANO

1 pound artichoke macaroni

SPINACH FILLING

2 10-ounce packages frozen chopped spinach
½ cup oil
2 cups soft artichoke-bread crumbs

½ cup minced parsley
½ cup grated Romano cheese
1½ teaspoons sea salt
1 teaspoon sage

BEEF FILLING

2 pounds lean ground beef
2 medium-size onions, chopped
1 clove garlic, minced or mashed
1 3-ounce can sliced mushrooms, drained
1 8-ounce can tomato sauce

1 6-ounce can tomato paste
1 cup water
1½ teaspoons mixed Italian seasonings
1½ teaspoons sea salt
½ teaspoon pepper

Cook macaroni according to directions on package; drain.

Thaw spinach; mix together with the other ingredients for Spinach Filling.

To prepare Beef Filling, lightly cook beef, onions, and garlic in large frying pan, covered, until crumbly. Add the balance of the ingredients in the order listed; stir until well blended. Cover; simmer gently for 1½ hours.

Grease a 9-by-13-inch pan; place half the macaroni in it. Top with half the spinach filling, and on that spread half the beef filling. Repeat this procedure with the balance of the macaroni, spinach, and beef fillings. Bake, uncovered, in a preheated moderate oven (350°) for 30 minutes.

Serves 10-12.

SQUASH KABOBS

2 small ripe acorn squash
12 small whole onions, peeled
¼ cup butter
1 teaspoon sea salt

⅛ teaspoon pepper
4 cloves, crushed
dash of nutmeg

Halve squash; peel; cut into 2-by-2-inch cubes. Combine butter, salt, pepper, cloves, and nutmeg; let stand for 15 minutes. Meantime, on lightly greased skewers, alternate squash cubes and onions; brush with half the seasoned butter. Wrap skewers in aluminum foil; place on hot barbecue grill, 6 inches from coals. Cook for 15-20 minutes, turning frequently, then open foil packages. Continue to cook until squash is tender. Remove from heat; brush with balance of butter mixture.

Serves 6.

GREEN AND GOLD SQUASH

2-3 medium-size zucchini
(about ¾ pound), scrubbed
and coarsely shredded
2 medium-size summer squash
(about ¾ pound), scrubbed
and coarsely shredded
1 medium-size onion, chopped
2 tablespoons oil
2 tablespoons chopped parsley

½ teaspoon sea salt
¼ teaspoon pepper
½ teaspoon oregano
3 eggs, slightly beaten
½ cup milk
1 cup shredded sharp Cheddar
cheese
½ cup cracker crumbs

In a large frying pan, sauté onion in oil until golden brown. Remove from heat; stir in shredded zucchini and squash, parsley, salt, pepper, and oregano. Beat eggs with milk until blended and add to vegetable mixture. Spoon about half the mixture into a buttered 1½-quart baking dish, and over it sprinkle half the cheese and half the crumbs. Make a second layer of the remaining vegetable mixture; sprinkle with remaining cracker crumbs and arrange the last of the cheese in a crisscross design on top. Bake, uncovered, in a preheated moderately slow oven (325°) for about 45 minutes.

Serves 6.

BAKED TOMATOES I

4 medium-size tomatoes
sea salt
pepper
2 tablespoons fresh soya-bread
    crumbs

2 tablespoons melted butter or
    margarine
1 tablespoon chopped parsley

Preheat oven to 450°. Wash tomatoes and cut in half crosswise. Sprinkle cut surfaces with salt, pepper, and bread crumbs; drizzle butter over top. Place in shallow baking pan. Bake for 10 minutes or until just tender. Sprinkle with parsley.

Makes 8 servings.

BAKED TOMATOES II

2 large tomatoes (about 1
    pound)
4 tablespoons butter or
    margarine
¼ cup finely chopped onion

1 teaspoon prepared mustard
½ teaspoon soy sauce
2 teaspoons chopped parsley
2 slices soya bread, torn into
    coarse crumbs

Preheat oven to 350°. Wash tomatoes; remove stems. Cut in half crosswise. Place, cut side up, in a small shallow baking dish. Heat 2 tablespoons of the butter in a small skillet and sauté onion until tender; stir in mustard and soy sauce. Spread on tomato halves. Melt remaining butter in same skillet and stir in bread crumbs and parsley. Sprinkle over tomatoes. Bake, uncovered, for 20 minutes, or until tomatoes are heated through and crumbs are golden brown.

Serves 4.

TOMATOES BAKED WITH ANCHOVIES

4 large tomatoes
2 medium-size white onions,
   sliced
1 2-ounce can anchovy fillets,
   drained
¼ cup grated Parmesan cheese

chopped parsley
2 tablespoons oil
2 cloves garlic, crushed
¼ cup capers
½ cup coarsely chopped ripe
   olives

Preheat oven to 400°. Wash tomatoes; remove stems. In each tomato make 4 even vertical cuts, being careful not to cut all the way through, so base of tomato is still intact. Arrange in a greased shallow baking pan.

In hot oil in small skillet, sauté onion and garlic, stirring, until tender (about 5 minutes). Rinse anchovy fillets and capers in cold water; drain. Spoon some of onion mixture into each cut in tomatoes (use about half); place an anchovy fillet in each cut. Top each tomato with capers and remaining onion mixture and sprinkle with Parmesan cheese. Bake, uncovered, for 15-20 minutes, or until tender. Sprinkle with chopped olives and parsley. Serve warm or cold, as an appetizer or salad.

CREOLE BAKED TOMATOES

2 medium-size tomatoes
   (about ½ pound)
¼ teaspoon sea salt
dash black pepper

2 tablespoons butter or
   margarine
½ cup finely chopped onion
1 clove garlic, crushed

SAUCE

1 tablespoon butter or
   margarine
1 tablespoon soya carob flour
1 cup light cream

¼ teaspoon hot sauce
½ teaspoon sea salt
½ cup chopped parsley

Preheat oven to 400°. Wash tomatoes; remove stems; cut in half crosswise. Place, cut side up, in greased small shallow baking dish. Sprinkle with ¼ teaspoon salt and pepper.

Heat butter in medium-size skillet and sauté onion and garlic over low heat until onion is tender. Spoon over tomatoes. Bake for 20-25 minutes, or until tomatoes are tender but not mushy.

Meanwhile, make sauce. In same skillet, melt butter; remove from heat; stir in flour, then cream. Bring to a boil, stirring constantly. Add salt, hot sauce, and parsley. Simmer, stirring, a few minutes longer.

Arrange tomatoes on serving platter; spoon sauce over top. Serves 4.

STEWED TOMATOES AND OKRA

2 tablespoons butter or margarine	1 10-ounce package frozen okra
1 medium-size onion, thinly sliced	1 1-pound can stewed tomatoes
	¾ teaspoon sea salt
	¼ teaspoon pepper

Heat butter in large skillet; sauté onion until tender (about 5 minutes). Add remaining ingredients. Cook gently, covered, for 15-20 minutes, or until okra is tender.

Serves 6-8.

BOILED TURNIPS

Allow 1 large turnip for each person. Peel turnips and boil in water in covered saucepan to which have been added salt, pepper, and a little white carob syrup. When turnips are tender, mash and season with additional butter or salt-meat drippings.

QUICK VEGETABLE CASSEROLE

2 10-ounce packages frozen cut green beans	1 3- or 4-ounce can mushroom pieces, drained
1 1-pound can bean sprouts, drained	1 10½-ounce can cheese sauce
1 4-ounce can water chestnuts, drained and sliced	1 meduim-size onion, chopped
	1 3½-ounce can fried onion rings

Cook green beans until barely tender, then drain. Toss lightly with bean sprouts, water chestnuts, and mushrooms. Turn into a greased shallow 2½-quart casserole.

Combine cheese sauce with onion; spoon over vegetables. Bake, uncovered, in a preheated moderate oven (350°) for 25 minutes. Top with fried onion rings and bake for 10 minutes longer.

Serves 6.

ZUCCHINI CUSTARD

2 pounds zucchini, scrubbed
and cut into small pieces
¼ pound butter or margarine
3 eggs
½ cup undiluted evaporated milk
2 tablespoons dry artichoke-
bread crumbs
1 teaspoon instant minced onion

1 teaspoon soy sauce
dash of liquid hot-pepper
seasoning
¾ teaspoon sea salt
⅛ teaspoon pepper
⅓ cup shredded Parmesan
cheese

In a large frying pan that has a tight-fitting cover, melt butter; add zucchini; cover, and cook over low heat, stirring occasionally, until tender (5 to 7 minutes). Remove from heat and set aside.

Beat the eggs and milk together; stir in the bread crumbs, onion, soy sauce, hot-pepper seasoning, salt, pepper, and about half the cheese. Combine with the zucchini, stirring until well blended. Turn into a buttered 1½-quart casserole. Sprinkle remaining cheese on top. Bake, uncovered, in a preheated moderate oven (350°) for 35-40 minutes.

Note: If the dish has been refrigerated between preparation and cooking, allow about 10 minutes more baking time.

Serves 4-6.

ZUCCHINI PARMESAN

4-5 small zucchini, thinly sliced
(about 3 cups)
2 tablespoons butter or
margarine

½ teaspoon sea salt
dash of pepper
2 tablespoons grated Parmesan
cheese

Place zucchini, butter, and seasonings in skillet. Cover; cook slowly for 5 minutes, uncovered. Turn slices, cook until barely tender (about 5 minutes more). Sprinkle with cheese; toss to coat pieces evenly.

Serves 6.

Pies and Pastries

SOYA CAROB PIE CRUST I

4 cups unsifted soya carob flour
2 cups plus 3 tablespoons
    vegetable shortening
3 teaspoons sea salt

½ cup water
2 tablespoons vinegar
2 eggs

Measure flour into a large bowl; add salt, stirring in; cut in shortening until mixture resembles coarse meal. Add vinegar to water. Beat eggs with a fork until lemon colored and add, with vinegar-water mixture, to bowl, mixing in well with a fork. Form dough into 5 balls, rolling each out separately. Follow instructions in individual recipes for filling and baking.

To freeze unbaked dough, place in pie pans; turn crust under, but do not flute. Do not wrap until frozen; freeze singly. Pans of frozen crusts may be stacked and stored in a single plastic bag.

Makes 5 9-inch crusts.

SOYA CAROB PIE CRUST II

2 cups soya carob flour
1 teaspoon sea salt

1 cup vegetable shortening
¼ cup cold water

Put flour and salt into mixing bowl; cut in shortening with pastry blender (or use fork or fingers). Add water, and mix lightly until well blended. With hands, form into 2 balls. Roll each out on lightly floured board and place in individual pans. Fill as desired.

Bake single-crust pie shells on center rack of preheated oven at 425° for 15 minutes, or until shell is light golden brown in color.

Makes 2 single crusts or a double crust. May be frozen.

Note: To freeze unbaked dough, place in pie pans; turn crust under, but do not flute. Do not wrap until frozen.

CHEESE CRUST FOR APPLE PIE

¼ pound (about 1 cup) grated yellow cheese
2 cups soya carob flour
½ teaspoon sea salt
dash of cayenne (optional)

½ cup vegetable shortening
¼ cup butter
6 tablespoons ice water
oil as needed
1 beaten egg white (optional)

Sift together dry ingredients; cut in shortening and butter until mixture is mealy. Mix in the cheese lightly. Add the water gradually, tossing to make a stiff dough. Divide in half and roll out on lightly floured board. Place bottom crust in 9-inch pie pan and brush very lightly with oil. Fill as desired; top with second crust; brush that with oil or egg white. (This makes crust crisp and it browns nicely.)

CREAM-CHEESE OR COTTAGE-CHEESE PASTRY

1¼ cups soya carob flour
¼ teaspoon sea salt
½ cup butter

4½ ounces soft cream cheese or cottage cheese

Measure salt and flour into mixing bowl; stir. Add butter and cheese, and with pastry blender, cut together until evenly blended. Gather together and press into ball. Wrap in plastic wrap and chill overnight, then roll out and use like any pastry. Bake unfilled shell in preheated moderate oven (425°) until golden brown.

Makes 1 9-inch crust.

COOKIE-DOUGH CRUST

1½ cups soya carob flour
½ cup finely chopped pecans
¼ pound soft butter

½ teaspoon lemon bits
¼ cup white carob syrup

Mix together flour, pecans, and butter. Add remaining ingredients, and mix in well. Press into bottom and sides of 9-inch pie pan. Chill until needed.

Note: Particularly good for cheesecake.

FRUIT-PIE CRUST

½ teaspoon sea salt
1 cup soya carob flour
¼ cup butter

1 tablespoon white carob syrup
   or 2 packets sugar substitute
1 egg yolk

Cream butter and sugar together; add egg, salt, and flour, mixing in well. Pat and press the dough ¼ inch thick to fit greased 9-inch pan. Place in refrigerator overnight, then fill with desired fruit mixture and bake in a preheated oven at 400°.

Note: This crust is particularly suitable for fruit pies as it does not absorb moisture and thus does not get soggy. Excellent with Apple Pie Filling, below.

Makes a single 9-inch crust shell.

APPLE PIE FILLING

5 firm tart apples, peeled,
   cored, and sliced
cinnamon as needed
3 tablespoons cream

½ cup white carob syrup
1 egg yolk, beaten
2 tablespoons butter, melted

Lay sliced apples in rows on any unbaked pie shell and sprinkle generously with cinnamon. Mix together cream, butter, and syrup; add egg yolk to it; pour over apples. Bake 20-30 minutes in a preheated hot oven (400°), or until crust is well baked and apples are soft.

APPLE PIE I

1 recipe Soya Carob Pie Crust II
    (*see* Index)
6 firm tart cooking apples
1 12-ounce can frozen,
    undiluted, unsweetened
    apple juice

1 teaspoon cinnamon
1 teaspoon nutmeg
3 tablespoons butter
1 packet sugar substitute
    (optional)

Prepare pastry. Line a 9-inch pie pan with it.

Mix together apple juice, cinnamon, nutmeg, and butter, and bring to a boil. Let boil until approximately 6-8 ounces of apple juice remain; cool. (If you prefer a sweeter pie, add sweetener to juice at this point.) Peel apples and cut into ¼-inch slices; place in prepared pastry shell. Pour juice over apples. Cover with top crust; prick top of pie 3 or 4 times with fork. Bake in pre-heated oven at 450° for 15 minutes, then reduce heat to 325° and bake for 45 minutes, or until golden brown. Serve hot or cold.

Very good topped with a slice of Cheddar cheese or with whipped cream.

Yield: 6-8 servings.

APPLE PIE II

1 recipe Soya Carob Pie Crust II
    (*see* Index)
6 firm tart cooking apples
1 teaspoon cinnamon

1 teaspoon nutmeg
½ cup white carob syrup
4 packets sugar substitute
3 tablespoons butter

Prepare pastry. Line a 9-inch pie pan with it.

Peel apples, core, and slice thinly; place in pie crust, sprinkle with cinnamon and nutmeg. Add syrup and sweetener, and dot with butter. Cover with top crust. Prick top of pie 3 or 4 times with fork. Bake in a preheated 425° oven for 15 minutes, then reduce heat to 350° and bake for 45 minutes longer, or until golden brown.

APPLE PIE III

½ recipe Soya Carob Pie Crust II
  (*see* Index)
3 cups coarsely chopped peeled
  and cored apples
1 cup white carob syrup
½ cup sugar substitute

3 tablespoons soya carob flour
2 eggs
½ cup melted margarine
½ teaspoon nutmeg
½ teaspoon cinnamon
1 teaspoon vanilla

Mix together syrup, sugar substitute, and flour. Add eggs, margarine, nutmeg, cinnamon, and vanilla, and mix well. Stir in chopped apples. Let filling stand while you prepare pie shell.

Line a 9-inch pie plate with the crust; pour filling into it. Bake in a preheated oven at 425° for 15 minutes; reduce heat to 350° and bake for 30 minutes longer, or until done.

To serve, let cool, then garnish with whipped cream sweetened with sugar substitute or carob syrup.

FRIED APPLE PIES

1 recipe Soya Carob Pie Crust II
  (*see* Index)
6 apples, peeled, cored, and
  coarsely chopped
¼ cup white carob syrup
¼ teaspoon sea salt

2 tablespoons melted butter
¼ teaspoon cloves
¼ teaspoon nutmeg
¼ teaspoon cinnamon
shortening as needed for frying

Peel, core, and coarsely chop apples, then cook apples for 10 minutes; stir in syrup, salt, butter, and spices. Cool. Prepare pastry and cut into 5-inch rounds (use the top of a 1-pound coffee can to do this). Put a spoonful of filling on half of each pastry circle within ½ inch from edge; fold the other half up over the filling to make a half moon. Seal pastry edges by pressing with tines of a fork or your thumb. Prick tops of pies 3 or 4 times with fork.

Heat shortening in large skillet to 350°. With a pancake turner, slide 3 or 4 pies at a time into the hot fat. Fry for 2-3 minutes (until golden brown on underside), then turn and fry other side. Lift out and drain on paper toweling. Serve warm or cold.

Note: If you prefer, the pies can be baked as turnovers on a cookie sheet. Bake in a preheated oven at 425° for about 25 minutes, or until golden brown.

Makes 8 pies.

BANANA CREAM PIE

1 Soya Carob Pie Crust II (*see* Index)	1 cup unsweetened pear or peach juice
2 large ripe bananas	2 egg yolks, beaten
3 tablespoons soya carob flour	1 tablespoon butter
1½ cups heavy cream	1 teaspoon vanilla
¼ cup white carob syrup	1 tablespoon carob syrup
¼ teaspoon sea salt	1 tablespoon lemon juice
1 teaspoon vanilla	

Prepare, bake, and cool 9-inch pastry shell. Blend flour and ½ cup of the whipping cream in heavy saucepan. Add ¼ cup carob syrup, salt, and vanilla. Stir in juice; add egg yolks; mix well. Add butter. Cook over direct heat, stirring constantly, until mixture thickens. Remove from heat; chill.

Whip remainder of cream until it forms peaks. Add vanilla and syrup. Fold ½ cup of the whipped cream into filling. Slice bananas, and sprinkle with the lemon juice to keep bananas from darkening. Pour ½ of filling mixture into baked pie shell; arrange bananas over it; spread rest of mixture over bananas; top with remainder of whipped cream. Makes a very rich, smooth pie.

BLUEBERRY PIE

1 unbaked 9-inch Soya Carob
   Pie Crust II (*see* Index)
1 16-ounce package frozen
   unsweetened blueberries
1½ tablespoons soya carob flour

2 tablespoons heavy cream
4 packets sugar substitute
3 tablespoons lemon juice
2 tablespoons butter
whipped cream for topping

Prepare pastry and line a 9-inch pie plate with it.

In saucepan, mix flour and whipping cream; then add blueberries, sweetener, lemon juice and butter. Heat at low temperature, stirring gently, until blueberries are thawed and butter is melted. Pour into prepared pie shell and bake in preheated oven at 400° for 40-50 minutes, or until crust is golden. Cool and top with whipped cream.

BLUEBERRY BANANA CREAM PIE

1 9-inch baked Soya Carob Pie
   Crust II (*see* Index)
1 package frozen unsweetened
   blueberries

2 medium-size bananas, sliced
7 packets sugar substitute
3 tablespoons lemon juice
½ pint heavy cream, whipped

In a saucepan, mix blueberries, 6 packets of sweetener, and lemon juice. Cook for 5 minutes, then remove from heat and chill. Fold in sliced bananas and half the whipped cream that has been sweetened with 1 packet of sugar substitute. Pour into prepared pie shell and top with remainder of whipped cream.

BUTTERMILK PIE I

1 9-inch chilled unbaked pie
   shell
6 eggs
2 cups white carob syrup
2 cups buttermilk

pinch of salt
¼ cup soya carob flour
1½ sticks (¾ cup) melted butter
2 cups dietetic or fresh ground
   coconut

Beat eggs; add syrup, and beat in well. Combine buttermilk, salt, and flour, and add to egg mixture. Add butter and coconut; mix in well. Gently stir in vanilla. Pour into prepared pastry shell. Bake in a preheated oven at 325° for 10 minutes, then reduce heat to 250° and bake for 1 hour longer, or until firm. Chill before serving.

BUTTERMILK PIE II

1 chilled unbaked 9-inch
   Soya Carob Pie Crust II
   (*see* Index)
2 eggs
¾ cup white carob syrup
1 cup thick buttermilk

pinch of sea salt
3 tablespoons carob flour
½ cup melted butter
2 teaspoons vanilla
1 teaspoon lemon extract

Beat eggs; add syrup, beating in well. Combine buttermilk, salt, and flour; add to egg mixture. Add butter, mixing in well. Stir in flavorings. Pour into prepared pastry shell. Bake in a preheated oven at 300° for approximately 1 hour, or until firm. Chill before serving.

BUTTERMILK CUSTARD PIE

2 9-inch unbaked pie shells
1½ cups white carob syrup
½ cup butter
3 eggs, separated

4 tablespoons soya carob flour
1 pint buttermilk
2 teaspoons vanilla

Cream butter and beat well with syrup and egg yolks. Add flour, mixing in well. Add buttermilk, stirring well. Add vanilla. Beat egg whites in a separate bowl until stiff, then fold gently into batter. Pour into prepared pie shells. Bake in a preheated oven at 350° for 45 minutes, or until custard is firm. Serve chilled.

CHESS PIE I

1 unbaked Soya Carob Pie Crust II (*see* Index)	5 eggs, separated
1 cup butter at room temperature	⅛ teaspoon sea salt
1¼ cups white carob syrup	½ teaspoon vanilla
	½ cup chopped nuts

Line a 9-inch pan with pie crust but do not prick it.

Cream butter until soft and smooth; add the 1 cup white carob syrup and blend in thoroughly. Add egg yolks one at a time, beating well after each addition. In a separate bowl, beat 2 egg whites until just stiff. Add to creamed mixture with salt, vanilla, and nuts, folding in well. Turn filling into prepared pastry-lined pan, spreading it smooth. Bake in a preheated oven at 450° for 12 minutes, then reduce heat to 350° and bake for 20 minutes more. Remove pie from oven.

Meantime, prepare a meringue from the 3 remaining egg whites. Beat them until stiff; add the ¼ cup syrup gradually, until the meringue is smooth and shiny. Spread meringue smoothly over pie, being sure it reaches the crust, touching it all around. Return pie to oven and bake 15 minutes longer, or until meringue is delicately browned. Cool before cutting.

CHESS PIE II

1 unbaked 9-inch Soya Carob Pie Crust II (*see* Index)	1 tablespoon cornmeal
½ cup butter	2 tablespoons soya carob flour
1 cup carob syrup	½ cup heavy cream
3 eggs	2 tablespoons lemon juice
	1 teaspoon vanilla

Cream butter; add syrup, mixing in thoroughly. Add eggs, one at a time, beating well after each addition. Mix cornmeal and flour with cream; add to syrup mixture, beating well. Add lemon juice and vanilla; beat in thoroughly. Pour into prepared pie shell. Bake in a preheated oven at 400° for 10 minutes, then reduce temperature to 350° and bake for 30-35 minutes longer.

MOCK CHOCOLATE CHESS PIE

1 unbaked 9-inch Soya Carob
    Pie Crust II shell (*see*
    Index)
3 eggs, well beaten
3 tablespoons carob powder
5 tablespoons undiluted
    evaporated milk

1 cup white carob syrup
1 tablespoon white vinegar
½ cup melted butter
1 tablespoon vanilla

Mix together carob powder and milk; add to beaten eggs, mixing in well. Add syrup, vinegar, butter, and vanilla; mix thoroughly. Pour into prepared pastry shell. Bake in a preheated oven at 400° for 10 minutes, then reduce heat to 350° and bake 30-35 minutes longer.

MOCK-CHOCOLATE CREAM PIE

1 9-inch baked Soya Carob Pie
    Crust II (*see* Index)
3 tablespoons soya carob flour
1½ cups heavy cream
½ cup carob powder

¼ cup white carob syrup
¼ teaspoon sea salt
1 teaspoon vanilla
2 egg yolks
1 tablespoon butter

In a saucepan, blend together flour, ½ cup of the cream, and carob powder. Add syrup, salt, vanilla, and fruit juice, mixing well together. Beat egg yolks separately and add, mixing in thoroughly. Mixture should be smooth. Add butter. Cook over direct heat, stirring constantly, until mixture thickens and reaches a boil; remove from heat. Chill.

Meanwhile, whip the remaining cream. When cooked filling has cooled, fold in half of the whipped cream; pour into prepared pie shell; top with remaining whipped cream.

MOCK CHOCOLATE PECAN PIE

1 9-inch unbaked Soya Carob
    Crust II (*see* Index)
2 eggs
⅓ cup white carob syrup
¼ teaspoon sea salt
1 teaspoon vanilla

3 tablespoons heavy cream
⅛ cup carob powder
1 tablespoon soya carob flour
1 tablespoon butter or margarine
1¼ cup halved pecans

TOPPING

(optional)
¾ cup heavy cream

1 tablespoon white carob syrup
    or 1 packet sugar substitute
1 teaspoon vanilla

Beat eggs; add syrup, salt, and vanilla, beating in well. Mix together cream, carob powder, and flour; add to egg mixture; beat well. Add butter, beating in well. Mix in pecans. Pour into prepared pie shell. Bake in preheated oven at 300° for 50-60 minutes. Serve with the whipped cream topping or with ice cream.

ENGLISH CHESS PIE

¼ pound butter
3 eggs
1 9-inch unbaked pie shell

1 cup white carob syrup
1 teaspoon vanilla

Melt butter. Add syrup; mix well. Cool slightly. Beat eggs until frothy; continue beating as you add spoonfuls of the butter-syrup mixture. Beat in vanilla. Pour into prepared pie shell. Bake in a preheated oven at 350° for 40 minutes.

Note: Do not substitute margarine for butter.

LEMON CHESS PIE I

1 unbaked 9-inch Soya Carob
    Pie Crust II (*see* Index)
½ cup margarine
1 cup carob syrup
1 tablespoon cornmeal

2 tablespoons soya carob flour
2 eggs
2 tablespoons lemon juice
¼ cup milk
½ teaspoon vanilla

Using wooden spoon, cream together margarine, syrup, corn-meal, and flour. Add the eggs, lemon juice, milk, and vanilla, beating all in thoroughly. Pour into prepared pie shell. Bake in preheated oven at 400° for 10 minutes. Reduce heat to 350° and bake 30-40 minutes longer.

LEMON CHESS PIE II

1 9-inch unbaked Soya Carob Pie Crust II (*see* Index)	1 cup white carob syrup
⅛ pound butter	4 eggs
4 packets sugar substitute	2 lemons, juice only
	1 scant tablespoon cornmeal

Cream butter; beat with sugar substitute and syrup. Add eggs, stirring until well worked in, but do not beat. Add lemon juice and cornmeal. Pour into prepared pie shell and bake in preheated moderate oven (350°) for 45 minutes or until set.

SOUTHERN CHESS PIE

1 9-inch unbaked Soya Carob Pie Crust II (*see* Index)	½ cup soya carob flour
1 cup butter at room temperature	¼ teaspoon sea salt
	4 egg yolks, beaten
1½ cups white carob syrup	1 cup undiluted evaporated milk
2 teaspoons vanilla	

Line pie pan with pastry.

Cream butter; gradually add syrup, beating in well. Stir in vanilla, flour, and salt, and beat until blended. Stir in egg yolks, then the milk, adding it gradually. Turn into pastry-lined pan and bake in preheated 450° oven for 10 minutes. Reduce heat to 350° and bake 25 to 30 minutes longer. Custard should be slightly soft in center when pie is removed from oven. After cooling, chill in refrigerator. Serve warm or cold.

CHERRY PIE

1 unbaked Soya Carob Pie
   Crust II (*see* Index)
¼ teaspoon almond extract
   unsweetened cherries
3 tablespoons heavy cream

2½ tablespoons soya carob flour
¼ teaspoon salt
¼ teaspoon almond extract
1 cup carob syrup
2 tablespoons butter

In a saucepan, blend cream with flour into a smooth paste.
Add salt, almond extract, syrup, cherries, and butter; heat 3-4
minutes. Pour into prepared pie shell. Bake in preheated oven at
400° for 40-50 minutes or until golden brown.

Makes 1 9-inch pie.

CRISSCROSS CHERRY PIE

1 recipe Soya Carob Pie Crust
   II (*see* Index)
2 #303 cans unsweetened red
   sour pitted cherries
1 envelope unflavored gelatin

½ cup cold water
2 tablespoons butter
3 tablespoons lemon juice
8 packets sugar substitute
¼ teaspoon sea salt

Prepare bottom crust for pie; reserve balance of dough for
latticed upper crust.

Sprinkle gelatin onto cold water to soften. Drain cherries;
pour into a saucepan. Add gelatin, butter, lemon juice, sugar
substitute, and salt to cherry juice. Boil until juice evaporates to
approximately 6 ounces. Add cherries; mix well. Pour into prepared pie shell. Crisscross with pastry. Bake in preheated oven
at 300° approximately 1 hour or until crust is golden brown.

For latticed upper crust: Roll out dough to rectangle; cut
into half-inch strips. Weave the strips into an openwork pattern
and lay across pie. Seal top to bottom crust.

COCONUT PIE I

1 9-inch Soya Carob Pie Crust
II (*see* Index)
1 tablespoon unflavored gelatin
½ cup cold water
4 eggs, separated
1 cup white carob syrup

pinch of sea salt
1 cup heavy cream
1½ cups fresh shredded coconut
1 teaspoon vanilla
1 packet sugar substitute

Prepare and bake pie shell.

Soak gelatin in water for 5 minutes. Beat egg yolks well, then add ½ cup of the syrup; add salt and half the cream; reserve other half for topping. Cook in double boiler until thick; let cool, then add the dissolved gelatin. In another bowl, beat egg whites until frothy; gradually add remaining syrup; continue beating until very stiff. Fold egg whites into the cooled custard mixture, then fold in 1 cup of the coconut and the vanilla. Pour into prepared pie shell; chill thoroughly in refrigerator. Just before serving, whip remaining cream and sweeten with sugar substitute. Spread whipped cream over top of pie and sprinkle with balance of coconut.

COCONUT PIE II

2 unbaked 9-inch Soya Carob
Pie Crusts I (*see* Index)
6 eggs

1½ cups white carob syrup
1 tablespoon melted butter
1 cup grated fresh coconut

Beat eggs well with syrup and butter. Add coconut. Pour into pie shells. Bake in a preheated oven at 350° for about 45 minutes or until custard is set.

Makes 2 pies.

EASY COCONUT PIE

1 9-inch unbaked **Soya Carob**
  Pie Crust I (*see* Index)
2 eggs
1 cup white carob **syrup**
½ stick (¼ cup) butter or
  margarine

1 small can undiluted
  evaporated milk
⅛ teaspoon sea salt
1 tablespoon vanilla
1½ cups fresh shredded coconut

Beat eggs thoroughly with syrup. Melt butter and blend into egg mixture. Add milk, salt, and vanilla. Stir in 1 cup of the coconut. Pour into prepared pie shell; sprinkle remaining coconut on top. Bake in a preheated oven at 350° for 45 minutes, or until custard is set.

COCONUT MACAROON PIE

1 9-inch unbaked Soya Carob
  Pie Crust II (*see* Index)
1 cup white carob syrup
2 eggs
½ teaspoon sea salt

½ cup soft butter or **margarine**
¼ cup carob flour
½ cup milk
1½ cups dietetic or fresh shredded
  coconut

Beat together syrup, eggs, and salt until mixture is lemon colored and thick. Add butter and flour; blend well. Add milk and 1 cup of the coconut. Pour into prepared pie shell. Top with remaining coconut. Bake in preheated 300° oven until lightly brown; reduce heat to 275° and bake until custard is firm (about 20 minutes longer).

FRENCH COCONUT PIE

1 unbaked 9-inch Soya Carob
  Pie Crust II (*see* Index)
3 eggs
1 cup white carob syrup

1 tablespoon soya carob flour
¼ cup buttermilk
1 teaspoon vanilla
½ cup fresh shredded coconut

Beat eggs; add syrup, stirring in well. Mix together flour and buttermilk in a separate bowl, then add to egg mixture. Add all remaining ingredients; mix well. Pour into prepared pie shell. Bake in a preheated oven at 325° for 45-50 minutes. Chill before serving.

COTTAGE CHEESE PIE

1 unbaked Soya Carob Pie
   Crust I (*see* Index)
2 cups cottage cheese
3 eggs
½ cup white carob syrup
5 packets sugar substitute

⅛ teaspoon sea salt
½ cup heavy cream
2 tablespoons soya carob flour
1 teaspoon grated lemon rind
1 tablespoon lemon juice
¼ teaspoon cinnamon

Mash cottage cheese well with a fork; set aside. Beat eggs lightly; add syrup and 4 packets of the sugar substitute, beating in well. Add cottage cheese, salt, cream, flour, lemon rind, and lemon juice, mixing in thoroughly. Pour into prepared pie shell. Mix cinnamon with remaining packet of sweetener and sprinkle over filling. Bake in a preheated oven at 350° for 40 minutes. Chill before serving.

FRENCH CREAM PIE

1 9-inch baked Soya Carob Pie
   Crust II (*see* Index)
1 cup heavy cream
⅔ cup soya carob flour
1 cup milk

1 cup white carob syrup
2 tablespoons butter
1 teaspoon vanilla
cinnamon as needed

Blend together cream and flour. Add milk and syrup; stir until well mixed. Cook mixture over medium heat until thick. Remove from heat; add butter and vanilla, and stir until butter is melted. Set pan in ice water; stir until mixture has cooled to lukewarm. Pour into prepared pie shell; sprinkle with cinnamon; chill.

CRANBERRY PIE

1 9-inch baked Soya Carob Pie Crust II (*see* Index)	1 cup plus 2 tablespoons carob syrup
3 cups raw cranberries	¼ teaspoon sea salt
1 cup hot water	2 eggs, separated
1½ tablespoons unflavored gelatin	whipped cream
¼ cup cold water	

In a bowl, soften the gelatin in cold water. Place the cranberries in a saucepan; add hot water. Cover and cook until soft; press through a sieve and place the pulp in the top part of a double boiler, over hot water. Add the cup of syrup, salt, and egg yolks that have been well beaten, and cook, stirring constantly, for 5 minutes, then add the softened gelatin and stir until dissolved.

In a separate bowl, beat the egg whites until stiff, to which have been added the 2 tablespoons syrup. When the cranberry mixture begins to set, fold in the egg whites. Pour filling into prepared pie shell and top with whipped cream.

CUSTARD PIE

1 unbaked 9-inch pie shell	1 quart milk
6 eggs	1 teaspoon vanilla
¾ cup white carob syrup	nutmeg (optional)
pinch of sea salt	

Combine eggs, syrup, salt, and vanilla. Scald milk; add to egg mixture; beat with rotary beater for 1 minute. Pour into prepared pie shell and sprinkle with nutmeg, if desired. Bake in a preheated oven at 450° for 15 minutes; then reduce temperature to 325° and bake for 30-35 minutes longer.

EGGNOG PIE

1 9-inch baked Soya Carob Pie
    Crust II (*see* Index)
1 envelope unflavored gelatin
2 cups eggnog
¼ cup white carob syrup
¼ teaspoon salt

1 cup whipped cream
1½ teaspoons vanilla
¼ teaspoon almond extract
2 tablespoons rum extract
nutmeg as needed

Mix gelatin with eggnog, syrup, and salt; set aside for 10 minutes, until gelatin softens, then warm over direct heat until gelatin dissolves. Chill until mixture mounds when dropped from a spoon (about 30-45 minutes). Fold in whipped cream and flavorings. Heap into prepared pie shell; dust with nutmeg. Chill 2-4 hours before serving.

LEMON-APPLE PIE

1 9-inch unbaked Soya Carob
    Pie Crust I (*see* Index)
1 cup hot water
1 tablespoon butter
1 egg, separated

1 cup white carob syrup
3 tablespoons soya carob flour
1 lemon, juice and grated rind
1 large apple, pared, cored,
    and grated

When placing pastry in pie plate, make a high fluted edge.

Melt butter in hot water. In a bowl, beat egg whites until stiff; add ¼ cup of the syrup; set aside. In a separate bowl, beat egg yolk; add flour, remaining syrup, lemon (rind and juice), apple, and hot-water-butter mixture; mix well. Fold in egg white. Pour into pastry-lined pan. Bake in a preheated oven at 425° for 15 minutes, then reduce heat to 350° and bake 45 minutes longer. Serve chilled.

LEMON CHIFFON PIE

1 9-inch baked Soya Carob Pie
   Crust I (*see* Index)
1 envelope unflavored gelatin
¼ cup cold water
1 cup plus 2 tablespoons
   white carob syrup

⅓ cup lemon juice
½ teaspoon sea salt
4 eggs, separated
1 teaspoon grated lemon rind
½ cup heavy cream, whipped

Soak gelatin in cold water in mixing bowl for 5 minutes. Meantime, combine 1 cup of the syrup, lemon juice, and salt in top of double boiler, over water. Beat egg yolks well, and add. Cook until smooth and thick, stirring constantly, then add to gelatin; stir until dissolved. Stir in lemon rind; chill until mixture sets.

Beat egg whites until stiff; beat in remaining carob syrup. Fold into cooked custard. Pour into prepared pie shell. Chill; top with whipped cream.

LEMON JELLY PIE

1 9-inch unbaked Soya Carob
   Pie Crust I (*see* Index)
3 eggs
1 cup plus 2 tablespoons white
   carob syrup

juice of 2 lemons plus grated
   rind of 1
¼ stick of (2 tablespoons)
   melted butter
½ cup heavy cream, whipped

Beat eggs slightly—just enough to blend yolks and whites; add 1 cup syrup, lemon (juice and rind), and mix well; then add butter. Pour into prepared pie shell and bake in preheated 300°-325° oven until filling is set and crust is delicately browned. Let cool. The filling will be of jellylike consistency. Top with whipped cream sweetened with remainder of syrup.

MILLIONAIRE PIE

1 9-inch baked Soya Carob Pie
   Crust II (*see* Index)
½ cup white carob syrup
½ cup heavy cream
3 tablespoons soya carob flour
2 egg yolks, beaten
¼ teaspoon sea salt

1 cup unsweetened pineapple
   juice, frozen concentrate
1 tablespoon butter
1 cup unsweetened juice pack
   crushed pineapple, drained
1 teaspoon vanilla
½ cup toasted chopped pecans

TOPPING

½ pint heavy cream, whipped
2 tablespoons white carob syrup

1 teaspoon vanilla

Blend the syrup, cream, egg yolks, and salt in a heavy saucepan. Slowly stir in pineapple juice; blend until smooth. Add butter, and vanilla. Cook over direct heat, stirring constantly, until mixture boils and thickens. Remove from heat; add crushed pineapple; chill.

For topping, whip together cream, vanilla, and syrup. Fold in ½ cup of this into chilled filling; fold in pecans. Pour into prepared shell; top with balance of whipped cream.

PECAN PIE I

1 9-inch unbaked Soya Carob
   Pie Crust II (*see* Index)
3 eggs
¾ cup white carob syrup

¼ cup melted butter
1 teaspoon vanilla
¼ teaspoon sea salt
1¼ cups coarsely broken pecans

Beat eggs slightly; add syrup, butter, vanilla, and salt; mix well. Add pecans. Pour into prepared pie shell; bake in a preheated oven at 400° for 10 minutes; then reduce heat to 350° and bake 25-30 minutes longer. Cool before serving.

PECAN PIE II

1 9-inch unbaked Soya Carob
   Pie Crust II (*see* Index)
½ cup butter at room
   temperature
1 cup white carob syrup
3 eggs

1 teaspoon vanilla
⅛ teaspoon sea salt
1 tablespoon brown-sugar
   substitute (optional)
1 cup coarsely chopped pecans

Cream butter until light and fluffy; add syrup, beating in well. Beat in eggs one at a time. Add remaining ingredients; mix well. Pour into prepared pie shell; apply a band of aluminum foil to edge of crust to prevent overcooking. Bake in a preheated oven at 375° for 40-50 minutes. Allow to cool thoroughly before serving.

PECAN PIE III

1 9-inch unbaked Soya Carob Pie Crust I (*see* Index)	⅛ teaspoon sea salt 1 teaspoon vanilla
3 eggs, slightly beaten	1 tablespoon soya carob flour
1 cup white carob syrup	1 cup coarsely broken pecans
3 tablespoons melted butter or margarine	

Combine eggs, syrup, butter, salt, and vanilla in mixing bowl. Add a small amount of mixture to flour and mix into a paste, then blend into filling mixture. Add pecans. Turn into prepared pie shell. Bake in a preheated oven at 325° for 1 hour or until firm. Cool before serving.

SOUTHERN PECAN PIE

1 9-inch unbaked Soya Carob Pie Crust II (*see* Index)	4 tablespoons butter 1 teaspoon vanilla
4 eggs	1½ cups coarsely broken pecans
1 cup white carob syrup	

Beat eggs so whites and yolks are just blended. Heat syrup and butter together, and slowly pour this mixture into eggs, stirring constantly. Add vanilla and pecans. Turn into prepared pie shell and bake in a preheated oven for about 45 minutes or until set. Cool before serving.

PINEAPPLE CREAM PIE

1 baked 9-inch Soya Carob Pie
    Crust II (*see* Index)
⅓ cup plus 2 tablespoons white
    carob syrup
1½ cups heavy cream
2 tablespoons soya carob flour
2 egg yolks, beaten

¼ teaspoon sea salt
1 cup frozen concentrated
    unsweetened pineapple
    juice
1 teaspoon vanilla
1 cup unsweetened crushed
    pineapple

Blend the ⅓ cup syrup with ½ cup of the cream, flour, egg yolks, and salt in a heavy saucepan. Slowly stir in pineapple juice; blend until smooth. Add butter and vanilla. Mix in crushed pineapple. Cook over direct heat, stirring constantly, until mixture boils and thickens. Remove from heat; chill.

Whip the remaining cream; to it add the vanilla and 2 tablespoons syrup; chill. Fold ½ cup of the whipped cream into the pie filling; pour into prepared shell. Top with remaining whipped cream.

HONEY PUMPKIN PIE

1 9-inch unbaked Soya Carob
    Pie Crust II (*see* Index)
2 eggs
1½ cups cooked pumpkin puree
¾ cup undiluted evaporated milk
¾ cup tupelo honey
¼ cup undiluted frozen
    unsweetened orange juice

¼ teaspoon ginger
1 teaspoon cinnamon
¼ teaspoon nutmeg
¼ teaspoon cloves
1 tablespoon boiling water

Line pie pan with prepared pastry, but do not prick.

Beat eggs well in 3-quart bowl; blend in next 6 ingredients. Place spices in a cup; measure in water; stir to a smooth paste, then mix thoroughly into pumpkin mixture. Turn into prepared pastry-lined pan. Bake in a preheated oven at 350° for 15 minutes, then reduce heat to 300° and bake about 25 minutes longer, or until custard tests done (a tester inserted in center will come out clean). Cool before serving.

GRANDMA'S SCORCHED PUMPKIN PIE

1 9-inch unbaked Soya Carob Pie Crust II (*see* Index)	¼ teaspoon ginger
1½ cups canned pumpkin puree	¾ teaspoon cinnamon
2 eggs	⅛ teaspoon nutmeg
¾ cup white carob syrup	2 tablespoons boiling water
¼ cup undiluted evaporated milk	½ teaspoon sea salt
	¼ cup heavy cream

Prepare pastry and fit into pie pan; trim edges with knife and crimp with fork (leaving edge flat), or flute with fingers. Do not prick.

Adjust oven rack so it is 4 or 5 inches above oven floor; preheat for 10 minutes at 425°.

Turn pumpkin into a 3-quart saucepan. Cook over direct heat, stirring constantly, until it is dried out and the natural sugar is in a slightly caramelized state (scorched but not burned). This should take about 9 minutes. Remove from heat.

In a large bowl, beat eggs just until whites and yolks are blended. In another bowl, blend together syrup, milk, spices, and water to make a smooth paste; mix well with eggs. Stir in pumpkin until blended, and add salt and cream, also until thoroughly blended. Pour into pastry-lined pan. Bake for 15 minutes at 425°, then reduce heat to slow (300°)—leave oven door open for a minute so heat will drop rapidly to desired 300°). Bake for about 25 minutes longer, or until all the custard is firm except for a small circle in the center. (This will set later.) Stand pie on cake rack; let cool to lukewarm before cutting.

Note: This is very good topped with ½ pint of whipped cream sweetened with 2 packets of sugar substitute.

RHUBARB PIE

1 recipe Soya Carob Pie Crust
   II (*see* Index)
1 20-ounce package frozen
   unsweetened rhubarb
3 tablespoons soya carob flour
1 cup white carob syrup

¼ teaspoon sea salt
2 tablespoons orange juice
2 tablespoons lemon juice
2 tablespoons butter
dash of nutmeg

Prepare pie crust and divide into two parts. Roll out shell for bottom crust and lay in pan. Do not prick. Roll out second part and cut into strips for lattice.

Put rhubarb into saucepan. In a bowl, thoroughly mix together flour, syrup, and salt; add orange and lemon juices, mixing well into a smooth paste. Add butter. Pour flour-juice mixture over rhubarb; heat for 3 minutes. Pour filling into unbaked pie shell; sprinkle with nutmeg. Top with lattice strips. Bake in preheated oven at 425° for 55-60 minutes, or until golden.

STRAWBERRY PIE I

1 9-inch baked Soya Carob Pie
   Crust II (*see* Index)
2 pints firm ripe strawberries,
   washed, hulled, and sliced
⅓ cup white carob syrup

1 envelope unflavored gelatin
¼ cup cold water
½ cup whipped cream
5 drops red food coloring

MERINGUE

2 egg whites

¼ cup white carob syrup

Combine strawberries and syrup; let stand for 15 minutes; strain juice from strawberries into saucepan. Add gelatin to water; let stand for 5 minutes; add to strawberry juice. Heat until gelatin is dissolved; cool. Add sliced strawberries to mixture; chill until it mounds when dropped from a spoon.

For meringue, beat egg whites until foamy; beat in syrup; continue to beat until meringue forms stiff, glossy peaks.

Whip cream. Fold strawberry mixture into meringue, then fold in 1 cup of the whipped cream, together with the food coloring. Pour into cooled crust. Top with additional whipped cream.

STRAWBERRY PIE II

1 9-inch baked Soya Carob Pie
   Crust II (*see* Index)
1 20-ounce package frozen
   unsweetened strawberries
3 tablespoons lemon juice
½ cup white carob syrup

4 packets sugar substitute
¼ teaspoon sea salt
2 tablespoons butter
¼ cup heavy cream
3 tablespoons soya carob flour

TOPPING

½ pint heavy cream, whipped
1 packet sugar substitute

1 teaspoon vanilla

Place strawberries in a large, heavy saucepan; add lemon juice, syrup, sugar substitute, salt, and butter. Cook for 5 minutes, stirring freuently. Mix together cream and flour; add to strawberries, and continue to cook, stirring constantly, for another 3-5 minutes. Turn into cooled pie shell, and let cool.

For topping, whip cream together with sweetener and vanilla until it stands in stiff peaks. Spread on cooled pie.

STRAWBERRY-PINEAPPLE CREAM PIE

1 9-inch baked and cooled Soya
   Carob Pie Crust I (*see*
   Index)
1½ cups fresh strawberries,
   washed, hulled, sliced, and
   sweetened with ¼ cup
   carob syrup
1 6-ounce can frozen
   unsweetened pineapple
   juice, thawed
1 8-ounce can unsweetened
   crushed pineapple

3 tablespoons soya carob flour
½ cup heavy cream
2 egg yolks, well beaten
¼ teaspoon sea salt
1 teaspoon vanilla
2 tablespoons butter
⅛ cup white carob syrup
½ pint cream, whipped with
   1 tablespoon carob syrup
   and 1 teaspoon vanilla

Blend flour and cream in heavy saucepan. Add egg yolks, salt, and vanilla. Stir in pineapple juice, butter, and syrup. Cook over direct heat, stirring constantly, until thickened, then remove from heat and chill.

Fold in ⅔ cup of the whipped cream. Fold in strawberries and crushed pineapple. Pour into prepared pie shell. Top with remainder of whipped cream.

Note: Do not substitute margarine for butter in this recipe.

Cakes and Icings

SOYA CAROB ANGEL FOOD CAKE I

1½ cups (approx. 16) egg whites
¾ cup unsifted soya carob flour
½ teaspoon sea salt
2½ tablespoons cold water

1½ teaspoons cream of tartar
1 cup white carob syrup
1 teaspoon vanilla
½ teaspoon almond extract

Whip egg whites in large bowl; add salt and water; whip until foamy. Add cream of tartar and whip until mixture will hold shape or stand in peaks. Whip in syrup, vanilla, and almond extract. Gently fold in flour. Pour batter into ungreased angel food cake pan. Bake in preheated oven at 350° for 40 minutes, or until cake springs back when touched. Invert cake pan on a rack until cake is cool.

SOYA CAROB ANGEL FOOD CAKE II

1½ (approx. 16) cups egg whites
1 cup soya carob flour, unsifted
½ teaspoon sea salt
2½ tablespoons cold water
1½ teaspoons cream of tartar

½ cup white carob syrup
7 packets sugar substitute
½ teaspoon almond extract
1 teaspoon vanilla
1 tablespoon lemon juice

Have all ingredients at room temperature. Preheat oven for 10 minutes at 350°.

Sift flour 6 times. Do not discard black specks; they are part of the flour. Place egg whites in large bowl; add salt and water; beat at medium speed with electric mixer until frothy. Add cream of tartar and beat until mixture will hold its shape or stand in peaks. Beat in syrup, sugar substitute, and lemon; add vanilla and almond extract. Gently fold in flour. Pour batter into ungreased 10-inch tube pan (preferably with removable bottom). Bake 40-50 minutes, or until cake springs back lightly at touch. Invert cake pan on rack until cake is cool.

ELSIE'S FRESH APPLE CAKE

2 cups soya carob flour
½ teaspoon soda
1 teaspoon sea salt
7 packets sugar substitute
3 eggs
1 cup oil and
   3 tablespoons melted butter

1 teaspoon vanilla
1 cup white carob syrup
2 cups peeled and finely
   chopped apples
1½ cups chopped pecans

Sift flour 5 times. Mix together all dry ingredients, including sugar substitute. Add eggs, oil, butter, vanilla, and syrup. Add apples and pecans. Bake in loaf or tube pan. Bake for 1 hour in preheated oven at 325°.

APPLESAUCE CAKE

½ cup shortening
¾ cup white carob syrup
1½ cups unsweetened applesauce
1 teaspoon baking soda

¼ teaspoon sea salt
1¾ cups soya carob flour
½ cup seedless raisins (optional)
¾ cup chopped pecans

Cream shortening and syrup together; add applesauce, soda and salt. Add flour, raisins, and nuts. Beat well (2 minutes). Pour into greased and floured 8-by-10-by-2-inch pan. Bake in oven preheated to 325° for 50 minutes. Turn out and cool on rack.

FIESTA BANANA CAKE

½ cup butter or margarine
1 cup white carob syrup
2 eggs
2 cups soya carob flour
1 teaspoon baking powder
1 teaspoon soda

1 cup buttermilk
1 cup mashed bananas
½ teaspoon sea salt
1 teaspoon vanilla
½ cup chopped walnuts or
   pecans

Sift dry ingredients together six times.

In a bowl cream butter and syrup; add eggs and beat well. Add ¼ cup of the buttermilk and bananas to creamed mixture. Beat 2 minutes, then add sifted dry ingredients and beat an additional minute. Add nuts, remainder of milk, and vanilla; mix well. Pour into a greased bundt cake pan. Bake in preheated oven at 325° for 1 hour or until done.

FRESH APPLE BUNDT COFFEE CAKE

12 ounces frozen unsweetened
    apple juice
½ cup milk
2 packages active dry yeast
½ cup warm water
¼ pound butter
5 packets sugar substitute
3 eggs

4 cups sifted soya carob flour
1½ teaspoons sea salt
1 cup chopped pecans
2 cups peeled and diced fresh
   apples
6 tablespoons fine dry bread
   crumbs

Boil apple juice until it is condensed to 6 ounces; cool. Scald milk; cool to lukewarm. Meanwhile, in a bowl, combine yeast and water. In another bowl blend butter, sugar substitute, and apple juice. Beat in eggs one at a time, blending after each one. Add softened yeast, milk, flour, and salt. Beat vigorously. Blend in nuts and apples.

Grease and flour 3-quart bundt pan; sprinkle bottom with bread crumbs. Pour batter into pan. Let stand 1 hour or until dough doubles in size. Bake in preheated oven at 325° for 30 to

35 minutes or until brown. Use a toothpick to test for doneness. Remove pan to a rack. Let stand 10 minutes. Invert to a bread board or platter.

LEMON BUNDT CAKE

1¼ cups butter	2½ cups soya carob flour
2 cups white carob syrup	2½ teaspoons lemon extract
7 eggs	

Cream butter and syrup together. Add eggs, one at a time, blending after each one. Sift flour six times. Add flour to creamed mixture; beat well (3 minutes). Add flavoring. Pour batter into greased bundt cake pan. Bake in preheated oven at 325° for 1 hour or until done. (Use a toothpick to test for doneness.) Cool 10 minutes before removing from pan.

PECAN BUNDT COFFEE CAKE

½ cup milk	3¾ cups sifted soya carob flour
6 tablespoons butter	3 teaspoons cinnamon
¾ cup white carob syrup	1½ teaspoons sea salt
3 eggs	1 cup chopped pecans
2 packages active dry yeast	½ cup chopped apricots
½ cup warm water	6 tablespoons fine bread crumbs

Scald milk; cool to lukewarm. Meanwhile, in a bowl, combine yeast and water. In another bowl blend butter and syrup. Beat in eggs one at a time. Add softened yeast, milk, flour, cinnamon, and salt. Beat vigorously. Blend in nuts and apricots. Cover bowl with a cheesecloth. Let stand 2 hours or until dough rises to twice its size. Pour batter into a greased and floured bundt pan, sprinkled with bread crumbs. Let stand 1 hour.

Bake in preheated oven at 325° for 30 to 35 minutes or until brown. (Use a toothpick to test for doneness.) Remove pan to a rack. Let stand 10 minutes. Invert to a bread board or platter.

GOLDEN BUTTER COFFEE CAKE

2½ cups soya carob flour
2 packages active dry yeast
¼ cup milk
½ stick (¼ cup) butter

4 packets sugar substitute
¼ teaspoon sea salt
1 egg

BUTTER GLAZE

½ cup butter
¾ cup sliced almonds
¾ cup white carob syrup

2 tablespoons water
2 teaspoons almond extract

To prepare dough:

In a large bowl, mix together 1 cup of the flour and yeast. In a 1-quart saucepan combine milk, butter, sugar substitute, and salt; heat until warm. Add to flour-yeast mixture. Add egg. Beat ¾ minute at low speed, scraping bowl constantly, then beat 3 more minutes at high speed. Add ½ cup flour and beat 1 minute. Stir in enough remaining flour to make a soft dough. Turn onto lightly floured surface; knead 8 to 10 minutes or until smooth and satiny. Place in buttered bowl; butter top. Cover with cheesecloth. Let rise over hot water until dough is doubled in size (45 to 60 minutes).

While dough is rising prepare Butter Glaze. In a 1-quart saucepan, over low heat, cook together butter and almonds, stirring constantly, until amber colored. Stir in syrup and water. Bring to a boil, cooking for 2 minutes; stir in extract.

Punch dough down and divide in half. Prepare each half as follows: divide dough into 8 equal portions and shape into smooth balls. Pour Butter Glaze into two 8-inch round pans and place balls of dough on top. Cover and let rise in a warm place until doubled in size. Bake in preheated 350° oven, 25 to 30 minutes. Invert immediately onto wire rack. Serve while still hot.

Makes two 8-inch coffee cakes.

LEMON BUTTERMILK CAKE

8 ounces whipped margarine
1 cup white carob syrup
3 tablespoons wheat germ
10 packets sugar substitute
4 eggs
3½ cups soya carob flour

1 teaspoon sea salt
2 tablespoons lemon juice
1 teaspoon lemon extract
½ teaspoon grated lemon peel
1 cup buttermilk
1 cup chopped walnuts

Cream margarine, syrup, and wheat germ together until fluffy. Add sugar substitute; continue creaming until mixture is light and fluffy. Add eggs, one at a time, blending well after each addition. Sift together flour, soda, and salt 4 times; add to creamed mixture. Mix in well lemon juice, lemon extract, lemon peel, and buttermilk. Add nuts. Turn batter into well-greased and floured 1-pound loaf pans. Bake in preheated oven at 350° for 1 hour or until cake springs back lightly at touch. Cool on rack.

CHEESECAKE I

1 9-inch Cookie-Dough Crust
   (*see* Index)
12 ounces cream cheese
2 eggs
½ cup white carob syrup
1 teaspoon vanilla

½ teaspoon lemon extract
½ teaspoon orange extract
¼ teaspoon orange bits
¼ teaspoon lemon bits
1 cup dietetic powdered coconut

Prepare Cookie-Dough Crust.

Have cheese and eggs at room temperature. Cream cheese until soft; add eggs, one at a time, beating well after each addition. Add syrup, blending in well, then add remaining ingredients and beat until well blended. Pour into prepared but unbaked crust. Bake in preheated oven at 350° for 35-40 minutes.

CHEESECAKE II

1 baked Cookie-Dough Crust
   (*see* Index)
1 8-ounce package cream chesee
¾ cup white carob syrup
1 envelope lemon or lime low-
   calorie gelatin

1 cup hot water
1 large can cold condensed milk
2 tablespoons lemon juice

Cream cheese and syrup together in large mixing bowl. Dissolve gelatin in water; add with lemon juice to creamed mixture. In a separate bowl, whip milk well; fold into mixture gradually. Pour filling into prepared crust; place in refrigerator and chill, or freeze until needed.

BLUEBERRY CHEESECAKE

1 9-inch unbaked Cookie-
   Dough Crust (*see* Index)

FILLING

1 8-ounce package cream cheese
2 large eggs

½ cup white carob syrup
1 teaspoon vanilla

TOPPING

1 15-ounce can unsweetened
   blueberries
3 tablespoons soya carob flour

⅓ cup white carob syrup or
   6 packets sugar substitute
2 tablespoons lemon juice

To make the filling, beat the cheese until fluffy, then thoroughly beat in eggs. Beat in syrup and vanilla. Spread mixture evenly into prepared crust; bake in preheated oven at 450° for 45 minutes or until crust is golden.

Prepare topping as follows: Strain blueberries, reserving juice, and to it add flour and syrup, mixing in well. Heat, stirring constantly, until mixture thickens, then add berries and lemon juice.

Remove from heat and let cool. Spread over pie, and chill for several hours before serving. Serve topped with whipped cream.

DELUXE CHEESECAKE

1 9-inch unbaked Cookie-Dough Crust (*see* Index)	¼ teaspoon sea salt
	1 lemon, grated rind only
5 8-ounce packages cream cheese	1 orange, grated rind only
	5 eggs plus 2 egg yolks
1¼ cups white carob syrup	¼ cup heavy cream
3 tablespoons soya carob flour	

Make Cookie-Dough Crust, and set aside.

Beat cheese until soft; blend in syrup. Mix together flour and salt; gradually blend into cheese, keeping mixture smooth. Add lemon and orange rinds. Add eggs and egg yolks, one at a time, beating them in thoroughly. Blend in cream. Pour into prepared crust. Bake in preheated oven at 450° for 15 minutes, then reduce temperature to 225° and bake for 1 hour longer. Remove from oven; cool in pan on rack, away from drafts; chill. Place on serving plate and decorate with whipped cream.

PENTHOUSE CHEESECAKE

1 9-inch Soya Carob Pie Crust I (*see* Index)	3 eggs, separated
	½ teaspoon vanilla
1 cup white carob syrup	½ teaspoon lemon juice
½ tablespoon soya carob flour	¼ teaspoon grated lemon rind
1 8-ounce package cream cheese	½ cup heavy cream

Cream cheese with syrup and flour. Add well beaten egg yolks, then vanilla, lemon juice and rind. Add the cream; fold in the stiffly beaten egg whites. Pour mixture into unbaked pie shell. Bake 45 minutes to 1 hour in preheated oven at 350°. Turn oven off. Open door and let cool for 1 hour.

COCONUT CAKE

¼ cup butter	2 eggs, beaten
½ teaspoon sea salt	1 cup half-and-half cream
¾ cup white carob syrup	1 cup soya carob flour
5 packets sugar substitute	1 cup grated coconut

Cream butter; heat with salt, syrup, and sugar substitute; add the eggs, half-and-half, and coconut, blending all in very well. Fold in flour. Pour batter into a greased and floured 9-inch layer-cake pan. Bake in preheated 325° oven for about a half hour or until cake springs lightly back when touched. Cool, and ice as desired.

Note: This recipe also makes good cupcakes. Fill paper-lined muffin tins two-thirds full and bake for 20 minutes at 350°.

GERMAN FRUITCAKE

¾ cup margarine	1 cup buttermilk
1¼ cups white carob syrup	1 teaspoon vanilla
5 eggs	⅔ cup Cherry Preserves
2 cups soya carob flour	(*see* Index)
½ teaspoon cinnamon	⅔ cup Pineapple Preserves
½ teaspoon allspice	(*see* Index)
½ teaspoon nutmeg	⅔ cup Apricot Preserves
¾ teaspoon soda	(*see* Index)
¼ teaspoon sea salt	5 cups chopped pecans

Cream margarine until fluffy; add syrup and blend well. Add eggs one at a time, beating well after each addition. Sift flour with spices, soda, and salt six times. Add to creamed mixture, mixing well. Stir in buttermilk, vanilla, then preserves, and nuts. Pour batter into tube pan that has been well greased and floured (or use two loaf pans). Bake in preheated oven at 350° for 30 minutes or until cake springs back when lightly touched. For Christmas cake, bake in October or November. Wrap tightly in clear food wrap or plastic bag, and store in freezer until ready to use.

MOIST FRUITCAKE

½ pound of butter	3 tablespoons lemon juice
8 packets sugar substitute	2 teaspoons vanilla
1 cup white **carob syrup**	2 teaspoons orange extract
5 eggs	4 cups crushed or broken
2 cups soya carob flour	pecans
1 teaspoon baking powder	2 20-ounce cans Candied
3 teaspoons lemon extract	Pineapple (*see* Index)

Cream butter, sugar substitute, and syrup; add eggs, one at a time, beating well after each addition. Sift 1½ cups of the flour with baking powder and add alternately with flavorings to creamed mixture. Sprinkle remaining flour over nuts and fruits; add to batter, mixing well. Coat bundt cake pan with non-stick vegetable spray, then flour, or place brown paper in bottom of the cake pan, greasing and flouring bottom and sides.

Place broiler pan containing water under cake pan in oven. Bake for 2 hours in preheated oven at 300°. Let cake stand overnight in pan. The next day, wrap cake in cloth and foil or plastic bag; store in refrigerator, or freeze.

Note: Do not substitute margarine for butter in this recipe.
Yield: 10-15 servings.

WHITE FRUITCAKE

1 cup butter	⅛ teaspoon sea salt
1 cup white carob syrup	2 cups chopped pecans or
4 eggs, well beaten	walnuts
1 ounce lemon extract	1 pound Candied Pineapple
2 cups soya carob flour	(*see* Index)
1 teaspoon baking powder	

Cream butter and syrup; add eggs, one at a time, beating well after each addition; add lemon extract. Sift flour with baking powder and salt 6 times; do not discard black specks, but add them to the flour each time. Add to creamed mixture, beating well. Add nuts and pineapple. Bake in a well-greased bundt or angel food cake pan in preheated oven for 2 hours at 300°. Test with toothpick.

WHITE CHRISTMAS FRUITCAKE

1 cup Cherry Preserves
   (*see* Index)
2 cups Candied Pineapple
   (*see* Index)
1 cup grated fresh coconut
1 cup chopped nuts
4 cups soya carob flour
½ pound butter

1½ cups white carob syrup
2 whole eggs
¼ cup liquid (water, milk, or
   fruit juice)
2 teaspoons baking powder
1 teaspoon mace
6 egg whites, beaten
1 teaspoon lemon extract

Place fruit and nuts in a bowl; add about 1 cup of the flour and gently mix with the fruit. Set aside. (This may be done a day early.)

Cream butter; add syrup, whole eggs, a small amount of the liquid, and blend well. Sift together mace, baking powder, and the remaining flour. Mix into the creamed mixture 1 cup of the sifted dry ingredients with the rest of the liquid. Fold in the beaten egg whites and add the rest of the dry ingredients, mixing well. Add flavoring. Last, work in the floured fruit and nuts. There is little or no danger that the dough will be too stiff. Bake in a preheated oven at 275° for 3 to 4 hours.

HONEY UPSIDE-DOWN CAKE WITH HONEY SAUCE

½ cup tupelo honey
¼ cup butter
4-5 unpeeled apples

Candied Pineapple or Cherry
   Preserves (*see* Index)
nut halves

Put honey and butter in a heavy medium-size skillet and slowly melt on top of stove. Core the unpeeled apples and cut them crosswise into ring slices ¾ of an inch thick, preparing enough apples to cover bottom of skillet. Add the apple rings to honey-butter mixture and simmer until apples are partially cooked, turning once. Place a small piece of Candied Pineapple or ¼ teaspoon Cherry Preserves into center of each apple ring. Add nut meats in the spaces around the apples. Pour the following batter over the hot mixture:

BATTER

½ cup butter
¾ cup tupelo honey
1 egg
½ cup milk
1½ cups soya carob flour or 1
    cup soya carob flour and
    ½ cup wheat germ

1 teaspoon baking powder
¼ teaspoon soda
½ teaspoon nutmeg
¼ teaspoon cinnamon
⅛ teaspoon ginger

Cream together butter and honey; add eggs and beat until smooth. Add milk, alternating twice with sifted dry ingredients. Pour in skillet and bake in preheated oven at 350°, 30 to 35 minutes. When done, turn upside down cake onto a large platter.

This may be served hot or cold, with sauce made from ½ cup honey combined with ½ cup butter and heated.

ELSIE'S JAM CAKE

1 cup butter
2 packets sugar substitute
1 cup white carob syrup
1 cup Pineapple Preserves
    (*see* Index)
1 cup Apricot Preserves
    (*see* Index)
1 cup Strawberry Jam
    (*see* Index)

5 eggs, separated
1 cup buttermilk
1 teaspoon soda
3 cups soya carob flour
1 teaspoon cinnamon
1 teaspoon allspice
1 cup grated nut meats finely
    chopped

Cream together butter and sugar; add jams and preserves. Beat egg yolks well; add to creamed mixture and beat until smooth. Mix soda with buttermilk and add alternately with flour, mixing well after each addition. Add the spices and nuts and mix well. Beat egg whites until stiff; fold in. Pour into 2 well-greased and floured 8-inch-round cake pans and bake in a preheated oven at 400° for 20 minutes, or until done. Cake will spring back lightly when touched. Frost with Caramel Frosting (*see* Index). Cool on rack.

EASY PROTEIN NUT CAKE

6 egg whites	2 teaspoons baking powder
6 egg yolks	¼ teaspoon sea salt
1 cup white carob syrup or 1 cup tupelo honey	3 cups ground pecans or walnuts
2 tablespoons soya carob flour	1 tablespoon vanilla or lemon extract

Beat egg whites until stiff but not dry. Beat egg yolks separately with syrup or honey until thick and lemon colored, and to them add flour, baking powder, and salt. Mix well, then add nuts, vanilla or lemon flavoring. Fold in egg whites. Bake in a preheated oven at 325° for about 1 hour. Serve topped with whipped cream.

Note: Makes a very good cake to freeze. Stays very moist.

OATMEAL CAKE

1 cup white carob syrup	1 teaspoon baking powder
½ cup boiling water	1 teaspoon soda
2 tablespoons lemon juice	7 packets sugar substitute
1 cup oatmeal	½ teaspoon sea salt
1 cup butter or margarine	1 teaspoon cinnamon
2 eggs	½ teaspoon nutmeg
1¼ cups soya carob flour	

Caramelize 1 tablespoon of the syrup; add water and lemon juice; add oatmeal; let stand for 20 minutes. In the meantime, cream margarine; add remainder of syrup and blend well. Add eggs, beating after each addition. Add oatmeal mixture to creamed mixture.

Sift dry ingredients together 6 times; add to creamed mixture and stir until just blended. Bake in an 8-by-11-inch greased pan. Bake in preheated oven at 350° for 30 minutes or until cake springs back when pressed with finger. Cool and frost with Coconut Frosting (*see* Index).

PEACH CAKE

6 ounces whipped margarine
1 cup white carob syrup
8 packets sugar substitute
1 teaspoon soda
½ teaspoon sea salt

1 teaspoon cinnamon
2 eggs
2 cups soya carob flour
1 cup fresh peaches, cut up

Cream together margarine, syrup, sugar substitute, soda, salt, and cinnamon. Add eggs one at a time, beating well after each addition. Add flour to creamed mixture and beat well (3 minutes). Add peaches. Pour into greased 8-by-10-inch pan. Bake 30 to 35 minutes in a preheated oven at 350°.

Icing

1 cup white carob syrup
1 cup condensed milk

¼ pound butter
1 teaspoon vanilla

Mix all ingredients and cook over medium heat until thickened, stirring constantly. Spread while still warm on cooled cake.

PINEAPPLE-CARROT CAKE

2 cups soya carob flour
1¾ teaspoons soda
2 teaspoons cinnamon
2 teaspoons baking powder
1 teaspoon sea salt
10 ounces (1¼ tubs) whipped margarine

1 cup white carob syrup
4 eggs
1 cup grated carrots
1 small can crushed unsweetened pineapple (drained)
1 cup chopped nuts

Sift all dry ingredients together 4 times and set aside.

Mix margarine, syrup, and sugar substitute; cream until fluffy. Add eggs one at a time, beating after each addition. Add dry ingredients; mix well. Add carrots, pineapple, and nuts. Pour into a greased and floured 13-by-9-by-2½-inch pan. Bake 30 to 35 minutes at 325° in a preheated oven, or until brown.

PRUNE CAKE

4 tablespoons butter
1½ cups white carob syrup
3 eggs
2 cups cooked prunes (cooked
    with ¼ cup carob syrup),
    mashed
1 cup prune juice

2¼ cups soya carob flour
1 teaspoon soda
1 teaspoon allspice
½ teaspoon sea salt
1 tablespoon nutmeg
1 teaspoon cinnamon
1 teaspoon ground cloves

Cream butter, sugar substitute, and syrup; add eggs one at a time, beating after each addition. Add prunes and prune juice, alternately with flour, which has been sifted with spices, salt, and soda 5 times. Bake in 2 well-greased and floured 9-inch-round layer cake pans for about 30 minutes in a preheated oven at 350°.

MOIST PRUNE CAKE

1 cup margarine
1½ cups white carob syrup
3 eggs, well beaten
1 teaspoon vanilla
2 cups soya carob flour
1 teaspoon soda
1 teaspoon sea salt

1 teaspoon nutmeg
1 teaspoon cinnamon
½ teaspoon allspice
1 cup buttermilk
1 cup chopped, stewed prunes
1 cup chopped nuts

Cream margarine and syrup; add eggs and vanilla, and blend well. Sift together 6 times flour, salt, soda, cinnamon, nutmeg and allspice. Add flour mixture alternately with buttermilk. Add prunes and nuts. Bake in greased and floured tube pan in a preheated 350° oven for 1 hour. Prick all over with fork and pour on topping.

TOPPING

1 cup white carob syrup
¼ pound butter

½ cup heavy cream
1 teaspoon vanilla

Caramelize 1 tablespoon syrup, then add rest of syrup, cream, butter and vanilla. Cook 3 minutes; pour over hot cake.

RHUBARB CAKE

2 cups diced raw rhubarb	1 teaspoon baking soda
10 packets sugar substitute	1 teaspoon cinnamon
1 cup white carob syrup	⅛ teaspoon sea salt
¼ pound butter	1 cup sour cream
1 egg	1 teaspoon vanilla
2 cups soya carob flour	

Mix rhubarb with ½ cup syrup and 5 packets sugar substitute; let set. Cream shortening and remaining syrup and sugar substitute. Add egg; mix. Sift dry ingredients 4 times. Add sifted dry ingredients alternately with sour cream and vanilla. Beat 2 minutes; fold in lightly rhubarb mixture. Pour into greased and floured 9-by-13-inch pan. Bake in preheated oven at 350° for 50 to 60 minutes, or until cake tests done.

Serve with whipped cream or Rhubarb Sauce (*see* Index).

CRUSTY POUND CAKE

1¾ cups butter	8 packets sugar substitute
4 cups soya carob flour, or a mixture of 3 cups soya carob and 1 cup all-purpose flour	⅛ teaspoon sea salt
	1 teaspoon baking powder
	1 teaspoon vanilla
8 eggs	1 teaspoon lemon extract
1½ cups white carob syrup	1 tablespoon frozen lemon-juice concentrate

Cream butter; work in flour (after sifting 3 times) until mixture is fine and mealy. In another bowl, beat eggs until thick and lemon colored; combine with syrup and sugar substitute; add to butter-flour mixture, beating in well. Add salt, baking powder, flavorings, and lemon juice. Beat for 15 minutes with rotary beater or 5 minutes with electric mixer. Bake in greased and floured 10-inch tube pan in preheated oven at 250° for 40 minutes, then raise heat to 325° and bake for another 40 minutes. Cake will be crusty. Cool on rack.

OLD-FASHIONED POUND CAKE

½ pound butter
1 cup white carob syrup
4 packets sugar substitute
2 cups soya carob flour
1 teaspoon baking powder

pinch of sea salt
5-6 eggs
2 tablespoons frozen orange-
    juice concentrate

Cream butter; beat well with syrup and sugar substitute; add flour and baking powder. Add eggs, one at a time, beating each in well. Add salt and orange juice. Beat batter for 15 minutes with rotary beater or 5 minutes with electric mixer. Bake in greased and floured pan in preheated oven for 1 hour at 325°.

SOUR CREAM POUND CAKE

1 cup butter
1½ cups white carob syrup
15 packets sugar substitute
3 cups soya carob flour
¼ teaspoon sea salt
6 eggs, separated

½ teaspoon soda
1 tablespoon lemon juice
1 teaspoon almond extract
1 teaspoon vanilla
1 cup sour cream

Sift flour and salt together; set aside. Cream butter, syrup, and sugar substitute. Add egg yolks, one at a time, beating well after each addition. Stir soda and lemon juice into sour cream; add, alternately with flour, to batter, blending well after each addition. Add flavorings. In a separate bowl, beat egg whites until stiff. Fold yolk batter into beaten egg whites. Pour into a greased and floured 10-inch tube pan. Bake in preheated oven at 300° for 1½ hours, or until lightly browned. Cool on rack.

SPONGE CUPCAKES

Note: To make these you must have kitchen scales. You will need the following:

6 eggs
white carob syrup

soya carob flour, unsifted
1 lemon, juice and rind

Weigh the eggs. Take the exact amount in weight of the syrup and half the amount in flour. Separate the eggs; beat the yolks well; beat in the syrup; fold in flour, lemon juice, and rind. Beat egg whites until stiff, then fold into batter. Line muffin tins with paper baking cups; fill two-thirds full with batter. Bake in preheated oven at 300° until cupcakes spring back when touched lightly.

Yield: 12 cupcakes.

TWO-EGG YELLOW CAKE

½ cup vegetable shortening	2 teaspoons baking powder
1 cup white carob syrup	¼ teaspoon sea salt
2 eggs	¾ cup milk
2 cups unsifted soya carob flour	1 teaspoon vanilla

Cream shortening with syrup. Add eggs; beat in well. Sift together dry ingredients. Add to mixture, alternately with milk and vanilla, folding in well. Pour batter into 2 greased and floured 8-inch pans or into 1 8-by-10-by-2-inch pan. Bake layers in a preheated oven at 350° for 25-30 minutes or until cake springs back lightly when touched; bake in loaf pan at same temperature for 35-45 minutes. Invert on cake rack to cool.

ICINGS

CARAMEL FROSTING

In a heavy skillet measure 1 cup syrup, ¼ pound of butter and 2 teaspoons vanilla. Cook over high heat until lightly browned (do not allow to brown too dark; stir constantly to keep from burning). Add ½ cup milk to the mixture slowly and cook until slightly warm. Beat until smooth. While still not thick enough to hold shape, smooth 1 tablespoon icing on each layer. This will soak in and hold the moisture in the cake. When the remainder of the icing has been beaten enough to hold shape, smooth again between the layer and frost the top and sides. This cake will be better several days after baking, as it will then be mellowed. Delicious on Elsie's Jam Cake (*see* Index).

COCONUT FROSTING

1 cup evaporated milk
¼ pound butter or margarine
1 teaspoon vanilla
1 cup chopped nuts

1 cup white carob syrup
3 egg yolks
1 cup coconut

Mix all ingredients together; cook over medium heat until thick, stirring constantly. Spread on cake. Very good on Oatmeal Cake (*see* Index).

COCONUT ICING

½ cup coconut milk or half-and-half cream
4 tablespoons white carob syrup

1½ cups grated coconut
2 egg whites

Mix ingredients with stiffly beaten egg whites and spread. Do not cook. Spread icing on Coconut Cake (*see* Index).

Cookies and Candy

COOKIES

APPLESAUCE COOKIES

2 cups soya carob flour
½ teaspoon sea salt
½ teaspoon each cinnamon, nutmeg and cloves
½ cup butter or margarine
1 tablespoon, plus 1 teaspoon

sugar substitute
1 teaspoon baking soda
1 cup unsweetened applesauce
1 egg well beaten
1 cup chopped nuts
1 cup raisins

Mix together unsifted flour, salt, and spices, and set aside. Cream butter and sweetener. Stir soda into applesauce; add egg. Combine with creamed mixture. Gradually add flour mixture, blending together well. Stir in nuts and raisins. Drop by teaspoonfuls onto a lightly greased cookie sheet. Bake in preheated oven at 375° for 15 minutes or until browned lightly.

Yield: 3 dozen.

BROWNIES

¾ cup tupelo honey
½ cup soft butter
2 tablespoons lemon juice
¼ teaspoon sea salt

2 teaspoons vanilla
1¼ cups soya carob flour
⅔ cup carob powder
1½ cups chopped nuts

Cream honey, butter, lemon juice, salt, and vanilla together until well blended. Combine the flour, powder, and nuts; add to honey and butter mixture; stir well. Pour into 8-inch square pan. Bake for 30 minutes in preheated oven at 350°. Cut into 2-inch squares.

Yield: 16 brownies.

CAROB BROWNIES

⅞ cup white carob syrup	2 teaspoons vanilla
½ cup cooking oil	1¼ cups soya carob flour
2 tablespoons lemon juice	⅔ cup carob powder
¼ teaspoon sea salt	1 cup chopped pecans

Beat syrup, oil, lemon juice, salt, and vanilla together until well creamed. Combine the flour, powder, and nuts; add to syrup and oil mixture, and stir well. Pour into 8-inch square pan. Bake for 30 minutes in a preheated 350° oven. Cut in 2-inch squares.

Yield: 16 brownies.

COCONUT CARAMEL CHEWS

½ cup butter	1 teaspoon baking powder
1 cup plus 2 tablespoons white carob syrup	½ teaspoon sea salt
2 eggs, separated	2 teaspoons vanilla
1¾ cups soya carob flour	1½ cups coconut
	1 tablespoon water

Cream together butter, 1 cup of the syrup, egg yolks, and 1 teaspoon of vanilla. Sift together 5 times flour, baking powder, and salt; include siftings. Add flour mixture to creamed mixture. Add ½ cup of the coconut. Mix well and turn into a 6-by-8-by-2-inch greased and floured baking pan. Beat egg whites until stiff, and add remaining vanilla. Caramelize remainder of syrup and add water. Add to egg whites and mix well. Add remaining coconut. Spread meringue over batter. Bake 30 minutes in preheated oven at 325°. Cool. Cut into squares.

Yield: 24 pieces.

REFRIGERATED COCONUT POPS

2 tablespoons white carob syrup	¼ teaspoon grated orange rind
1 3-ounce package softened cream cheese	1 teaspoon chopped walnuts
¼ teaspoon grated lemon rind	¼ cup toasted coconut

In a bowl blend 1 tablespoon syrup, cheese, grated rinds, and walnuts. With a teaspoon form into 12 tiny balls. Add remainder of syrup to fresh ground coconut, toasted and cooled. Roll balls in toasted coconut.

Yield: 1 dozen.

A LITTLE COOKIE

½ cup white carob syrup	½ teaspoon sea salt
½ cup butter	1 egg
2 cups soya carob flour	1 teaspoon vanilla
½ teaspoon baking powder	

Cream syrup and butter together; add dry ingredients, egg, and vanilla. Roll out and cut with cookie cutter. Bake in preheated 350° oven for 10 minutes or until brown.

Yield: 3 dozen.

HONEY COOKIES

1 cup butter	3 cups soya carob flour
1 cup brown sugar substitute	1½ teaspoon soda
2 eggs	⅛ teaspoon sea salt
¼ cup tupelo honey	1 cup walnuts (optional)
1 teaspoon vanilla	

Cream butter; add sugar substitute and cream together. Add eggs and beat at high speed for 5 minutes. Add honey and vanilla. Sift together flour, soda, and salt; fold gradually into egg mixture, then mix well. Form dough into rolls; chill 2 or 3 hours. Slice and place on greased cookie sheet. Bake in preheated oven at 350° for 10 to 15 minutes.

For variety try adding 1 cup walnuts to dough mixture, before baking. Dip baked cookies into Pineapple Glaze.

Yield: 4 dozen.

PINEAPPLE GLAZE

⅛ cup tupelo honey   ⅛ cup pineapple juice
2 teaspoons vinegar   2 tablespoons butter

Simmer all ingredients in saucepan for 5 minutes. Cool to lukewarm. Dip cookies into glaze and let set for a while.

LEMON THINS

⅛ cup white carob syrup   1 teaspoon lemon extract
4 packets sugar substitute   2 teaspoons lemon juice
⅛ cup butter   1 cup soya carob flour
2 tablespoons wheat germ   1⅛ teaspoon baking powder
1 egg   ⅛ teaspoon sea salt

In mixing bowl, combine syrup, sugar substitute, butter, and wheat germ. Cream until fluffy. Add egg and beat well. Add flavoring and lemon juice. Combine flour, baking powder, and salt, sifting together 5 times. Add to creamed mixture. Drop by teaspoonfuls 1½ inches apart on greased and floured cookie sheet. Bake in preheated oven at 375° for 8-10 minutes or until delicately browned.

Yield: 2 dozen.

LEMON REFRIGERATOR COOKIES

2 cups soya carob flour   1 cup white carob syrup
⅛ teaspoon soda   1 teaspoon vanilla
¼ teaspoon sea salt   2 eggs, beaten
⅛ cup butter   ⅛ cup chopped nuts
⅛ cup vegetable shortening

Have ingredients at room temperature. Have baking sheet ready. Preheat oven 10 minutes before baking; set to moderately hot (400°).

Sift flour, salt, and soda together 5 times; do not discard any of the flour. Cream butter and shortening until smooth; add syrup, blending thoroughly. Stir in vanilla, then the eggs, one at a time, and beating after each addition until well blended. Add flour in 3 portions, mixing well after each. Stir in nuts.

Chill dough until stiff, then divide in half and place on 2 sheets of waxed paper. Quickly shape into 2 uniform rolls about 2 inches in diameter, then roll up in the paper. Lay on piece of cardboard to keep level and store in refrigerator until very firm, from 3 to 6 hours. If roll flattens out the first hour, quickly re-mold into round rolls. When firm, slice with a sharp knife into ¼-inch thick cookies. Keep thickness uniform for perfect baking. Place 1 inch apart on baking sheet. Bake 7-9 minutes to a pale golden color. Remove from pan to cake rack to cool thoroughly before storing in an airtight container with waxed paper between layers.

Yield: 3 dozen.

OATMEAL COOKIES

1½ cups soya carob flour	½ cup white carob syrup
½ teaspoon baking soda	8 packets sugar substitute
¼ teaspoon sea salt	1 egg
½ teaspoon cinnamon, ginger and nutmeg	¼ cup milk
1 cup margarine	1¾ cups quick cooking rolled oats
	1 cup chopped walnuts

Sift together flour, soda, salt, and spices; set aside. Cream shortening with syrup and sugar substitute in a large bowl. Beat in egg and milk. Sift in flour mixture, blending well to make a thick mixture. Fold in rolled oats and walnuts. Drop by teaspoonfuls 3 inches apart on a greased cookie sheet. Bake in preheated oven at 375° for 10-12 minutes until lightly golden.

Yield: 2 dozen.

ORANGE THINS

1¼ cups white carob syrup	1 teaspoon grated orange peel
1 cup butter	(optional)
5 tablespoons wheat germ	2 cups soya carob flour
2 eggs	2¼ teaspoons baking powder
2 teaspoons orange extract	¼ teaspoon sea salt

In mixing bowl combine syrup, butter, and wheat germ; cream until fluffy. Add eggs and beat well. Add flavoring and orange peel. Combine flour, baking powder, and salt, and sift 5 times. Add to creamed mixture, mixing well. Drop by teaspoonfuls 1½ inches apart on greased and floured cookie sheet. Bake in preheated oven at 375° for 8 to 10 minutes or until delicately browned.

Yield: 6 dozen.

PEANUT COOKIES

Soya powdered milk	½ cup dietetic peanut butter
1 cup raw peanuts, chopped	½ cup tupelo honey

Use enough soya powdered milk to make stiff dough. Mix in peanuts. Roll in waxed paper and chill overnight. Cut into slices.

Yield: 2 dozen.

PECAN MACAROONS

4 egg whites	½ teaspoon sea salt
2 cups white carob syrup	1 teaspoon vinegar
1 teaspoon vanilla	2 cups pecan meats, chopped

Set egg whites and syrup on back of stove (very low heat or just warm surface); add vanilla, salt and vinegar. Beat until quite stiff; add pecans, then drop by teaspoon on well greased baking sheet. Bake in slow preheated oven (325°) for—or until done.

Yield: 3 dozen.

PECAN SANDIES

1 cup butter	1 tablespoon water
¼ cup white carob syrup	2 cups flour
2 teaspoons vanilla	1 cup chopped pecans
¼ teaspoon sea salt	

Cream butter and syrup; add vanilla, salt, and water. Add flour gradually, and mix well. Add pecans. Form into small balls. Place on ungreased cookie sheet. Bake in preheated oven at 300° for 20 minutes or until delicately browned.

Yield: 3 dozen.

SHORT'NIN' BREAD
(THE KIND THAT "MAMMY'S LITTLE BABY" LIKES)

¼ cup white carob syrup	¼ teaspoon sea salt
2 tablespoons brown sugar substitute	1 teaspoon vanilla
½ pound butter	1 teaspoon cinnamon (optional)
	2 cups soya carob flour

Mix syrup, sugar substitute, salt, butter, and cream well. Add vanilla and cinnamon, then flour, and mix well. Place on floured surface and pat to ½-inch thickness. Cut into desired shapes and bake in preheated oven on cookie sheet in moderate oven (325° to 350°) for 20 to 25 minutes.

Yield: 3 dozen.

VANILLA COOKIES

1⅜ cups soya carob flour
½ teaspoon sea salt
1 teaspoon baking powder
½ cup butter or margarine

1 cup white carob syrup
2 teaspoons vanilla
2 eggs

Sift together 4 times flour, salt, and baking powder and set aside. Cream butter; add carob syrup. Cream well. Stir in vanilla, then beat in eggs, one at a time until mixture is fluffy. Stir in flour, mixing until smooth. Drop by teaspoonfuls 1½ inches apart onto greased and lightly floured cookie sheet. Bake in preheated oven at 375° for 7 to 8 minutes or until delicately browned. Remove from cookie sheet immediately to cake rack to cool.
Yield: 4 dozen.

VANILLA WAFERS

½ cup white carob syrup
½ cup butter
2 tablespoons wheat germ
1 egg
1 teaspoon vanilla

1 cup soya carob flour
1⅜ teaspoons baking powder
⅛ teaspoon sea salt
4 packets sugar substitute

In mixing bowl combine syrup, butter, sugar substitute, and wheat germ. Cream until fluffy. Add egg; beat well. Add vanilla. Sift together 5 times flour, baking powder, and salt; add to creamed mixture, mixing well. Drop by teaspoonfuls 2 inches apart on a greased cookie sheet. Bake in preheated oven at 375° 8-10 minutes or until brown.
Yield: 3 dozen.

WALNUT COOKIES

2 eggs
1 cup white carob syrup
⅔ cup sifted soya carob flour

¼ teaspoon baking powder
¼ teaspoon sea salt
1 cup finely chopped walnuts

Beat eggs until light in color. Add syrup and beat until thick. Add sifted dry ingredients and nuts. Mix well. Drop by scant teaspoonfuls onto greased cookie sheet. Bake in 400° preheated oven for 5 minutes. Let stand ½ minute before removing. Store in airtight container.

Yield: 5 dozen.

WALNUT OATMEAL COOKIES

½ cup white carob syrup	1 teaspoon vanilla
8 packets sugar substitute	1 cup soya carob flour
¼ cup butter	1½ teaspoons baking powder
2 tablespoons heavy cream	¼ teaspoon sea salt
2 tablespoons wheat germ	¾ cup minute oatmeal
1 egg	1 cup chopped walnuts
2 tablespoons lemon juice	

In a small mixing bowl, combine syrup, sugar substitute, butter, cream, and wheat germ. Cream until fluffy. Add egg and beat well. Add lemon juice and vanilla. Sift together 5 times flour, baking powder, and salt; add to creamed mixture. Add oatmeal and nuts, and mix well. Drop by teaspoonfuls 2 inches apart on a greased cookie sheet. Press down. Bake in preheated oven at 300° 10-12 minutes or until golden brown.

Yield: 4 dozen.

CANDY

ALMOND-BUTTER CRUNCH

1½ cups blanched almonds	¼ cup water
water (to cover almonds)	⅛ teaspoon sea salt
2 tablespoons butter	¼ pound butter
1 cup white carob syrup	½ teaspoon soda

Place almonds in saucepan and add enough water to cover; bring to a boil. Reduce heat and simmer 2 minutes. Drain. Split almonds. In jelly roll pan melt 2 tablespoons butter; add almonds. Toast in oven stirring occasionally, for 8-10 minutes. In another pan combine syrup and ¼ cup water; cook slowly until candy thermometer registers 225°. Add salt, butter, and nut mixture. Cook to 290° or 295°. Cook until mixture begins to caramelize; add baking soda, stirring in at once; pour onto buttered cookie sheet. Allow to cool. Break into pieces and store in tightly covered container.

CARA COA CHOCOLATE NUT CARAMELS

½ cup heavy cream	¼ pound butter
5 tablespoons cara coa	1 teaspoon vanilla
1 cup white carob syrup	1 cup chopped nuts

Mix cara coa with cream. Add syrup and butter. Cook and stir over medium heat until mixture reaches firm ball stage. Add vanilla and nuts. Remove from heat. Beat about five minutes. Pour into well-buttered 8-inch square pan. When cold, cut into squares and wrap each cube individually in plastic wrap.

Yield: 3 dozen.

VANILLA CARAMELS

2 cups white carob syrup	2 cups heavy cream
⅛ teaspoon sea salt	1 teaspoon vanilla
¼ pound of butter	1 cup chopped nuts

Combine syrup, salt, butter and 1 cup of the cream; boil to soft ball stage, stirring constantly. Add remaining cream slowly, while cooking. Cook an additional 45 minutes or until mixture makes a firm pliable ball when a small amount is dropped into cold water. Add vanilla and nuts. Pour into an 8- or 9-inch square pan. Let stand 12 hours. Cut into 1-inch squares. Wrap each cube individually.

Yield: 3 dozen.

DIVINITY

2 cups white carob syrup
¼ teaspoon sea salt
½ cup water
2 egg whites

1 teaspoon vanilla
2 cups coarsely chopped nuts
1 cup coconut meal

In saucepan, mix syrup, salt, and water. Cook, stirring until a small amount dropped into cold water forms a firm ball. Beat egg whites until stiff but not dry. Pour mixture over egg whites, slowly, beating constantly. Add vanilla and beat until mixture holds its shape. Add nuts and coconut meal. Spread in 9-inch buttered square pan. When firm cut into squares.

Yield: 3 dozen.

PEANUT BRITTLE

1 cup white carob syrup
¼ cup water
2 cups raw peanuts

¼ pound butter
⅛ teaspoon sea salt
1 teaspoon soda

Combine syrup and water in a heavy 2-quart saucepan. Cook slowly until candy thermometer registers 225°. Add nuts, butter, and salt. Cook to 290° to 295°. Cook until mixture begins to caramelize. Add baking soda quickly, stirring in at once. Pour onto buttered cookie sheet. Allow to cool. Break into pieces; store in tightly covered container in deep freeze.

PECAN COCONUT BARS

1 cup white carob syrup
¼ cup water
2 cups pecans
¼ pound butter

2 cups fresh ground toasted coconut
½ teaspoon soda

Combine syrup, water, pecans, and butter. Cook on top of stove at medium heat until mixture begins to caramelize. Add coconut and soda; mix well. Turn onto greased cookie sheet; cool. Cut into bars.

Yield: 18 bars.

ORANGE PECANS

2 cups white carob syrup
1 tablespoon soya carob flour
½ cup milk
1 tablespoon butter

juice of 1 orange
1 teaspoon grated orange rind
juice of 1 lemon
4 cups pecans

In saucepan, mix syrup and flour, then add milk and butter. Bring to boil. Add orange juice, grated orange rind, and lemon juice. Cook until mixture forms a soft ball when dropped in cold water. Cool slightly, without stirring; then pour over pecans. Beat until thick and nuts tend to separate. Pour mixture onto lightly buttered platter. Separate into serving-size pieces, pulling with 2 forks. Allow 2 pecans to each piece.

Yield: 36 pieces.

CANDIED PINEAPPLE

2 20-ounce cans sliced pineapple. Drain well. Place in a quart jar. Cover with tupelo honey or white carob syrup and let set overnight. Place in 2-quart pan; cook over open flame at low temperature, stirring constantly until all liquid is condensed.

WALNUT CRUNCH

2 cups white carob syrup
⅛ cup water
¼ cup heavy cream
⅛ teaspoon sea salt

¼ pound butter
1 teaspoon vanilla
2 cups toasted walnuts

Caramelize 1 tablespoon of the syrup; add water, cream, and remainder of syrup. Add salt, butter, and vanilla. Cook at medium heat on top of stove, stirring constantly. Add walnuts. Cook until candy reaches hard ball stage. Pour into well-buttered 8 by 12-inch pan. Allow to cool. Remove from pan and break into pieces.

Jams and Jellies

APRICOT PRESERVES

3 cups prepared apricots	4 tablespoons lemon juice
¾ cup white carob syrup	½ bottle **Certo**
12 packets sugar substitute	

To prepare fruit: In a saucepan add enough water to cover 1 pound dry apricots; let stand overnight. Drain, reserving liquid. Grind apricots or chop fine. Mix with liquid.

To the measured fruit in saucepan add syrup, sugar substitute, and lemon juice. Mix well. Place over medium heat and boil for 2-3 minutes, stirring constantly; stir in Certo at once. Cook 2 minutes, stirring constantly. Pour into sterilized glasses.

Yield: 1½ pints.

PINEAPPLE PRESERVES

2 20-ounce cans unsweetened sliced pineapple, drained and cut into small pieces	unsweetened pineapple juice
1 6-ounce can frozen	2 cups tupelo honey
	¾ bottle **Certo**

To the measured fruit in large saucepan, add frozen pineapple juice and honey. Bring to a rapid boil, stirring constantly. Boil 5 minutes; add Certo and continue to boil 3-4 minutes. Remove from heat. Ladle into sterilized glasses.

Yield: 1 quart.

CHERRY PRESERVES

1 20-ounce package   4 packets sugar substitute
   frozen unsweetened   1 cup white carob syrup
   cherries   ⅓ bottle Certo
2 tablespoons lemon juice

To the measured fruit in saucepan, add lemon juice, sugar substitute, and syrup. Cook over medium heat 10-15 minutes, stirring constantly. Add Certo; continue to boil 2-3 minutes. Remove from heat. Ladle into sterilized glasses.

Yield: 1 pint.

STRAWBERRY JAM

1 quart fully ripe strawberries,   1½ cups white carob syrup
   washed and hulled   ⅓ bottle Certo
3 tablespoons lemon juice

Crush strawberries in a large saucepan, so that each berry is reduced to pulp. Add lemon juice and syrup. Cook over high heat, stirring constantly until mixture boils hard. Stir in Certo. Bring to a full rolling boil, that cannot be stirred down. Boil hard 1-2 minutes, stirring constantly. Remove jam from heat. Ladle quickly into sterilized glasses.

Yield: 6 glasses.

BLUEBERRY JELLY

1 cup blueberry juice   1 cup white carob syrup
3 tablespoons lemon juice   ⅓ bottle Certo

To the measured juice in heavy saucepan, add lemon juice and syrup. Place over high heat and bring to a boil, stirring constantly. Boil 5 minutes; stir in Certo. Then bring to a rolling boil and boil hard 2 minutes. Remove from heat and pour quickly into sterilized glasses.

Yield: 2 glasses.

CHERRY JELLY

1½ cups cherry juice   1½ cups white carob syrup
2 tablespoons lemon juice   ½ bottle Certo

To the measured fruit juice in heavy saucepan, add the lemon juice and syrup. Place over high heat and bring to a boil, stirring constantly. Boil 5 minutes. Stir in Certo; then bring to a rolling boil and boil hard 2 minutes. Remove from heat and pour quickly into sterilized glasses.

Yield: 3 glasses.

ELDERBERRY JELLY

2 cups elderberry juice   ½ bottle Certo
2 cups white carob syrup

In saucepan combine juice and syrup. Bring to a rapid boil, stirring constantly. Boil 3-4 minutes. Stir in Certo at once. Then bring to a full rolling boil and boil hard for 2 minutes. Remove from heat and pour quickly into sterilized glasses.

Yield: 4 glasses.

ELDERBERRY-APPLE JELLY

1 6-ounce can frozen   elderberry juice
  unsweetened apple juice   1½ cups carob syrup
6 ounces unsweetened   ½ bottle Certo

Mix juices and syrup in heavy saucepan. Bring to a rolling boil. Boil 3-5 minutes. Add Certo; boil 1-2 minutes, stirring constantly. Remove from fire. Pour quickly into sterilized glasses.

Yield: 3 glasses.

HONEY APPLE JELLY

1 12-ounce can frozen   1½ cups tupelo honey
   unsweetened apple juice   ½ bottle Certo

Mix apple juice and honey in heavy saucepan. Bring to a boil; boil 3-5 minutes. Add Certo and bring to a full rolling boil and boil for 2 minutes. Remove from heat and pour into sterilized glasses.
Yield: 4 glasses.

HONEY PINEAPPLE JELLY

2 6-ounce cans frozen   1½ cups tupelo honey
   unsweetened pineapple   ½ bottle Certo
   juice

To the pineapple juice add honey. Place over high heat and bring to a boil. Boil 3 minutes, stirring constantly. Add Certo, continue boiling 1-2 minutes. Remove from heat and pour into sterilized glasses.
Yield: 4 glasses.

Ice Cream, Puddings, and Other Desserts

ICE CREAM

3 eggs
¾ cup plus 2 tablespoons white carob syrup
1 tablespoon vanilla (or 1 teaspoon vanilla and ⅛ teaspoon lemon extract)
¾ teaspoon sea salt
1 12-ounce can evaporated milk
1 pint half-and-half coffee cream
2 cups powdered milk
1½ cups whole milk

Beat eggs, add syrup and continue to beat until well blended. Add vanilla, salt, evaporated milk, and cream. Dissolve powdered milk into whole milk. Add to mixture and beat well. Turn into freezer. Last, add enough extra milk to come within 5 inches of top of freezer can.
Yield: 1 gallon.
Note: You may add any fruit sweetened with carob syrup or sugar substitute before adding last milk. Or you may use 3 or 4 bananas, sliced, and chopped nuts if desired.

BANANA NUT ICE CREAM

4 cups milk
14 packets sugar substitute
2 bananas, mashed
1 tablespoon vanilla
½ teaspoon sea salt
juice of 4 oranges
juice of 4 lemons
1 cup pecans, chopped
4 cups heavy cream

Thoroughly mix milk, cream, sugar substitute, bananas, vanilla, and salt. Freeze until mixture begins to congeal. Stir in fruit juices and nuts. Continue freezing until firm.
Yield: 1 gallon.

241

COUNTRY-STYLE VANILLA ICE CREAM

4 eggs	4 cups heavy cream
1¼ cups white carob syrup	2 tablespoons vanilla
4 cups milk	½ teaspoon sea salt

In a large mixing bowl beat eggs until foamy; add syrup; beat until thickened. Add milk, cream, vanilla, and salt; mix thoroughly. Chill and freeze.

Yield: 1 gallon.

EASY ICE CREAM

3 eggs	1 12-ounce can evaporated milk
1½ cups white carob syrup	1 teaspoon sea salt
1 tablespoon vanilla	1 quart half-and-half cream

Beat eggs until they are light in color; add syrup and beat at high speed until mixture is thick. Add vanilla, salt, and evaporated milk, beat 10 seconds. Add cream and mix thoroughly. Freeze.

Yield: 1 gallon.

HOMEMADE ICE CREAM

3 eggs	packets sugar substitute
1 tablespoon vanilla	1 pint heavy cream
½ teaspoon sea salt	1 quart whole milk
1 cup white carob syrup or 14	1 16-ounce can evaporated milk

Blend the eggs with vanilla, salt, and syrup (or sugar substitute) until smooth. Mix in the cream, whole milk, and evaporated milk. Pour into container. Freeze according to freezer instructions.

Yield: 1 gallon.

PEACH ICE CREAM

3 cups mashed fresh peaches
3 tablespoons fresh lemon juice
1 cup white carob syrup or 14
    packets sugar substitute
4 cups milk

3 cups heavy cream
1 tablespoon vanilla
¼ teaspoon almond extract
¼ teaspoon sea salt

Combine peaches and lemon juice in a large bowl; add syrup or sugar substitute; stir well.

In another large bowl combine milk, cream, vanilla, almond extract, and salt. Add peach mixture; stir well. Chill and freeze. Yield: 1 gallon.

FRESH PEACH ICE CREAM

2 cups fresh crushed peaches
    (about 7 medium size)
½ cup white carob syrup or 14
    packets sugar substitute
    (for peaches)
¼ teaspoon almond extract
¾ cup white carob syrup

2 tablespoons soya carob flour
⅛ teaspoon sea salt
2½ cups heavy cream
2 eggs, slightly beaten
1½ cups milk
2 teaspoons vanilla

Peel and pit peaches; cut into chunks and crush (with potato masher or electric blender). Add sweetener and almond extract; cover and refrigerate.

In a heavy saucepan, blend syrup, flour, salt, ½ cup of the cream, and eggs. Mix well. Add the milk slowly and cook over low heat, stirring constantly until mixture coats the spoon, about 7 minutes. Remove from heat; cool. Add vanilla and remainder of cream to cooled custard; blend well. Pour into two freezer trays.

Freeze until frozen ½ inch around edges of trays. Remove from trays to chilled bowl and beat with electric beater until smooth and fluffy. Fold in crushed peaches. Return to trays and freeze until firm. Yield: 2 quarts.

STRAWBERRY ICE CREAM

1 quart ripe strawberries, washed and hulled	2 cups milk, scalded
⅓ cup white carob syrup (for berries)	6 eggs
⅓ cup soya carob flour	3 teaspoons vanilla
¼ teaspoon sea salt	4 cups heavy cream
	1½ cups white carob syrup

Mash strawberries with ⅓ cup syrup; let stand while preparing custard.

Add flour, salt, and ½ cup of the milk in top of double boiler; mix well, then blend in remaining milk. Cook over simmering water, stirring constantly, about 5 minutes, or until thickened. Cover; cook 5 minutes longer. Beat eggs slightly; stir into hot mixture and cook 2 minutes longer. Cool; add vanilla. Blend in cream and strawberry mixture.

Freeze according to directions of manufacturer of your ice cream freezer. After ice cream freezes, paddle can be removed and freezer packed with ice and salt. Ice cream will keep 3-4 hours with this packing or may be set in deep freeze.

Yield: 2 quarts.

VANILLA ICE CREAM

2 cups milk	¼ teaspoon sea salt
½ cup white carob syrup	4 cups light cream
4 tablespoons vanilla	

Scald milk; add salt, cream, and syrup, and stir well. Stir in the vanilla. Cool and turn into freezer.

Yield: 2 quarts.

Note: For variety, add ripe peaches, bananas, strawberries, or most any other fruit.

CARA COA HOT FUDGE SAUCE

¼ cup cara coa powder
½ cup heavy cream
¼ teaspoon sea salt

¾ cup white carob syrup
1 teaspoon vanilla

Mix ingredients well in heavy saucepan. Bring to a boil and boil for 1 minute. Spoon desired amount over well-frozen ice cream.

Yield: 1 cup.

PEACH SHERBET

1½ cups buttermilk
¾ cup white carob syrup
1 teaspoon vanilla
⅛ teaspoon sea salt

2 cups crushed fresh or frozen peaches
1 unbeaten egg white

Mix together buttermilk, syrup, vanilla, sea salt, and peaches, stirring well. Turn into freezing tray and freeze until almost hard. Transfer to a mixing bowl. Add egg white and beat with electric beater until fluffy. Return to freezer tray and freeze until firm and ready to serve.

Yield: 1 quart.

PINEAPPLE ICE

juice of 4 lemons
1 small can crushed unsweetened pineapple

3 egg whites
1 cup white carob syrup
5 cups water

Mix lemon juice and pineapple, two of the beaten egg whites, the syrup, and the water. Stir well. Pour into sufficient number of refrigerator ice trays to accommodate the contents, leaving plenty of room for the third egg white, which should be whipped until stiff and stirred into each tray after the mixture has slightly hardened. Serve frozen.

Serves 4.

BLACK RASPBERRY ICE

2 teaspoons unflavored gelatin	1½ cup concentrated unsweetened
¾ cup cold water	black raspberry juice
¾ cup white carob syrup	¼ cup lemon juice
2 egg whites	½ teaspoon grated lemon rind

Sprinkle gelatin over ¼ cup of the water and let soften 5 minutes. Combine remaining water with ½ cup of the syrup and heat to boiling. Remove from heat; add gelatin and stir until dissolved. Cool. Beat egg whites until they form peaks; fold in remaining syrup, fruit juices, and lemon rind. Combine with gelatin mixture. Pour quickly into clean can of ice cream freezer and freeze to stiff mush.

Yield: 2 quarts.

STRAWBERRY ICE

1 pint fresh strawberries,	juice of ½ lemon
measured after hulling	½ cup water
¾ cup white carob syrup	

Crush berries; add syrup, lemon juice, and water. Press mixture through sieve, or blend in blender. Pour into freezing trays and freeze until slightly hardened. Remove from tray and beat until creamy. Return quickly to freezing tray and allow to finish freezing.

Serves 4.

BAKED CUSTARD

3 cups milk	3 eggs, slightly beaten
¼ cup white carob syrup	1 teaspoon vanilla
¼ teaspoon sea salt	dash of nutmeg

Scald milk with syrup and salt; stir slowly into beaten eggs; add vanilla. Pour into custard cups, sprinkle with nutmeg. Set in a shallow baking pan of hot water. Bake in preheated oven at 325° until done, about 30 minutes. Bake until knife inserted in center comes out clean. Do not overbake. Cool and serve.
Serves 6.

BAKED INDIAN PUDDING

1 quart hot milk	¾ cup carob syrup
½ cup cornmeal	2 tablespoons butter or
1 teaspoon sea salt	margarine
¼ teaspoon cinnamon	

Combine milk, cornmeal, and salt. Cook until thickened (about 15 minutes), stirring constantly. Remove from heat and stir in remaining ingredients. Pour mixture into an 8-by-8-inch baking dish and bake in a preheated oven at 275° for 2 hours.
Serves 6.

PEACH PUDDING

20 fresh peaches (about 4 pounds)	1 cup soya carob flour
1 cup white carob syrup	½ cup butter

Reserve one peach for garnish. Wash and peel peaches. Cut into quarters and drop into mixture of ½ cup syrup and 3 tablespoons flour. Turn into baking dish (10-by-6-by-2 inches). Mix remaining syrup and flour; cut in butter to crumblike consistency. Sprinkle over above mixture. Bake in preheated moderate oven (375°) for 1 hour or until peaches are tender and crumbs are brown.
Serves 6.

BAKED CINNAMON APPLES

3 tart apples   1½ teaspoons cinnamon
3 prunes, seeded   ¼ teaspoon allspice
3 tablespoons butter   3 tablespoons white carob syrup

Wash apples; do not pare. Use apple corer to remove cores. Stuff bottom of holes with prunes. Fit apples in covered casserole, prune side down. Fill holes in top of apples with mixture made from blended butter, spices, and syrup. Place cover on casserole. Preheat oven 8-10 minutes before baking; set to moderate (350°). Bake until apples are tender, 40-50 minutes.

BAKED APPLES

6 medium apples   12 teaspoons white carob syrup
Frozen unsweetened apple juice   6 teaspoons butter
    or cider, thawed

Wash apples, cut in half lengthwise; then with paring knife, cut out a narrow wedge to remove core. Dip cut surface of apple in apple juice or apple cider. Place halves, cut side up, snugly together in a shallow baking dish, 2-by-8-by-12 inches. Place 1 teaspoon syrup and ½ teaspoon butter in each half. Preheat oven 8-10 minutes. Bake at 350° until tender, about 40-50 minutes.

FRIED APPLES

6 tart apples   3 tablespoons butter
¼ cup white carob syrup

Use slightly green tart apples. Wash, but do not pare. Cut into quarters, remove core, stem and blossom ends. Cut into lengthwise slices. Sauté gently in butter 4-5 minutes, until apples are puffed and very wet with juice. Turn fruit over with a pancake turner. Pour syrup over apples. Cover; reduce heat and cook for 2 minutes. Serve hot with bacon or sausage or for dessert.

CHERRY COBBLER

2 tablespoons butter	¼ teaspoon sea salt
1 16-ounce can unsweetened cherries	¾ cup flour
	½ cup white carob syrup
1 tablespoon lemon juice	1 level teaspoon baking powder
7 packets sugar substitute	1 cup milk

Combine butter, cherries, lemon juice, sugar substitute, and salt in saucepan. Heat, then pour in shallow baking dish. Mix flour, syrup, baking powder, and milk. Pour over cherry mixture. Bake at 300° in preheated oven until golden brown.

Serves 6.

BLUEBERRY MOUSSE

1 20-ounce package frozen unsweetened blueberries	1 cup white carob syrup
	3 tablespoons lemon juice
2 cups water	2 cups heavy cream

Cook blueberries in water 15 minutes. Pour into blender and blend 2 minutes. Add syrup and lemon juice to blueberries. Return to heat and cook for 5 minutes. Remove from heat and cool.

Divide mixture between 2 ice trays and put into freezer. In 1 hour, stir with spoon. Repeat at intervals until mixture begins to set. When whole tray is partially frozen, whip cream very stiff and stir some into frozen mixture in each tray. Return to freezer; stir occasionally while mousse is hardening to be sure cream does not separate. Let freeze overnight. Serve in sherbet or parfait glasses.

Serves 8.

CREAM-CHEESE MOUSSE

1 envelope orange flavored low-calorie gelatin
1 cup unsweetened pineapple juice
1 cup unsweetened orange juice
2 tablespoons lemon juice
8 ounce soft cream cheese
⅓ teaspoon almond extract
¼ teaspoon sea salt
1 cup heavy cream, whipped
¾ cup toasted slivered almonds

Turn refrigerator control to coldest setting. Add gelatin to pineapple juice; heat, stirring, until gelatin is dissolved. Cool. Add orange and lemon juice. Blend cheese with almond extract, salt, and almonds. Stir in gelatin mixture; fold in cream; pour into freezing trays and freeze until firm.

Serves 6.

PINEAPPLE MOUSSE

1 cup heavy cream
1 cup unsweetened pineapple juice
1 envelope lemon flavored low-calorie gelatin
⅛ teaspoon sea salt
3 tablespoons lemon juice
1¼ cups unsweetened crushed pineapple

Chill cream thoroughly. Heat pineapple juice to simmering. Remove from heat, add gelatin, and stir until gelatin dissolves. Add salt, and cool. Then add lemon juice and pineapple. Chill until thick.

Remove cream to a cold bowl and beat until stiff. Fold lightly but thoroughly into pineapple mixture. Turn into chilled refrigerator tray; set refrigerator at coldest temperature and freeze for several hours, or until firm. Return controls to normal refrigerator temperature to ripen until ready to serve. Serve in chilled dishes.

Serves 8.

Beverages

BANANA MILK SHAKE

2 large bananas	supplement
5 cups cold milk	¼ cup whipped cream
4 tablespoons protein	1 tablespoon finely chopped nuts

Put bananas, milk and protein supplement in blender. Blend until thoroughly mixed. Pour banana mixture in jar and chill well. Then pour into 6 tall, chilled glasses. Top with whipped cream and garnish with nuts before serving.

EGGNOG I

2 eggs	½ cup heavy cream
¼ cup white carob syrup	freshly ground nutmeg
dash of sea salt	1 tablespoon rum extract
2 cups milk	

Beat eggs, syrup, and salt. Add milk and mix well. Pour in top of double boiler. Cook over hot water with frequent stirring until mixture barely coats a metal spoon. Chill. Stir in flavoring. Fold in stiffly whipped cream. Pour immediately into glasses and add dash of nutmeg.

Yield: 6 servings.

EGGNOG II

4 egg yolks
¼ cup white carob syrup
3 cups milk, chilled
1 cup cream, chilled

1½ teaspoons vanilla
¼ teaspoon sea salt
freshly ground nutmeg

Beat egg yolks until very thick and light in color. Add syrup, beating it thoroughly. Stir in milk, cream, vanilla, and salt. Serve immediately in glasses with a dash of nutmeg.

Yield: 4-5 servings.

HOT APPLE CIDER EGGNOG

½ cup heavy cream
½ cup white carob syrup
¼ teaspoon cinnamon
2 eggs, separated

1 cup unsweetened apple cider
½ teaspoon sea salt
⅛ teaspoon nutmeg
3 cups hot milk

Beat cream until stiff and set aside. Put remainder of ingredients, except egg whites and milk in electric blender jar. Blend 30 seconds. Add milk slowly to mixture. Beat egg whites until stiff. Pour milk mixture slowly over egg whites and fold together. Serve hot with additional whipped cream. The nutmeg can be reserved and sprinkled on cream topping if desired.

Yield: 1 quart.

LEMON EGGNOG

4 egg yolks
½ cup white carob syrup
⅜ cup lemon juice
¼ teaspoon sea salt

¼ teaspoon grated lemon rind
½ cup heavy cream
3 cups chilled milk
nutmeg

Beat egg yolks until thick. Add syrup, lemon juice, salt, and rind. Beat until thick and light in color. Whip cream and fold into lemon mixture. Pour into tall glasses. Add milk to almost fill glasses. Stir well. Add a dash of nutmeg. Serve at once.

Yield: 4 servings.

EGG PINEAPPLE PUNCH

2 eggs
⅛ teaspoon sea salt
1 cup chilled unsweetened
   pineapple

⅓ cup white carob syrup
1 quart chilled milk
½ cup heavy cream

Beat eggs, syrup, and salt until thick and light colored. In top of double boiler, scald 1 cup of the milk and stir well into the egg mixture. Return to double boiler, stir, and cook 3 minutes longer. Chill. Just before serving, stir in rest of milk and pineapple. Beat cream until stiff, then add to pineapple mixture and stir until foamy. Pour into tall glasses. Serve at once.

Yield: 4 servings.

PARTY PINK PINEAPPLE PUNCH

1 46-ounce can unsweetened
   pineapple juice
1 cup cranberries, cooked,
   strained, and blended
1 cup fresh lemon juice

1 cup white carob syrup or
   sugar substitute to taste
2 quarts dietetic lemon-lime
   soda

Have ingredients well chilled. Combine and stir well.

YULETIDE PUNCH

1 pound cranberries
water to cover
2 cups white carob syrup
½ cup lemon juice

3 small fresh limes, sliced thin
1 package unsweetened frozen
    strawberries
4 quarts water

Cook cranberries with water to cover in covered saucepan about 10 minutes or until skin pops. Put berries through a seive and discard skins. Add syrup to water in pan and cook about 1 minute to dissolve syrup. Let stand until cold. Combine all ingredients in a punch bowl, adding ice cubes or crushed ice a few minutes before serving. Float lime slices on top.

Suggested Menus
and Calorie Countdowns

SUGGESTED MENUS

BREAKFAST

Orange juice
Smoked ham*
Eggs

Soya Carob Bread, toasted
Honey-Pineapple Jelly
Decaffeinated coffee or milk

MIDMORNING SNACK

Boiled egg

LUNCH

Eye of Round Roast
Asparagus with Cheese Sauce
Soy Beans

Cucumber Salad
Cheese Cake with Cookie Dough
Crust

AFTERNOON SNACK

Dietetic peanut butter

DINNER

London Mushroom Broil
Green Beans with Onions
Baked Carrots with Toasted

Sesame Seed
Greek Salad I or II
Apple Pie

BEDTIME SNACK

Nuts

---

*Not sugar-cured.

BREAKFAST

Smoked bacon
Eggs
Soya Carob Yeast Bread, toasted
Honey-Apple Jelly

Oatmeal
Orange juice
Decaffeinated coffee

MIDMORNING SNACK

Peach

LUNCH

Mexican Salad
Cucumber-Avocado Salad

Blueberry Pie
Weak tea or decaffeinated coffee

AFTERNOON SNACK

American cheese

DINNER

Butter Baked Chicken
Cauliflower with Cheese Sauce
Broccoli Piquant

Crisscross Cherry Pie
Milk

BEDTIME SNACK

Cheese Ball

BREAKFAST

Soya Carob Pancakes
Elsie's Pancake Syrup
Smoked bacon

Orange juice
Decaffeinated coffee

MIDMORNING SNACK

Peanuts

LUNCH

Salmon-Cheese Casserole
Garden Salad Mold
Pecan Sandies

Peaches and Cream
Milk

AFTERNOON SNACK

American cheese

DINNER

Mexican Round
Oven Baked Soy Beans
Soya Carob Bread

Avocado Ring Salad
Pineapple Cream Pie
Decaffeinated coffee

BEDTIME SNACK

Milk

BREAKFAST

Orange juice	Breakfast Muffins
Smoked ham	Blueberry Jelly
Scrambled eggs	Decaffeinated coffee

MIDMORNING SNACK

Peanut Butter

LUNCH

Beef and Olive Casserole	Pineapple-Carrot Cake
Artichoke-Avocado Salad	Decaffeinated coffee

AFTERNOON SNACK

Boiled egg

DINNER

Barbecued Sirloin Steak	Garden Salad Mold
Green Beans with Onion	Rhubarb Cake
Cauliflower with Cheese Sauce	

BEDTIME SNACK

Milk

BREAKFAST

Smoked ham   Pineapple Preserves
Eggs   Decaffeinated coffee
Soya Carob Yeast Bread, toasted

MIDMORNING SNACK

Swiss cheese

LUNCH

Italian Spaghetti   Pecan Pie
Lettuce and tomatoes with   Decaffeinated coffee
  vinegar and oil

AFTERNOON SNACK

Orange

DINNER

My Favorite Roast   Fruit Salad Supreme
Tropical Carrots   Cara-Coa Hot Fudge Sundae
Swiss Chard and Green Onions   Decaffeinated coffee

BEDTIME SNACK

Milk

BREAKFAST

Smoked bacon   Soya Carob Bread, toasted
Soft scrambled eggs   Honey-Apple Jelly
Oatmeal   Decaffeinated coffee

MIDMORNING SNACK

Nectarine

LUNCH

Salmon-Cheese Casserole   Oatmeal Cake
Cranberry Salad   Decaffeinated coffee or milk

AFTERNOON SNACK

Cheese Dip with Sesame Chips

DINNER

Ham Loaf   Green Salad mold
Italian Green Beans   Millionaire Pie
Creole Baked Tomatoes   Decaffeinated coffee or milk

BEDTIME SNACK

Nuts

BREAKFAST

Apple juice
Eggs

Smoked bacon
Bundt Pecan Coffee Cake

MIDMORNING SNACK

American cheese

LUNCH

Hamburger Pot Pie
Cucumber-Sour Cream Mold

Banana Nut Ice Cream
Decaffeinated coffee

AFTERNOON SNACK

Boiled egg

DINNER

Tenderloin Plus
Fried Carrots
Soy Beans

Cabbage-Carrot-Apple Salad
Cranberry Pie
Decaffeinated coffee

BEDTIME SNACK

Protein milk shake

CALORIE COUNTDOWNS

1100-CALORIE DIET (APPROXIMATE)

BREAKFAST

		CALORIES
Smoked bacon, crisp fried, drained	2 slices	98
Egg, large, poached	1	81
Orange juice, unsweetened	4 ounces	56
		———
		235

MIDMORNING SNACK

Large boiled egg	1	81

LUNCHEON

Smoked ham, baked	4 ounces	215
Mushrooms, sautéed in 1 teaspoon butter	¼ cup	43
Green beans, fresh cooked	½ cup	15
Pineapple, fresh sliced	4-ounce slice	30
		———
		303

MIDAFTERNOON SNACK

Dietetic peanut butter	1 teaspoon	33

DINNER

Shrimp on ice, average size	10	100
Shrimp sauce	1 ounce	8
Saltine crackers	3	50
Lettuce wedge	⅛ pound	7
Vinegar for lettuce	to taste	0
Grandma's Scorched Pumpkin Pie (*see* Index) cut wedge ⅙ of pie-size	1	308
		———
		473
		———
Total for Day		1125

BEDTIME SNACK

Protein tablets	8	Negligible

BREAKFAST

		CALORIES
Smoked bacon, crisp fried,	2 slices	98
drained	1	81
Egg, large poached	4 ounces	56
Orange juice, unsweetened		
		235

MIDMORNING SNACK

Nectarine, average size	1	30

LUNCHEON

Shrimp on ice, average size	15	150
Seafood Sauce (*see* Index)	2 ounces	16
Saltine crackers	3	50
D-zerta whip	4 ounces	120
		336

AFTERNOON SNACK

Cheese	½ ounce	50

DINNER

Beef tenderloin, broiled	5 ounces	320
Green beans, boiled and drained		16
with ¼ tablespoon butter	½ cup	25
Cucumbers with vinegar	10 slices	10
		371

BEDTIME SNACK

Egg, large boiled	1	81
Total for Day		1073

BREAKFAST

		CALORIES
Smoked bacon, crisp fried, drained	2 slices	98
Egg, large, boiled or poached	1	81
Orange juice, unsweetened	4 ounces	56
		235

MIDMORNING SNACK

Peanuts, roasted	10 only	50

LUNCHEON

Baked chicken breast, seasoned with Elsie's Barbecue Spice (*see* Index)	6 ounces	310
Cucumber	10 slices	10
Green beans, boiled	½ cup	16
with ¼ tablespoon butter		25
Apricots, canned unsweetened with liquid from can	½ cup	54
		415

MIDAFTERNOON SNACK

Fresh peach, average size	1	35

DINNER

Rump beef roast, lean only	5 ounces	296
Asparagus, seasoned with ¼ ounce American cheese melted in 2 ounces liquid to make a sauce; also sea salt and pepper	6 spears	20
		25
Lettuce, ⅛ pound wedge with vinegar	1	7
		348

BEDTIME SNACK

Dietetic peanut butter	1 teaspoon	33
Total for Day		**1116**

BREAKFAST

CALORIES

Smoked bacon, crisp fried, drained	1 slice	49
Egg, large, boiled or poached	1	81
Orange juice, unsweetened	4 ounces	56
		186

MIDMORNING SNACK

Nectarine, average size	1	30

LUNCHEON

Tuna, water pack	6 ounces	216
with 3 teaspoons Poppy Seed Dressing (*see* Index)		18
Apple, peeled	¼ segment	17
2-inch square Strawberry Pie (*see* Index)		120
		371

MIDAFTERNOON SNACK

Tomato juice	4 ounces	23
Chicken, baked light meat	2 ounces	103
		126

DINNER

Steak, broiled, lean only	4 ounces	274
Swiss chard, cooked and drained	½ cup	25
with 1/16 tablespoon butter and sea salt and pepper		7
Pineapple, fresh, size 3½-by-¾	1 slice	44
		350

BEDTIME SNACK

Dietetic peanut butter	1 teaspoon	33
Total for Day		1094

BREAKFAST

		CALORIES
Smoked bacon, crisp fried, drained	1 slice	49
Egg, large, poached or boiled	1	81
Orange juice, unsweetened	4 ounces	56
		186

MIDMORNING SNACK

Dietetic peanut butter	1 teaspoon	33
½ apple, average size	½ apple	33
		66

LUNCHEON

Steak, broiled, lean only	4 ounces	274
Cabbage, white, boiled in small amount of water and drained and seasoned with ⅙ tablespoon	½ cup	17
butter, sea salt, and pepper		13
Strawberries, fresh, sweetened with sugar substitute and 1 teaspoon lemon juice	½ cup	30
Whipped cream to top straw- berries	2 tablespoons	53
		387

MIDAFTERNOON SNACK

Boiled egg	1	81

DINNER

Catfish, baked or broiled	5 ounces	280
Lemon juice	1 tablespoon	4
Yellow squash, boiled and drained	¼ cup	8
seasoned with sea salt, pepper, and ⅙ tablespoon heavy cream		26
Cabbage, raw, shredded	½ cup	12
seasoned with ½ tablespoon sour cream and ½ tablespoon lemon juice, sugar substitute, sea salt, and pepper		15
		4
		349

BEDTIME SNACK

Nectarine, average size	1	30
Total for Day		1099

BREAKFAST

Smoked bacon, crisp fried, drained	1 slice	49
Egg, large, boiled or poached	1	81
Orange juice, unsweetened	4 ounces	56
		186

MIDMORNING SNACK

Peanuts, roasted	10 only	50

LUNCHEON

Pork loin, roasted, lean only	4 ounces	290
Carrot, baked, average 5½-by-1	1	21
with ⅛ tablespoon butter and ¼ teaspoon sesame seed, sea salt, and pepper		7
Fresh cantaloupe	8 ounces	34
		352

MIDAFTERNOON SNACK

American cheese	½ ounce	76

DINNER

Chicken, baked seasoned with Elsie's Barbecue Spice (*see* Index)	6 ounces	310
Broccoli, cooked and drained	½ cup	12
seasoned with ⅛ tablespoon butter, sea salt, and pepper		20
Dietetic canned pear	½ segment	25
topped with cottage cheese	1 tablespoon	17
		384

BEDTIME SNACK

Dietetic peanut butter	1 teaspoon	33
Total for Day		**1093**

BREAKFAST

		CALORIES
Smoked bacon, crisp fried, drained	2 slices	98
Egg, large, poached	1	81
Orange juice, unsweetened	4 ounces	56
		235

MIDMORNING SNACK

Nectarine, average size	1	30

LUNCHEON

Cooked lobster, meat only	8 ounces	216
Lemon juice	1 tablespoon	4
Butter	1 tablespoon	100
Large tossed salad:		
Lettuce	¼ pound	14
Tomato, average size	½	11
Radishes, raw, small	4	7
Carrot, raw, average	¼	6
Asparagus, green, canned	6 spears	20
seasoned with ⅛ tablespoon		
butter, sea salt, and pepper		12
		390

MIDAFTERNOON SNACK

Apple, peeled, average size	½	33

DINNER

Rump beef roast, lean only	5 ounces	296
Green beans, boiled, drained,	½ cup	16
cooked with a dot of butter and		
average ⅛ raw red pepper, sea		
salt and pepper		2
2 Pecan Sandies (*see* Index)		90
		404
Total for Day		1096

Index